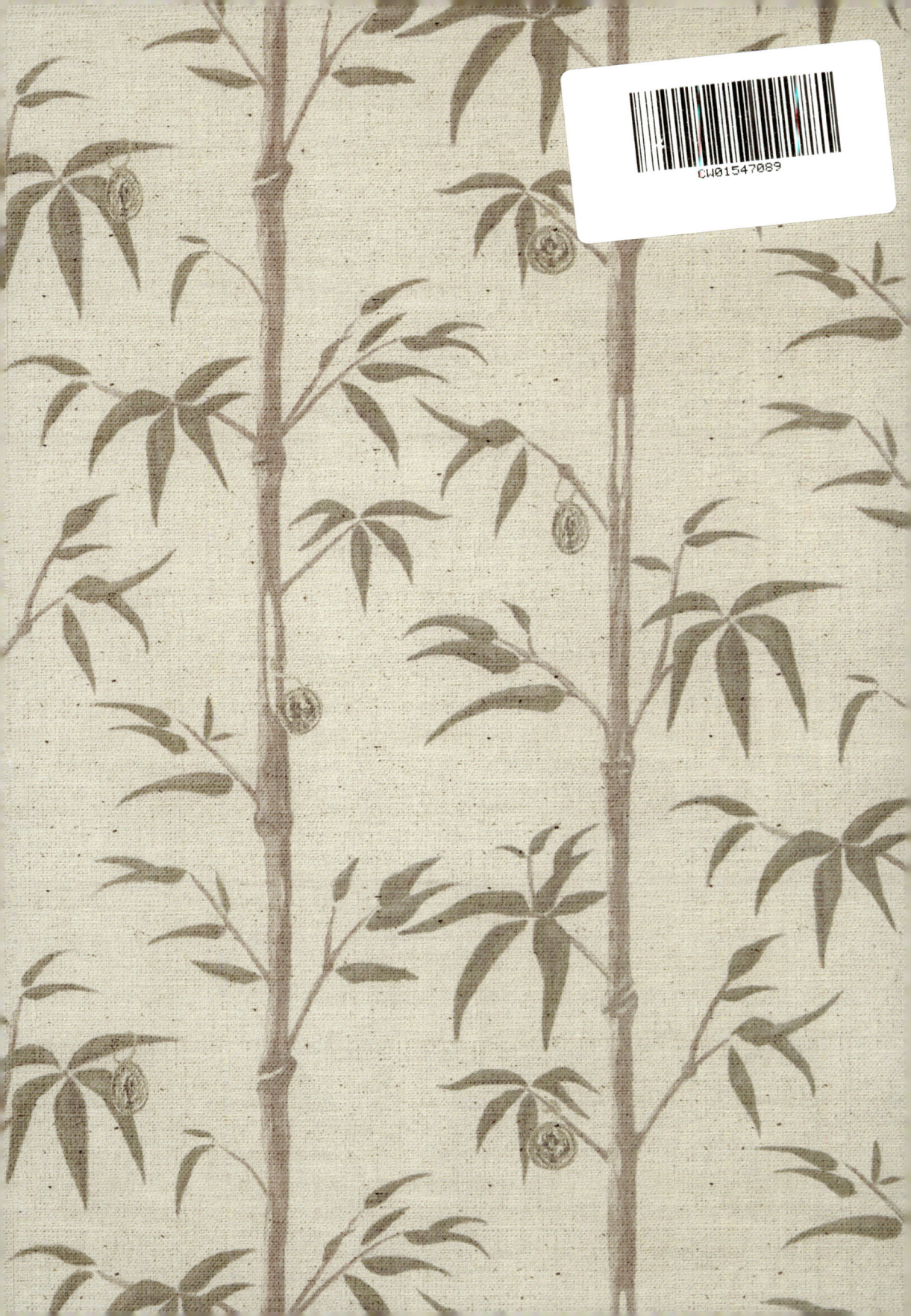

You Are Home

You Are Home

Heritage, authenticity and the beauty of your space

Africa Daley-Clarke

First published in Great Britain in 2025 by Orion Spring,
an imprint of The Orion Publishing Group Ltd
Carmelite House, 50 Victoria Embankment
London EC4Y 0DZ

The authorised representative in the EEA is Hachette Ireland,
8 Castlecourt Centre, Dublin 15, D15 XTP3, Ireland (email: info@hbgi.ie)

An Hachette UK Company

10 9 8 7 6 5 4 3 2 1

Copyright © Africa Daley-Clarke 2025

The moral right of Africa Daley-Clarke to be identified as
the author of this work has been asserted in accordance
with the Copyright, Designs and Patents Act of 1988.

All rights reserved. No part of this publication may be
reproduced, stored in a retrieval system, or transmitted
in any form or by any means, electronic, mechanical,
photocopying, recording, or otherwise, without the
prior permission of both the copyright owner and the
above publisher of this book.

A CIP catalogue record for this book is
available from the British Library.

ISBN (Hardback) 978 1 3987 1427 4
ISBN (eBook) 978 1 3987 1428 1

Designed by Hart Studio
Photography by Kasia Fiszer
Printed in China

www.orionbooks.co.uk

To my beloved children, may this book serve as a testament to the depth of my love for you and the endless possibilities that await you. Never forget that joy is your birthright. I hope you always find solace in the knowledge that home, in its purest form, resides within our hearts, forever yours to return to. With all my love, Mama

And to my dear papa, though you are no longer with us, your presence is felt in every word, every page and every heartbeat. Your wisdom, strength and enduring belief in me continue to inspire. This book is dedicated to you, a tribute to the man who instilled in me the importance of reading, and taught me the power of resilience and the beauty of chasing dreams. Love, Princess Africa

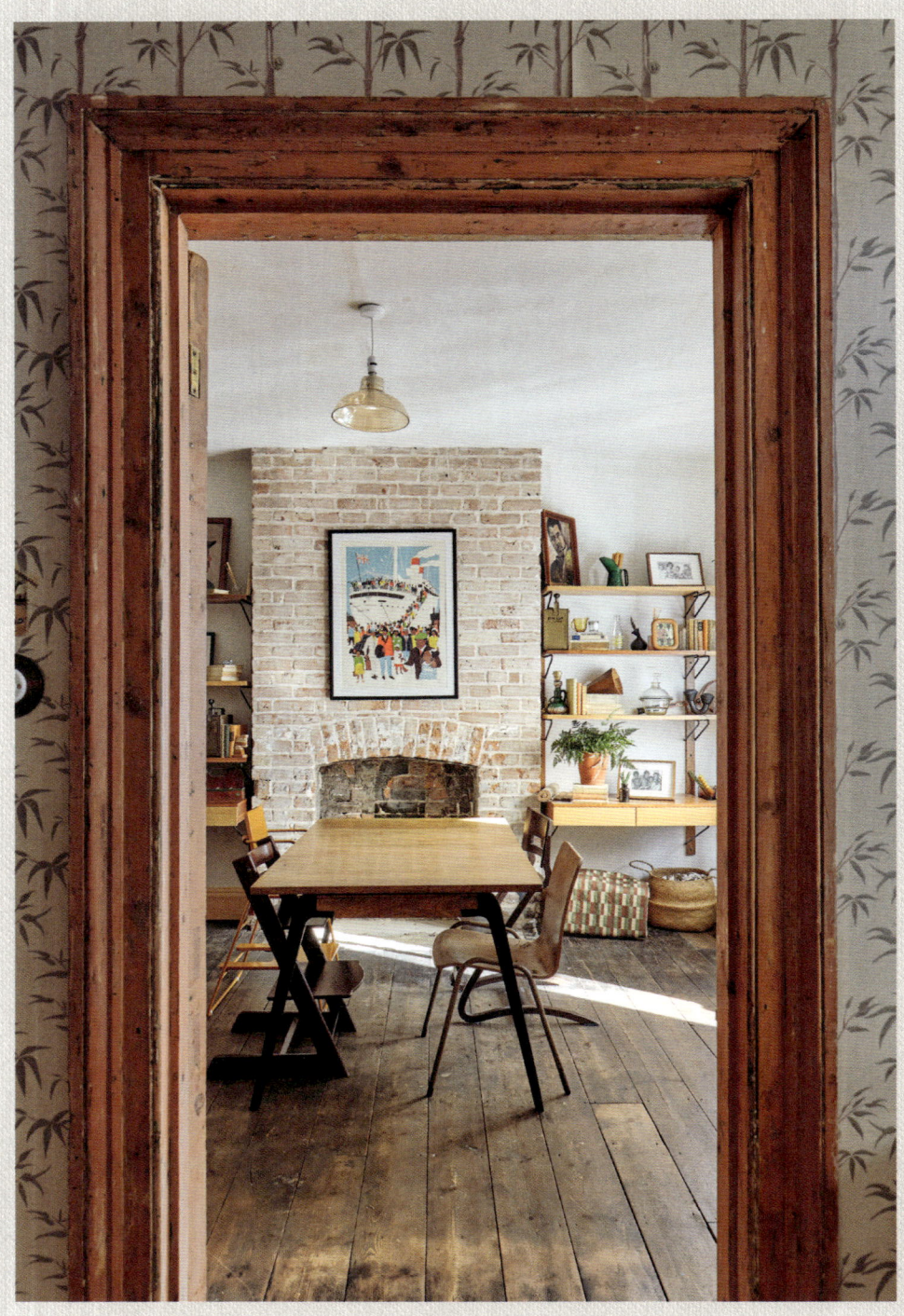

Contents

Foreword 9

LIVE 21
Chapter 1: Making a House a Home 26
Chapter 2: Who Lives Here? 41
Chapter 3: Who Works Here? 55
Chapter 4: The Perfect Home Does Not Exist 68

EMBRACE 83
Chapter 5: Finding Your Own Taste and Style 89
Chapter 6: Your Home as a Whole 107
Chapter 7: Easy Updates 126

SOURCE 145
Chapter 8: Process and Provenance 153
Chapter 9: Sourcing Materials 170
Chapter 10: Pre-loved: Sourcing (and Selling) Second-hand 193

CREATE 207
Chapter 11: Creativity in Your Home 211
Chapter 12: Where to Start, Where to Spend 226
Chapter 13: Care and Maintenance 240
Chapter 14: Creating Connection 250

Afterword 264
Acknowledgements 266
Further reading 270

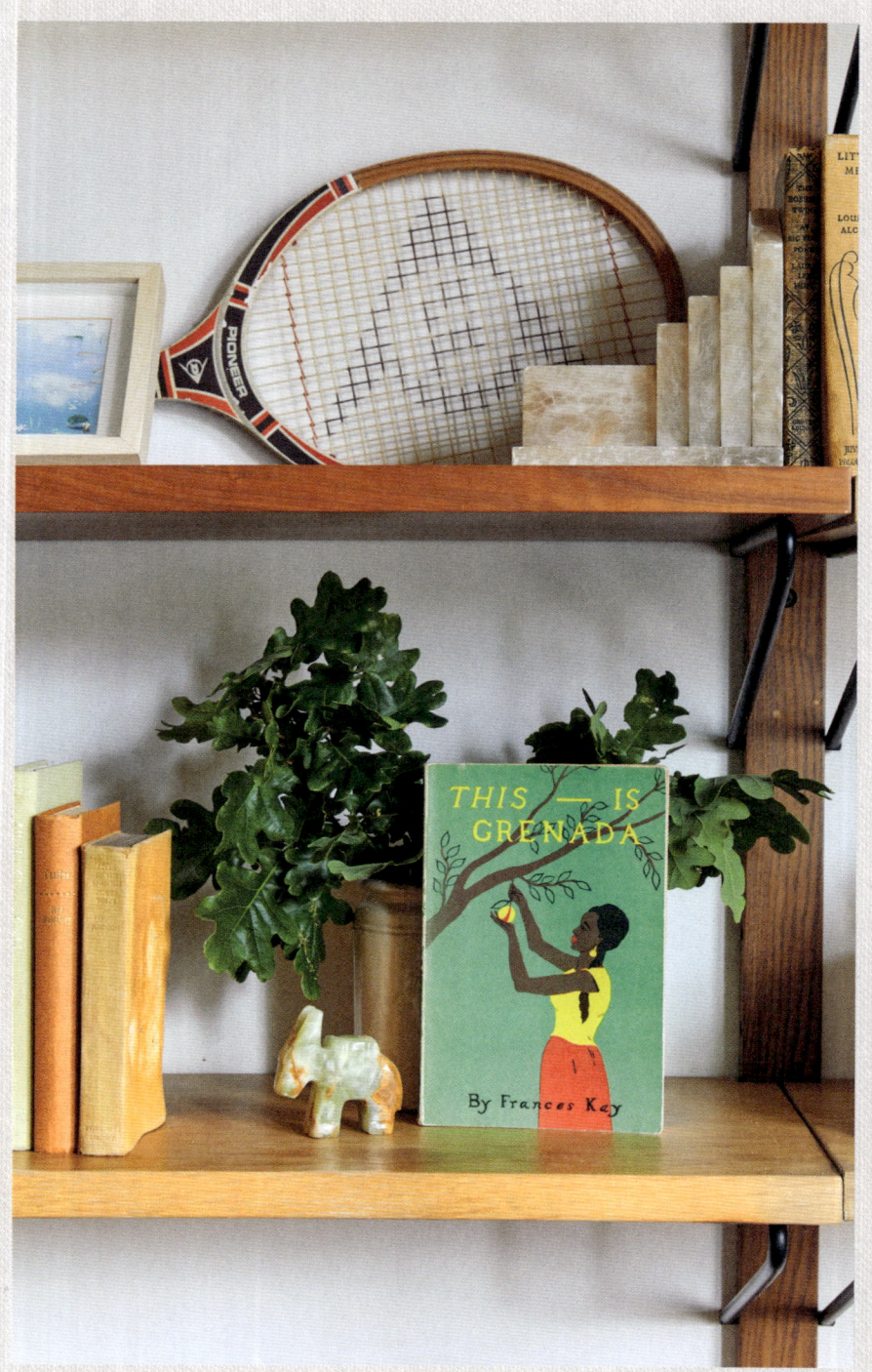

FOREWORD

In the middle of writing this book, a family emergency meant that I was called home unexpectedly. Not home to the fixer upper I share with my husband and children by the Kent coast, and not the childhood home a couple of hours away in London, where I grew up and where my mum and siblings still reside. This time, going 'home' meant travelling thousands of miles to Carriacou, a thirteen-square-mile island northeast of Grenada in the Caribbean.

I wasn't born on this tiny island, so picture-perfect with its white sands swept by lapis-blue waves, and its timber-frame houses painted in every shade. Nor were my parents, who both hailed from West Yorkshire before being lured towards the buzz of England's capital. It was three of my grandparents who began their lives in the West Indies, coming to Britain in the late 1950s as part of the Windrush generation, encouraged by an invitation from the British government, who needed workers to help rebuild the post-war economy. My grandparents were promised opportunities in Britain that were scarce back home: a secure job, a chance to raise a family and set up home. And so they packed up their bags (and dreams) dressed in their finest clothes, and were filled with anticipation for that 'better' life. But the resistance that met them in Britain meant that the road was not an easy one. They worked earnestly to adapt to British culture, often stifling aspects of their own character and heritage in the process, toning down innate parts of themselves (and, in turn, their homeland) in the hope of being accepted. A small price to pay, they reasoned, for the grand idea of a new home.

I visited Carriacou once as a baby, but not again until a temporary relocation in my early teens, and so, until I went back, my knowledge of my ancestral homeland was all gathered second-hand through stories from my extended family. Still, there was never any doubt that Carriacou was home. Music, games and recipes from this place had stayed with me; it was faraway, almost fantastical, but somehow central to my identity, and I couldn't really explain why. A sense of push and pull towards this motherland was always there. Eventually, my dad, who for decades worked gruelling sixteen-hour shifts six days a week in London, realised his dream of retiring to Carriacou, a place that was always 'home' for him, despite not having been born there.

You Are Home

When I hastily travelled to the island that hot, humid July, it was to bury my much-loved father – Papa – who had died suddenly in a swimming accident. My need to return was primal: to tangibly connect to the land he had tended as a smallhold farmer, to see the market where he'd sold his produce each week, to touch the home he had created there. My husband and four small children came too and, in the midst of stifling grief, of pain so profound, something quite magical happened. In a place where everyone looked like us, where they didn't stand out for their skin tone, hairstyles or names, a place that shared their heritage, my children blossomed. They weren't (implicitly or overtly) held up as a stereotype, or a curious minority representing a monolith; instead, they were truly seen. Both for their unique spirit and their individuality. And they could sense this. It was the same feeling my husband and I had worked hard to create for them within the sanctuary of the four walls of each home we had built over the years: a deep pride in who they are and where they come from. On this short but essential trip, seeing themselves represented and receiving affirmation from revered locals who would bound across the road with excited purpose to greet them, made them stand a little taller. They were home.

While writing a book about creating a home that reflects not just our superficial tastes, but also our deeper values, I have learnt all over again that home is a feeling rather than a location. Home is more than a wallpaper choice or a new sofa or a kitchen extension; it is a place where we hope to find ourselves feeling safe, seen, affirmed, and we can find that feeling in the most unexpected places.

Foreword

Welcome

You Are Home is a guide to creating a space that nourishes and supports you – one that lifts your mood when you turn your key in the front door and offers you a refuge from the world outside. Because if I've learnt one thing, it's that when you live in a nurturing environment that reflects your unique and indomitable spirit, you have the foundation to thrive in all areas of your life.

The world as we know it has experienced a seismic shift in recent years. Many of us are now paying more to rent or own homes where the square footage has shrunk, despite wages stagnating and remaining the same, despite bills continuing to rise. This means our homes have never had to work harder for us. Kitchen tables (if you are fortunate enough to have one) are doubling as desks, spare bedrooms are a thing of the past and outdoor space is a luxury for the relative few. With all this in mind, you might wonder why and how we should devote energy to our homes, especially when it feels like all our resources are being directed into simply staying afloat. I believe, however, that building a home that uplifts you is more crucial now than ever.

I've met so many people who have felt lost and disenfranchised by the constant barrage of images of unrealistic, 'perfect' homes – social media has a lot to answer for. Even the most design-savvy creatives are often wracked with indecision when it comes to their own homes, no longer sure of what they like or don't like, or what they actually need on a day to day basis. Having moved many times and having worked in homewares retail before becoming a freelance art director, I know how daunting it can be to carve out a home from scratch, especially one that reflects your individuality and allows you to flourish. But when you summon the creative energy to improve your surroundings, you will see the benefits manifest in so many other ways, because essentially you're making an investment in your wellbeing. This doesn't have to mean spending a lot of money – 'investment' also means your time, your attention, your consideration.

In this book, we'll be exploring different concepts of home, why it's time to rethink our options when it comes to our living spaces and how thinking outside the box may help us secure our needs. Woven throughout are personal stories, including many of my own, that will bring these different possibilities of being to life. I'll be offering plenty of practical advice on how to maximise your surroundings in order to create a home you'll be proud to live in. Whether you're in a temporary set-up, renting long-term, living in your family home or setting down roots, this is an inclusive guide that proves it's possible for everyone to create a unique home they love.

It's easy to fixate on attaining your dream house at some point in an imagined future, rather than putting thought into your current space. So many of us put off investing in our homes unless we own them but I'm adamant to change that mindset (especially given that home ownership is in decline among younger generations). Later, I'll be showing you how to find your style (not mine or anyone else's!), rather than mindlessly copying transient trends, and how to embrace individuality at home by drawing on your own story and family history. We'll look at how micro-changes like carving out more storage, revamping tired bathrooms and adding affordable textiles can have a transformative effect.

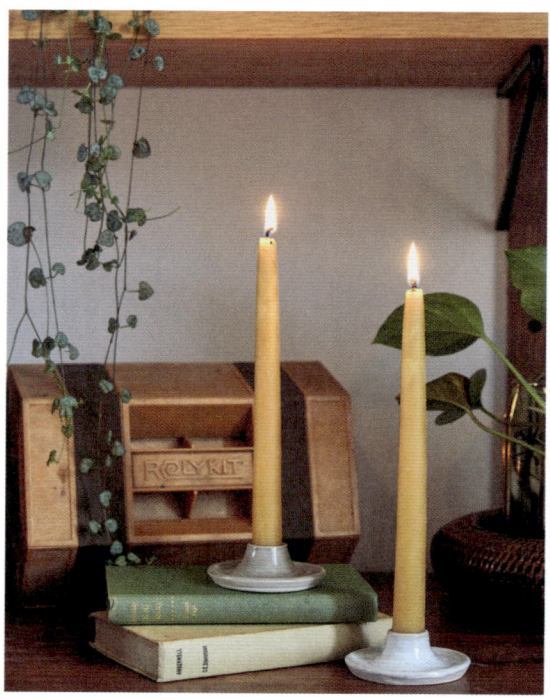

Foreword

My journey of home

Home has meant many things to me over the years, but it was setting up my own home that really put me on a trajectory towards my own definition. I'd watched my peripatetic parents create many types of home for us over the years – from an overcrowded high-rise block to a Housing Association maisonette in a Victorian conversion in London in one of the priciest postcodes in the country. Moving from one place to another on repeat had slowly instilled in me an increasingly abstract idea of home, and so I understood that home was less about the physical space and more about how I wanted to feel.

In my mid-teens, after a tumultuous period in my family home, I eventually packed up my few possessions and left. After craving and romanticising the freedom I imagined would come from creating a home by and for myself and being responsible for where I lived – and how I lived – it was now actually happening. It was terrifying to make so many big life decisions without adult advice but thrilling too. My first bid for independence – untethered and answerable only to myself, and on a quest to determine what home meant for me.

For the next four years, I went on to live in high-pressure, precarious scenarios with little to no security. I was back in a high-rise flat, this time in North London. AstroTurf had been fitted throughout the communal areas, brick-effect wallpaper adorned the walls and a cellophane cone ensured that the light in the shared areas gave off an aggressive red glare, day or night. I was subletting a room with someone who had, let's say, a relaxed approach to the law. My wellbeing was suffering, as was my flatmate's, and we were experiencing mental health crises simultaneously – it was not a healthy atmosphere. And yet the independence from my family home gave me the type of breathing room I hadn't experienced before. Sure, the décor was a long way from *World of Interiors*, but part of that space was mine, and the feeling that that instilled in me was revelatory. It was as if a part of my brain had been freed up by not having to navigate my difficult family situation – my drive and ambition flourished as a direct result.

I got to work on transforming my boxy, low-ceilinged bedroom into the haven I needed. I painted the walls and ceiling a shade of green intended to complement the bright white laminate I'd inherited. A new arty friend from sixth form added a mural of a cherry tree. I set to work dotting photos of my family around the mural's branches, and, although I was too stubborn to admit that I should have ordered a tester pot of that green (which ended up being a little nauseating), I felt so proud of the result. Instead of lamenting the lack of proper working lighting in the room I lit candles, which had a soothing, cocoon-like effect. These were not expensive interventions, but they were incredibly effective. Within these confines, I was able to drown out the heady scents and sounds seeping in under my door from the chaotic carousel of new flatmates and the neighbourhood outside. And, as I had seen my mum and grandma (creative magpies both) do during my childhood, I continued to decorate and reinvent the space several times over the next few years.

Of course, I knew that wasn't my long-term home. It was so far from being even adequate accommodation for someone vulnerable and on the cusp of adulthood, and such a leap from my imagined first step into DIY domesticity. Rather than being a resident of a like-minded and convivial flatshare, it was more of an everyone-for-themselves situation. I'd keep a plate and cutlery in my bedroom, washing them after each quickly prepared meal, rather than play roulette with the tower of dirty dishes in the shared kitchen sink. My flatmate and I were usually playing a losing game of chicken over the washing-up. He'd work his way through every item of crockery and cutlery in our cupboards, allowing the detritus to pile high before I inevitably caved in and deep-cleaned his mess.

But in spite of all that, I found something invigorating about having my own space. I instinctively knew there was value in investing my energy into elevating my otherwise shabby little bedroom. Even as a teenager, long before the visual inspiration of Instagram and Pinterest became mainstream, I recognised that there can be a mirror effect between our surroundings and our mood. My mental health took several turns for the worse over those years, and I was even hospitalised on more than one occasion, but I truly believe that in those dark times it was the sanctuary of my bedroom and the peace it brought that kept me going. Against the odds, I had created my first home, and it was grounding me with resilience to face the uncertainty around me.

A home with soul

How would you like to live? This is a question I'll be coming back to throughout the book, and the answer will be unique to you, so I won't be answering it, you will. This simple, unassuming question might be harder to sum up than you think, but unlocking your feelings around what home means to you will really help you focus on your space in a way that'll best serve your needs as an individual or more.

Your home needs to support and nurture your wellbeing by helping you replenish your 'cup' after each day and ensure you're revived enough to take on the next. Creating a home that nourishes its inhabitants will come down to the feelings that fill it and the values you want to uphold. How your home *feels* – by which I mean its atmosphere, flow and function – is more important than anything else, including how it looks. If it feels good to you, it will naturally look aesthetically pleasing. And if you are driven to distraction a thousand times a day, tripping over shoes and bags or repeatedly searching for your house keys in a hurry, it's just not going to feel great.

I believe that every room, large or small, has untapped potential and I'd like this book to help you realise the opportunities within your space, however imperfect it may seem right now. I'll hold your hand as you get into the zone of your creative process, I'll show you how to gauge your needs, how to prioritise affordable furnishings and how to approach small, fulfilling DIY projects if you fancy having a go. Throughout the book, you'll notice an emphasis on longevity and sustainability (even if you'll be moving on again before long). This has become central to my mindset around creating a home. Investing in better-quality pieces often means savvy prioritising and a bit of extra effort, and this can be hard in our impulsive 'click-to-buy' culture. I'm also on a journey of creating a home myself – an ongoing work-in-progress – and I'll share with you the invaluable tips I've gathered over the years from expert tradespeople and makers, to help you maintain your home and everything in it.

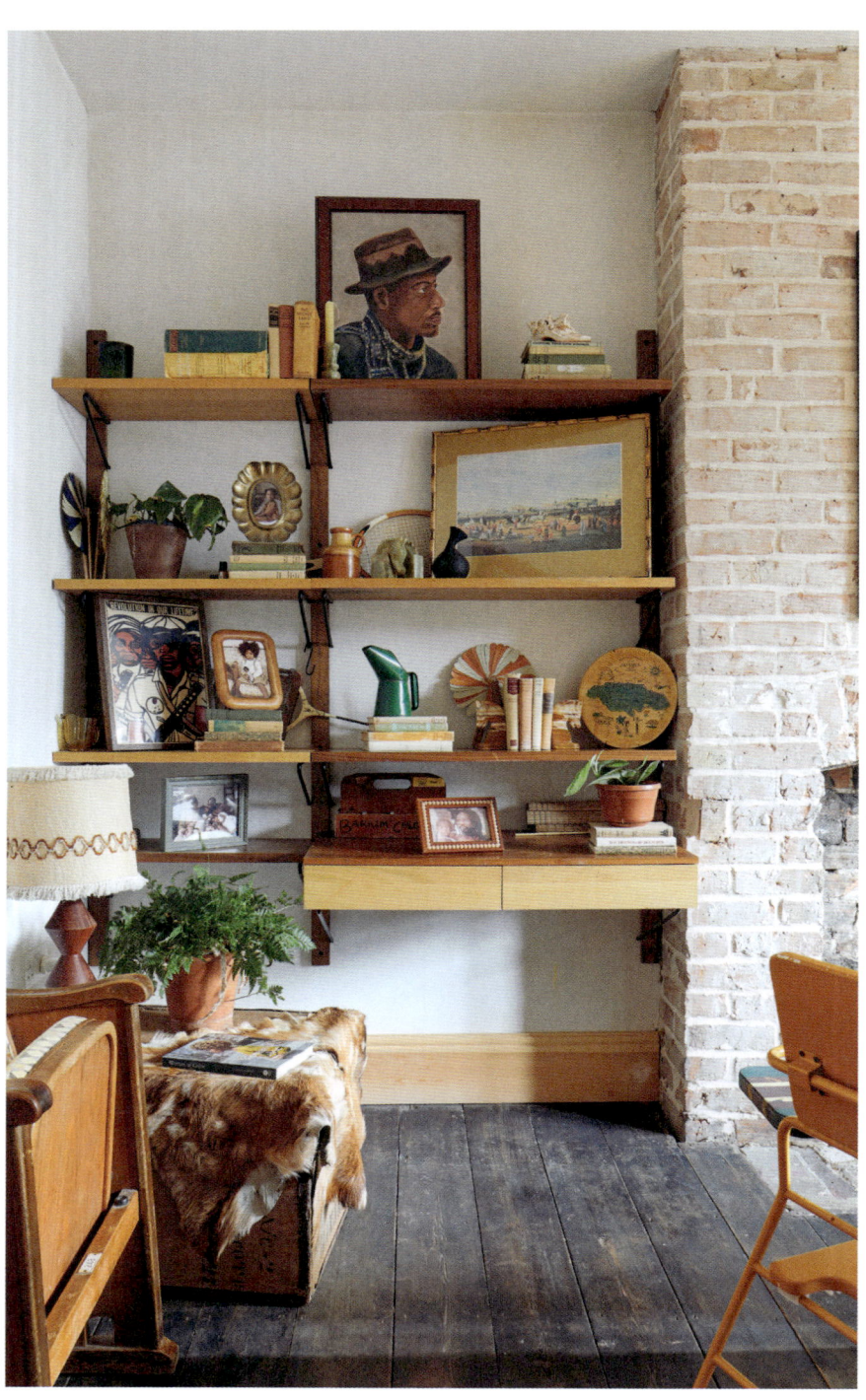

Foreword

Heritage and personality in our homes

I'm a passionate believer in making our homes reflect our personal heritage and tapping into what that means for you, even if you have thus far never felt particularly connected to your past. Part and parcel of this involves developing an interest in the provenance of everything that comes into your space and being conscious of its history. It's why a chipped mug handmade by someone you love will always bring more joy than a pristine one bought from a superstore off the motorway. In the Source section, we look in detail at how you can respect makers, source items for your home that you'll love (often at rewarding prices) and carve out a space that transcends fads.

For me, bringing my heritage into my home has meant drawing on my immigrant backstory. Throughout history, some of the most significant advancements in Western interior and architectural design have been shaped by the contributions of immigrants and marginalised communities. A compelling example is the influence of 'Black culture' on mid-century modern design. Originally popularised by a predominantly white, upper-middle-class demographic, this design movement was reinterpreted and enriched by Black people, who infused it with unique cultural elements. This reinterpretation not only broadened the movement's appeal but also democratised it, making mid-century modern design more accessible and resonant with a wider audience. Similarly, in the realm of fashion, the fusion of Jamaican youth culture and English working-class skinhead style gave rise to one of the most iconic and enduring fashion movements in the UK – rude boy style. This powerful blend of influences not only embodied the defiance and energy of both groups but also created a unique fashion statement that resonated across cultural boundaries, leaving a lasting impact on British fashion. We should never forget how much immigrant stories contribute to who we are today, and how much our lives and identities are intertwined with each other. By cherishing the meaningful pieces we have in our homes, we can create a stronger connection between ourselves and our cultures – a reminder of where we've been, who we are now and all that has come before us.

Let's continue to strive for our own sense of home, to create spaces with soul, regardless of the circumstances that have brought us there. Let's create a place we can call our own, with a feeling of permanence (even if the reality is more transient) that reflects our experiences along the way. By cultivating an appreciation for the past, embracing both its beauty and its flawed nature, let's be inspired by history. Let's be mindful of the spaces we inhabit, as they can cultivate a sense of security and joy for generations to come, and – in the case of families like mine, where those homes may not be assets to be passed down – remember, it's the mindset that becomes the valuable heirloom.

Non-native English speakers sometimes remark on the language's many idiosyncrasies, like the way in which we often describe our emotional state as being 'in a good place' (or not, as the case may be), as if our wayward feelings are embodied in a physical location. These semantic eccentricities make sense to me, reminding me that home extends beyond our immediate surroundings. Creating communities and the feeling that someone has our back is, of course, far more important than the cushions we choose to scatter on our sofa. Feeling connected to the place we're in, being rooted to our wider environment, having someone nearby to call on when the chips are down and someone you can help in turn has been shown to boost the quality and even longevity of life. This feeling of belonging underpins everything that home means to me, and to most of us. In the final section, Create, we look at how community starts with us, and how to establish meaningful connections with those around us, even if we live far away from family and close friends.

Using this book

You Are Home is divided into four parts – Live, Embrace, Source, Create – each tackling a key aspect of my approach to creating a home that helps you flourish. These four sections will encourage you to consider what you need from your home, how you can be true to your tastes, how to mindfully choose the things that go into it while supporting independent makers and how to foster a community around your home. Rather than preaching a didactic list of dos and don'ts, I hope to give you lots of ideas, highlight some materials and processes you might like to use (and some that may be best avoided) and encourage you to think creatively about your space. My wonderful friend and colleague Kasia Fiszer's photography adorns the pages of this book, bringing to life the story on each page; I know you'll love her work as much as I do.

While there are some serious issues covered in this book, like how we, as a society, must work towards a more respectful and considered approach to consumption, overall I would suggest that you don't take decorating your home too seriously. Have a go, get it 'wrong', avoid being overly tasteful and instead, concentrate your efforts on creating a *feeling* that you love, rather than stressing over the finished 'look'. You might already be a dab hand at bringing life and style to a room, be able to identify iconic Italian lighting by designer (I confess, I can't!), or you may be a complete beginner who doesn't know one end of a paintbrush from the other. Either way, I want you to be ambitious for your home so that it offers you the sanctuary to help you live well every day. This is a book for anyone who wishes to elevate their space, to create a home that reflects its inhabitants – welcome, all of you.

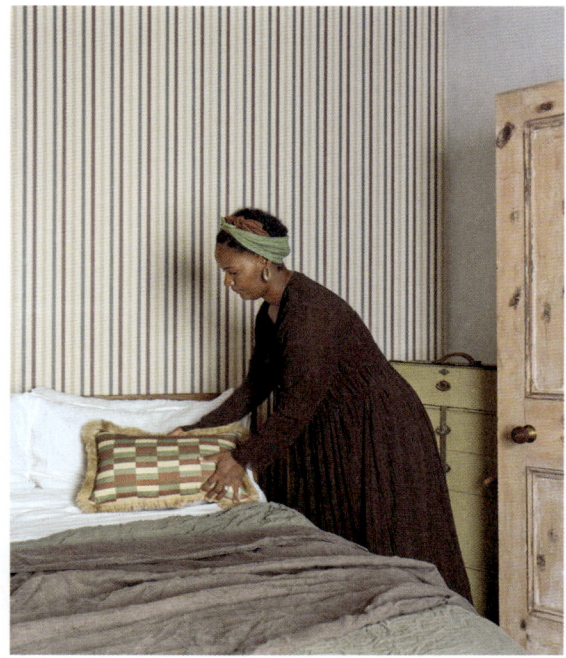

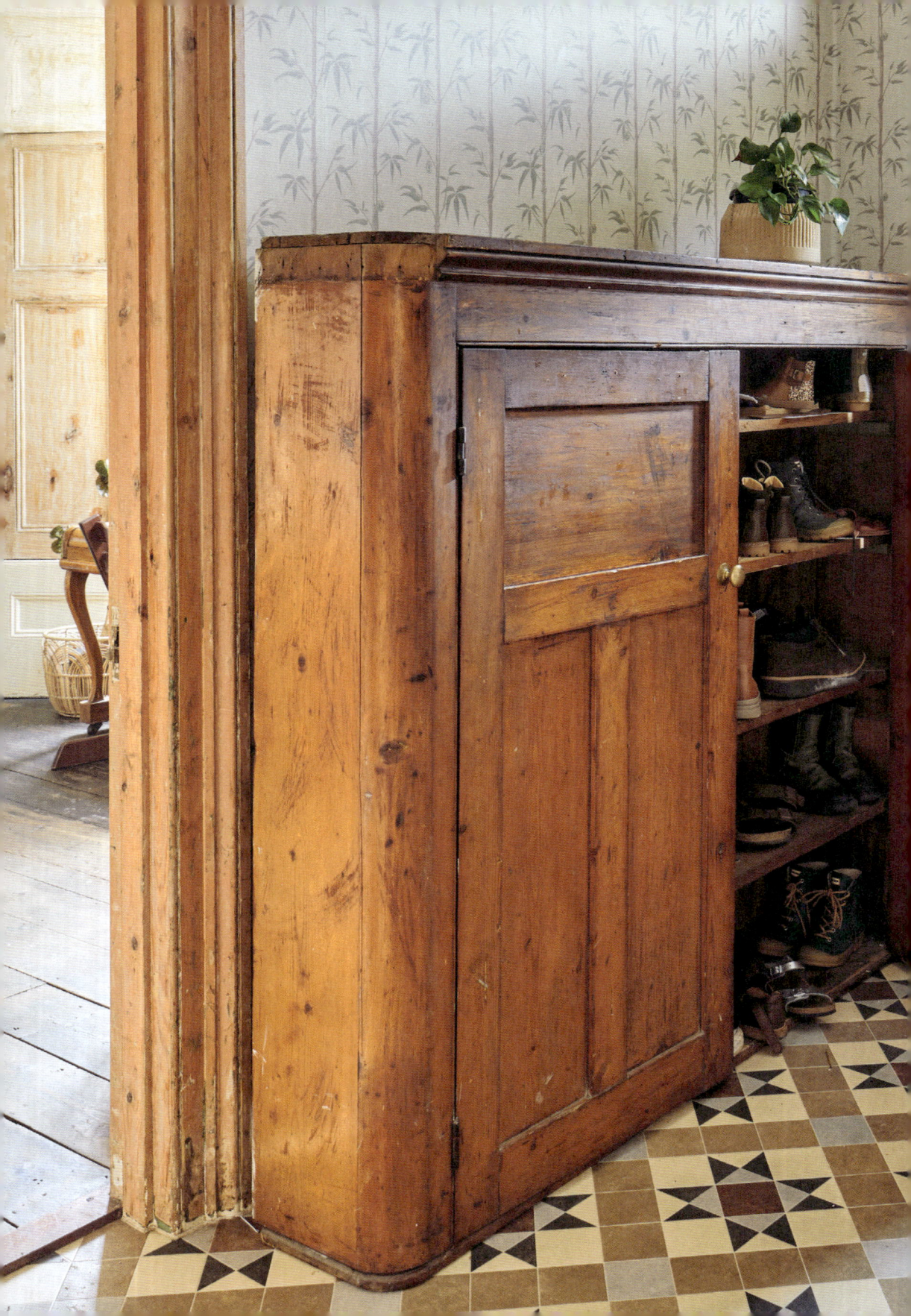

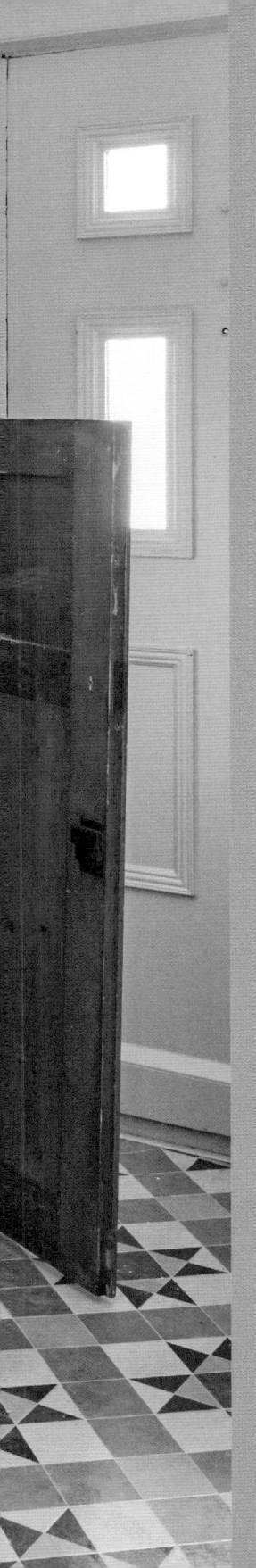

LIVE

The idea of home is my guiding compass – it transcends physical boundaries and is an evolving story. I have moved frequently and was often forced to do so at crucial points in my life when I was unprepared for the change, leaving me quite vulnerable. Despite the challenges that come with creating a home in unfamiliar territory, I have found real peace in carving out safe spaces, even in the most temporary environments. Home should ideally be a place of emotional safety where you can remove your armour at the door and be your authentic self without judgement or fear. Somewhere that supports security, identity, and comfort; holds memories and stories; and is where you can seek solace.

Let's take the time to slow down, so you can examine not just where you live but how you live, and whether it is working for you. In the upcoming chapters, we will explore our emotional connection to home and move away from the one-size-fits-all idea to celebrate the many varying ways to thrive there. We will look at what makes a home, and how to create one that roots you to your place in the world.

My changing homes

Aged twenty-one, with a secure job that came with a pay rise, I applied for a new housing scheme for working professionals through my local council and secured a flat within a development in Central London. The rent was 50 per cent of my income – a stretch on my salary – but it brought security. I sublet my old room for the final months of the tenancy agreement to save an impossible double rent scenario, and never looked back. Now that I finally had my own private space, there was no deep breath before opening the front door. No darting eyes, quickly counting the trainers piled up by the door to work out how many strangers might be in my home. No stench of mould from stacks of unwashed dishes in the sink. No debt to pay off every time I topped up the gas meter because the previous tenant had fiddled it, leaving me to foot the bill now that it had been corrected. My bedroom had a working light. I had a monthly electricity bill. And, above all, I felt safe. The relief that came with that safe space changed the trajectory of my life, and the thought of going back to a chaotic flatshare propelled me to excel in my career. Failure was no longer an option.

Around this time, I met my husband, J, who moved into my home. We soon married and a few months later welcomed our firstborn into our one-bedroom flat. Two years on and our second child joined us. After seven years in the home that had changed my life for the better, and eighteen months as a family of four (and the added possessions that come with that!), we relocated to a two-bedroom maisonette in Islington. My home life felt as if it had come full circle, as we were now within walking distance from the second home I'd ever lived in. My children attended a great local pre-school – one that I used to pass every morning on my way to primary school as a child. We were living our wildest dreams, carving out a lovely life, with a routine and predictability that my own childhood had often lacked. Our children were loved and thriving and that felt like a big marker of success in our books.

And then things changed. Redundancy, the Covid pandemic, and the birth of our third child. We had to think on our feet to get through the rollercoaster. Life had never been busier but the sanctuary that we'd built saved our sanity. A flurry of good fortune followed, including a segue into a new field for my husband and a pivot into self-employed advertising and consultancy for myself, following the growth of my social media presence. Never did we think we'd be in a position to secure our own home, but somehow we saved enough for a deposit and found a three-bedroom house on the

Kent coast in need of lots of TLC. For the first time in our lives, we could look forward to a home with some permanence. A lot was at stake – leaving a secured tenancy with affordable rent, and a network of friends and family close by. We reminded ourselves that home is a place, but it can also be an experience, an energy, a feeling. And when it is the latter, home can be found anywhere, in any place. We took the plunge and headed for the coast, to a new home and a new life.

Home should sustain and revive us. It should be a world away from perfection, where ownership isn't glorified and renting isn't demonised; it shouldn't be about fetishising homewares or maxing out credit cards. It's not about putting yourself under massive pressure to keep everything tidy all the time (I've got four kids, so that's certainly not happening!). Unique, authentic spaces are not perfect; they do (and should) take time – and I hope I can offer a little inspiration for why we should make the best of what we've got throughout all of life's stages. We all know that feeling of 'Oh no, back to this mess,' when we walk through our front door, and how different it feels to the shoulder-drop relief of 'I am so glad to be home.'

Let's make you glad to be home, wherever that is.

CHAPTER 1

MAKING A HOUSE A HOME

In setting up several homes myself – first as a single person, then as part of a couple, and later as a mother – it was always vital to me to carve out a peaceful home amid what was often a chaotic time. When life was tumultuous, returning to a calming space that represented me was what kept me going. I believe that feeling connected to our space, in a way that celebrates our unique identity, is what transforms it into a true home. When there is a disconnect between us and our environment, it creates a feeling of unease that can filter into other aspects of our life.

Over the years, I've thought a lot about how a house (or flat, mobile home, narrow boat, bedroom or any other space) becomes more than its four walls and begins to feel like home. How is that feeling captured? Is it something physical that happens once you've unpacked your boxes? Or does it take longer? Have you ever lived somewhere which never felt like home, despite all efforts to make it so? This chapter is about unravelling that, understanding the essence of home and how you might go about capturing that in your space. I'll be posing some questions to help you gain an understanding of how you're feeling about your space at this moment in time. There are no right or wrong answers here; by becoming more aware of our environment, we can better understand our needs.

Thinking of home

What feelings does the word 'home' evoke for you? Are these feelings different now, for better or worse, than they have been in the past? Is there a scent or sound that transports you to the home of your childhood? Does 'home' mean bricks and mortar? Or does it mean family members, neighbours, a geographic location, community, a place of worship or something else entirely? You might have cosy memories – warm kitchens with delicious things cooking on the stove; a feeling of being relaxed and secure among people who care for you – or, thinking of home might bring up more challenging recollections. Don't be afraid to go at your own pace when considering your emotional associations with your home.

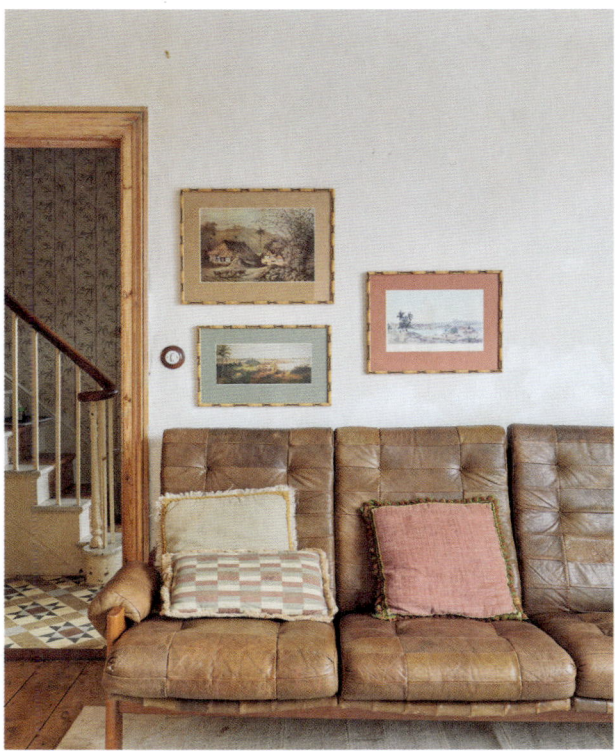

Home should be a place of refuge, where you feel comfortable being yourself without pretence or effort. The sanctuary of home is often especially important for those who experience marginalisation and discrimination, because home accommodates authenticity without demanding the mental energy of code-switching and self-censorship. When I lived in that dodgy flatshare years ago, every time I put my key in the front door I'd inhale sharply and feel a deep tug in my shoulders; my jaw would clench in anticipation of who or what mess I'd find on the other side. This feeling would quickly melt away once I had passed through the second door to my bedroom, where I'd immediately relax, seeing the familiarity of my own things in my own space. It was a safe place to recover from external pressures. Does your home allow you to let your guard down, or is it a source of stress?

As you read this book, think about the feelings you currently hold towards your home and consider how they might be expanding or diminishing your quality of life.

When I asked myself this question, these were the answers that came up for me.

Africa's list

- Safety
- Privacy
- Authenticity
- Relaxation
- Comfort
- Affirmation of our identity

Security

We humans do not do well with unpredictability. For the most part, we like to feel an element of control (even if, logically, we know that so much is beyond it and that fate often laughs at our plans). We all have the right to feel secure in our homes, even if they are transient spaces. Security means different things to us all: some people will feel more secure renting rather than owning a home as they are not locked into a decades-long loan and subject to unpredictable interest rates (the word 'mortgage' literally means 'death pledge'). They are also free to relocate easily for the sake of work, necessity or pleasure, should they so choose. Others find that the idea of a permanent home, with their name on the deeds, boosts their feeling of security. For others still, staying in or returning to their original family home might be the ultimate comfort. Similarly, many long to live in their home town, while for others that would feel like a prison. We all perceive security in different ways.

Have you considered what brings you a feeling of security? You might even like to write a list in a notebook. I have found it insightful and empowering to become curious about my feelings, even if I don't have all the solutions worked out yet. If you share your home with others and are finding it difficult to communicate your wants and needs, reckoning with your concept of security can also be a great place to start.

What brings me a feeling of security?

- A space that clearly belongs to us as a family
- A space that reflects us in how it looks, smells and feels
- A space that captures our taste and values, no one else's
- Family photographs and keepsakes
- A sense of community around us

For me, achieving that all-important sense of security has not necessarily come down to renting or owning, but to agency. I've been fortunate to have lived in spaces that really felt like home, in no small part because I've been permitted (even when renting) to make changes so that it worked for me and our family at the time. I felt great security in the lovely maisonette J and I rented through our local housing association, largely due to the five-year tenancy we secured (though we left after two). We moved there with our two older children, aged three and one (our third child arrived a few months later), and although the flat was rather dishevelled, it represented a real feeling of safety and permanence. That feeling gave us the confidence and motivation to put a huge amount of effort into renovating our home, to make it work for and reflect us.

The homes that made me

When I was a child, my mum, siblings and I moved every few years (including a brief stint in a hostel). Each home was steadily more presentable than the previous one, and each was a stark contrast to my dad's home, where my siblings and I spent our weekends and school holidays as my parents separated. The first home, and the only one that my parents ever shared together, was in a twenty-storey council high-rise in Mornington Crescent, not far from Central London. Fragmented memories from that time feature a small and busy environment with a permanent warm and earthy scent. Towering money trees in outgrown pots in every corner and ska and lovers rock vibrating through each room. The air was constantly thick with fraught anxiety – which I suppose was hard to avoid in a home of late-teen parents with financial worries.

From there, we moved a mile or so north, to a dilapidated Victorian maisonette just off leafy Camden Road. No more piss-drenched lift, no dodgy stairwells to navigate when said lift was out of order, and, for the first time, a small bit of outside space in the form of a balcony. We had landed on our feet. It was a street with a confronting imbalance of wealth – affluent families living in some of the priciest houses in the country cheek by jowl with social housing where there were many on the breadline. Despite this, there was a real sense of community. Our flat was wedged between my two best friends, Megan and Sudeka, both second-generation immigrants of Jewish and Bengali descent respectively. We would put on singing performances for our elderly neighbours on hot summer days who would crane out of the windows giving us raucous applause. It was a community that had everyone's back, and even at a young age I appreciated that my single mum could count on their back-up if she needed it. Our dog, Toots, a beautiful mongrel bought for a tenner from another neighbour one night, would walk herself each day and on the rare occasion she'd be gone too long, we could rely on our neighbours to let us know where they'd spotted her last.

Once I had been accepted into a good secondary school (a postcode lottery system), we moved again – this time to a recently renovated Georgian maisonette in Bloomsbury that we rented from a housing association. We had an extra bedroom that I shared with a much younger brother and sister. The

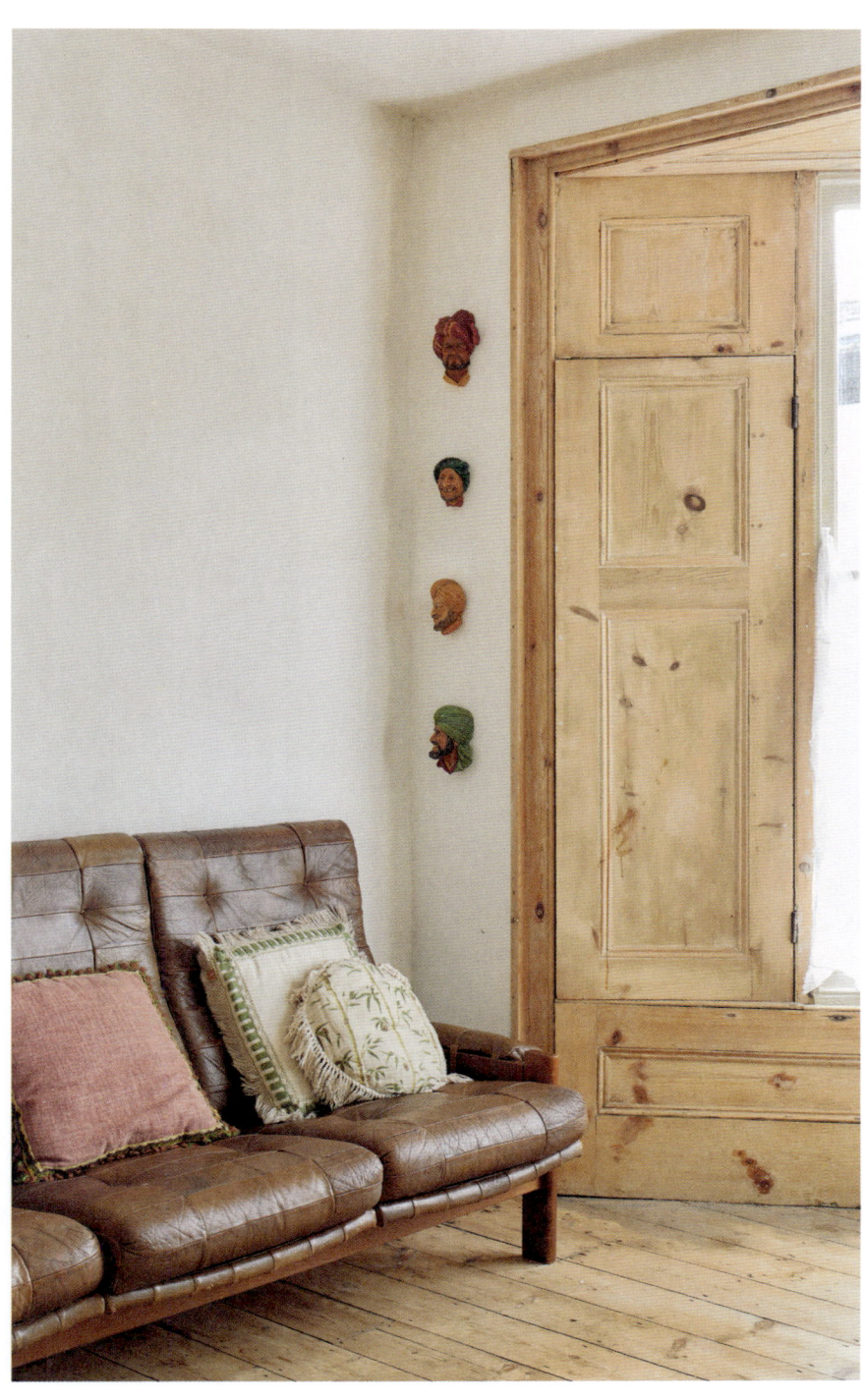

area felt like a new world, full of private garden squares, Dickensian cobbled streets and sprawling office buildings, and the beautiful, historic park of Coram's Fields became our new backyard. What we'd gained in space though, we lost in community, and I missed the friendships and camaraderie of inner Camden. Though my mum seemed to know just about everyone in our new neighbourhood (such were her Yorkshire ways!), our shiny new home had come at a cost of the social connection we'd left behind.

A few years later we relocated to my final childhood home – a nearby terraced Georgian house. It was beautiful, its two-hundred-year heritage permeating every nook and cranny, telling stories of its many inhabitants over the years. Births, marriages, deaths – it had seen them all as life unfolded, year in, year out. As a child I read voraciously, and I liked to think that this house was the type of home an author would have thrived in. It sowed a seed, making me think about the home I would one day create, and I lived there until I left home a few years later. Even at a young age, I recognised the privilege that the relatively presentable last two homes had afforded me.

When you think of your childhood home(s), what kind of feelings emerge? Have you noticed a similarity, or indeed difference, between how you've established your home as an adult and the home where you grew up? I have found it interesting; the conventions J and I have carried over from our own childhoods and ones we have left in the past – sometimes this has been conscious, other times not. To give you some inspiration here are some of my own thoughts.

In my childhood home	In my own home
Only adults were catered for	*A sense for our children that they are at the centre of our home*
Adults made all the decisions	*Children are involved in age-appropriate decisions*
Children should be seen and not heard	*Children's thoughts and voices matter*

Home is a feeling

I'm sure you've been to other people's homes and immediately picked up on a vibe, whether consciously or not. Homes where you feel at ease before you've even taken off your coat. It might be light-filled or just obviously cared for, or it might be harder to pin down why you're feeling like you want to stay a while. It's not necessarily that you love the décor or that it's super tidy. It could be just a sense that it's a joyful home, with good people contributing to the uplifting energy. Likewise, you've undoubtedly stepped into homes that feel less welcoming, where you'd rather not stray too far from the front door so you can head back out again soon. Perhaps they're neglected spaces that hint at the occupant's state of mind, or quite the opposite – an obsessively curated home, so polished and on-trend you're afraid you'll spill something on the perfectly plumped armchair. When you arrive home after a busy day, what feeling do you currently get when you turn your key in the door? Is this different to the feeling you would like to have?

My maternal grandma's house in Yorkshire is very much the welcoming kind, and there's a joy that fills my bones whenever I visit her. Her home is a part of my history, absorbed into my DNA and its energy is something I've tried to replicate in all the homes I've created as an adult. It was at her house that we spent most school holidays, and although her personal tastes were different, it was clear why my mum was so skilled at tailoring spaces to suit her. My grandma, a white-presenting woman of Irish–Armenian decent, settled down with my Black grandfather back in 1960s West Yorkshire, at a time when their rental choices were severely restricted because of their interracial relationship. For much of my mother's very early years, their family rented a single room with only a coal fire for heat output, and it wasn't uncommon for my grandfather's gambling habit to leave the family without heating.

After a short while, my grandma secured a home for the family that became the scene of a terrible house fire. Young children, accessible matches and flammable furniture. My family went through something no one deserves to experience. Aged just twenty-four (and once all her family were safe), my grandma leapt from the blazing building, shattering both of her hips. The burns and injuries she sustained were so severe that she spent close to two years in hospital. Throughout this time, my mum and her siblings were separated and distributed among various white foster families. It was a distressing time. The extensive damage to that house resulted in it being knocked down.

The house that my grandma lives in now has been home to my mother and all her siblings. It's been the backdrop of so many school holidays, and all four of my children are carving out memories there too. After facing such a harrowing, life-altering experience, my grandma has made a point of creating a uniquely nurturing home that supports her at every turn. A hub of warmth, memories and safety within four cosy walls, and a masterclass in what home means. So much of my approach to making a home – and much of the advice in the upcoming chapters – comes from my grandma, and I feel hugely indebted to her for that.

One thing I have always loved about my grandma's home is that every time we visit, she's revived another room, constantly keeping her home at its best, and she couldn't care less what anyone else thinks about her decorating choices. I'm inspired by her total confidence. Despite living on a state pension, she prioritises her surroundings and is always looking for ways to improve them, and in turn her mood. These choices owe nothing to trends or Pinterest, just to her personal taste. I try to keep that self-belief in mind in my own home.

Identity

When J and I moved to our last home in London – the maisonette in a beautifully appointed double-fronted Victorian villa that we rented from a local housing association – we were beyond excited to start transforming a tired space into a loving home for our two little children. I reference this flat a lot throughout the book because it really felt like we'd come 'home'. The house was split into three flats, carved up and reconfigured crudely to maximise the number of tenancies, and our sliver was on the floor in between another family and an older gentleman. Still, we felt like we'd hit the jackpot.

Shortly after getting the keys, I remember skipping back from my job as an interiors showroom manager, talking giddily to Instagram stories about everything I had planned for our new home. The kitchen posed the biggest challenge. Originally just a landing, it was 2.8m × 2.8m and needed to house the white goods along with enough storage and surface space for a growing family. Unphased, I told my then (modest) audience that I'd always dreamt of having a range cooker, and, believing this to be our long-term home, I was determined to make it happen.

The online response shocked me. Many people made short work of expressing their distaste at me, a young Black woman, daring to dream about an item that in their minds was meant for a very different type of person, in a very different home, at a very different stage in their life. I'll never forget one woman brandishing me 'inauthentic', saying she was 'surprised that I'd succumbed to losing my identity' trying to obtain such an object. The comments lingered in my mind longer than most as they truly puzzled me. It was my paternal grandmother – the stoic, Black matriarch of the family – who had etched the range cooker's value into my mind. She and my grandfather arrived in Huddersfield, West Yorkshire, from the West Indies in the late 1950s. There, they raised my dad and his six siblings in a home that ticked every immigrant cliché of that era. There was the clear plastic tablecloth covering the dainty lace one on the dining table. The forbidden 'best' china, trapped inside the prized display cabinet. Waxed fruits collecting dust in the oversized mid-century wooden fruit bowl, and hard-to-miss nods to British culture dotted throughout their modest home. My grandmother's most prized possession? A classic range cooker in British Racing Green. This cooker not only represented my grandparents' grit, determination and hard work but also their unrequited love of Britain and their eternal quest to seek validation from it. When my paternal grandparents retired back to Carriacou in 2000, they packed up a shipping container filled with a lifetime of amassed treasures and transplanted them to their new self-build home. Taking centre stage, some forty years later, is my grandmother's range cooker. The heart of their home, continuing its life of service on warmer shores.

And so when we moved to the maisonette, I trawled online marketplaces to secure our very own perfect range cooker (with a £280 price tag) and J and I took the existing kitchen back to brick and rebuilt it all to encapsulate this nod to my grandmother, my connection to her and to my history. When we finally relocated from Islington to the Kent coast, I smiled watching our trusty range cooker winched from its enclave and hauled down two flights of stairs, knowing that its next voyage would hopefully be its last as it moved to its rightful home.

Is there an object or set of objects that truly represent home to you? It might be an old leather sofa that has been worn to shiny smoothness by multiple generations, or a piano, or perhaps it's something more practical, such as a rice cooker on the kitchen counter that always means 'home'. For some people, a home doesn't feel like a home without plants, or even a pet! If you want to create a particular feeling in your home, think about the homes that you have loved and felt safe in – not necessarily the décor, although that can be inspiring – think about how that feeling of safety was created. What is your range cooker equivalent? I think we all have one, if not more.

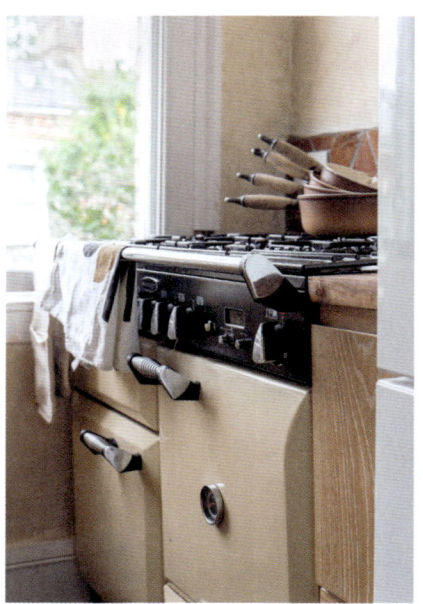
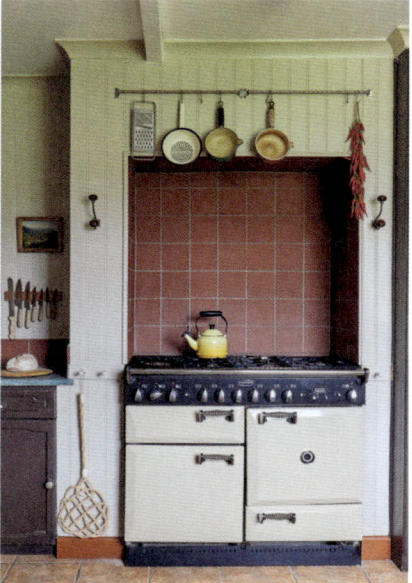

Connection

What happens when you're making a home far away from your homeland? Is it possible to capture the feeling of home in another town, country or even continent? How does leaving your home behind influence how you establish roots elsewhere?

The universal pride that many immigrants have in their homes is a real testament to the power of identity and the strength of our cultural heritage. This isn't unique to Caribbeans. My Irish friends and family share a similar joy in the seemingly trivial. They tell me of their grandparents' homes, in some of which still hang pictures of President John F. Kennedy on his visit to Ireland in 1963 (shortly before his assassination) – the proud fourth-generation emigrant-done-good, returning 'home' to a hero's welcome.

Ask a grandmother who has migrated from afar why she covers her table in plastic. Or an uncle why he continues to uphold the custom of removing shoes at the front door. There are habits that transcend and bind immigrants no matter which corner of the world they come from. I've observed these practices throughout my life in various homes around my local community and it is this connection that links us together, helping to shape a shared understanding of who we are and where we've been. In Camden, I'd often follow my nose, mesmerised by the many delicious and varying cuisines wafting from kitchen windows, with families often cooking the dishes of their homelands, following recipes they grew up eating or adapted – riffs depending on the local ingredients they could find. Caribbean, Bengali, Ghanaian, Polish, Brazilian – a seemingly endless mix of multiculturalism. Cooking is, of course, another prominent way to stay connected with our homeland, and this pride is a part of our identity that links us to generations gone by and the generations to come. That's the beauty of forever being an immigrant. No matter how long someone has been here, we each own a piece of our past and proudly carry it with us, remaining connected to the lands we came from and allowing future generations to share in its ritual too, no matter which corner of the world they travel to.

In our home, we've aimed to replicate a colour palette that is reminiscent of our Caribbean heritage. We've chosen warm hues, texture, natural materials and lots of plants. This hint of the Caribbean is not necessarily something that's immediately visible to visitors, but it has meaning for us as a family.

While it is always possible to go to a big furniture superstore and buy everything brand new, this can sometimes leave a home feeling a little soulless. I have found that creating a space that feels like it belongs to an individual, or a family, means reflecting who you are and where you are from. Family photographs can do this, as well as objects that have been passed down or collected from places that are meaningful to you. Not all of us have family heirlooms to inherit, but even a couple of shells collected from a beach can mean a lot if they have a story or a memory attached.

How can you find small ways – or big ones – for your home to signal where you have come from and what that means to you?

Our history through the objects in our home

For my Grenadian grandparents, the deep sense of pride they attach to material possessions is because to them, often enough, these signify success. This viewpoint has been really instilled in me as a third-generation immigrant, but the 'success' part is something I've tried to intentionally give less power to over the years. The importance of your home and the possessions you place there cannot be overstated. To the uninitiated, it might seem like there's a materialistic obsession with the accumulation of 'things' in an immigrant home, but it goes far beyond that (in my family's case, at least). Having more than just the basics to function represents security and, in turn, belonging to some degree, like the sacrifice of leaving home was worth it. When you have taken the radical step to leave behind your home of origin in search of better opportunities (some people with a spring in their step, others begrudgingly), creating a life with tangible markers of success can validate that decision.

If you have ever left home to move to another part of the world and were only able to take the items that fit into your suitcase or backpack with you, your connection to these items can become even stronger. These pieces become valuable, not just for their practical purposes but also as symbols of something much deeper: a link to your culture, and, if you've moved abroad, a shared history through generations of migration. It's why many might save a dinner set or cherished set of glassware for special occasions, or why others relish cleaning

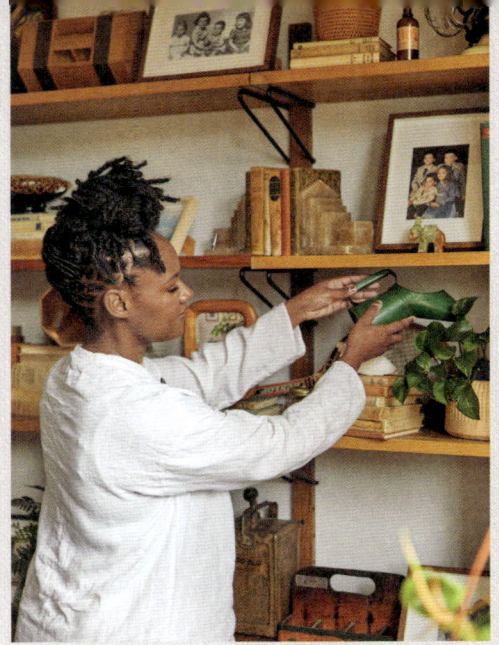
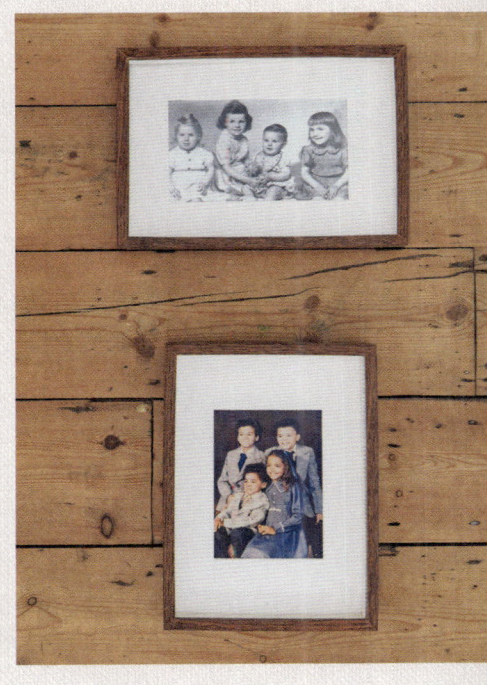
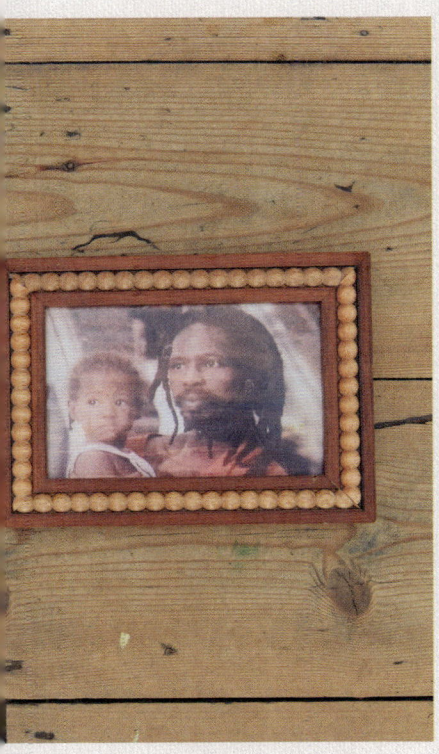
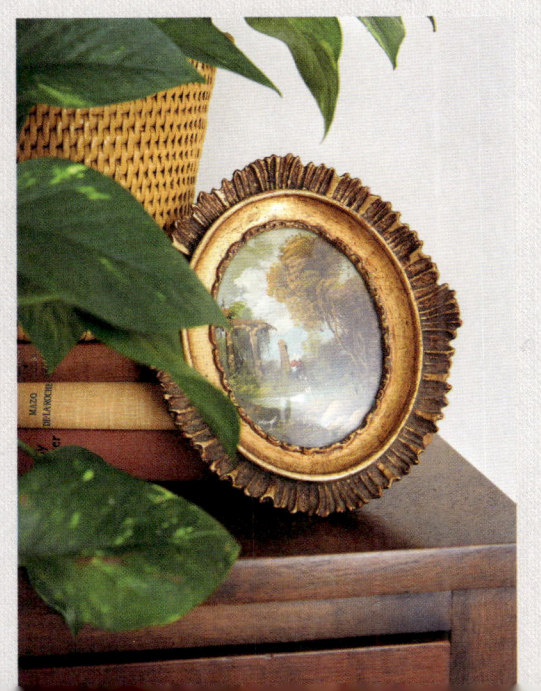

and caring for furniture that has been passed down through the family, or why a treasured book of photographs from days gone by might remind us of the people who came before us.

For many immigrants, the bonds formed with certain possessions once away from home are even deeper than before. By keeping them, we are reminded of our unique identity and are able to express our pride for where we come from. This is shared among many of those who have experienced similar journeys.

I believe a home should sing your personality to the rafters. Whatever your heritage, it's so important to tap into your own taste or style (you do have one, even if you're not sure of it just yet!) as well as your personal history. Your home is yours, not anyone else's, and you should feel that every room is full of meaning and memory. It doesn't matter if that meaning isn't exactly what's on the pages of the latest interiors magazine – home is a place that reflects you and evolves with you.

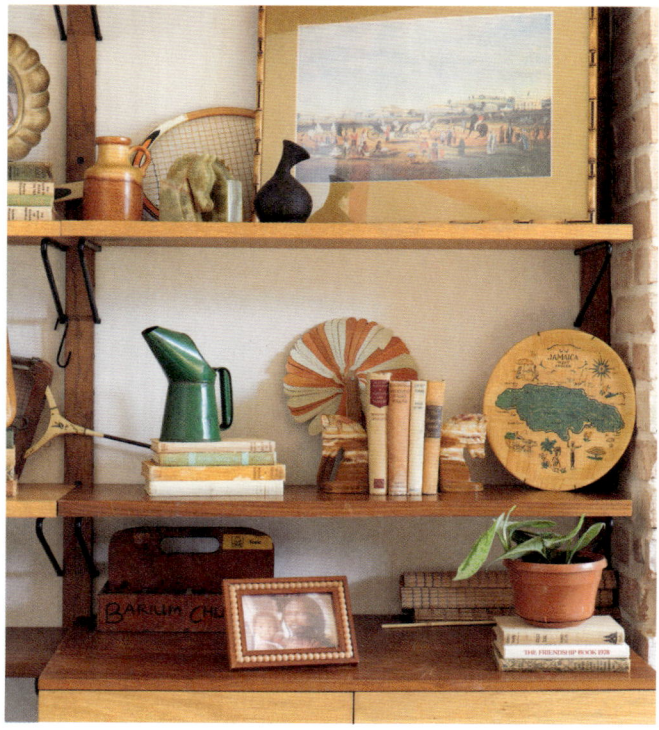

CHAPTER 2

WHO LIVES HERE?

When it comes to creating a home, 'Who lives here?' is the very first question we should ask ourselves. The minimalist home of a single architect is going to look very different to a home with three children under seven – neither is 'better', they will just have different priorities in making a space feel like home. There are many beautiful ways to set up home, and there really is no such thing as the perfect arrangement, only the perfect arrangement for you. Recent world events have been a catalyst for reshaping the way many of us are now approaching our home set-ups. With a rise in living costs at the forefront of our minds, people are having to be creative and re-evaluate ways to live that suit their age, stage of life and of course budget.

From living off-grid or in eco-villages to professional house-sitting – moving from home to home with no fixed abode – more and more people, are rethinking the types of home that work best for them, whether out of freedom or necessity. This shift to a broader approach to living has so many benefits, not least because it presents more choice and opportunity. Something else to be gained is more diverse communities, leading to fairer, kinder and more tolerant societies. Our lives can become so enriched by not just *proximity* to but also *integration with* other cultures. Even as a kid, I saw the value of growing up in and around key hubs for migration, with London being a home away from home for economic migrants as well as refugees.

Diverse home set-ups are composed of all sorts of variation, from age and ability to religious or political beliefs and many other factors. Think of an exchange in which an elderly person, who has come to need help with everyday tasks but wishes to live independently, opens their spare room to someone needing a low-/no-rent home, who wants to give their time and assistance to a person in need. Experiencing a different way of living comes unexpectedly for many, and though there can undoubtedly be challenges, there are upsides too.

Growing up in social housing, I knew there were people out there who owned their homes, but I had no idea that private renting existed. As far as I was concerned, there were those of us on the breadline and those who owned their homes outright. I don't think I even understood the concept of a mortgage until my late teens! An early foray into the working world very quickly amended that limited viewpoint. It was eye-opening to discover so many different ways of owning or occupying a home.

Asking 'Who lives here?' is, for me, the question that comes before any paint charts or furniture decisions. Before you can begin to decide how each room in your space will be used, you need to be clear on who lives there, and what their needs and priorities are, as well as who may be visiting your home either regularly or infrequently.

Who lives here every day?

We are a family of six, in a home with three bedrooms – and we feel so lucky to have this space to ourselves after living in much smaller flats previously. How many people live in your home? If there's more than two of you, write it down! I would suggest you also include people who spend a lot of time in your home, even if they don't live there, such as close family who visit regularly or a childminder who is often at your home. The key is to understand how many people are in your space and how they might be using it (and factor in any pets if you have them). Ask yourself what the different needs and priorities of those people might be within the home.

For example, here's our family:

- **Africa:** working from home 3 days a week, commuting to London 1 day a week, making family lunches, creating content for online platforms
- **J:** working outside the home 5 days a week, gardening, DIY projects, cooking evening meals for family

- **Oldest child:** at school 5 days a week, needs space for homework, loves dancing so needs lots of room to move, happiest outdoors
- **Second child:** at school 5 days a week, has autism and needs a quiet space to retreat to when necessary, loves crafting and being outside
- **Third child:** at school 5 days a week, total whirlwind who wants to be near everyone, doesn't like being confined to one space, loves being in the garden
- **Youngest child:** not yet at nursery, needs a dedicated space near my desk to play safely while I'm working from home

Your priorities will look very different, I am sure, and priorities for each family member or home sharer (and even just for yourself if you live alone) will change and evolve. So, this is an exercise you can come back to regularly, to ensure that your home continues to reflect who you are as your circumstances change.

One decision we made with our priorities in mind worked out really well for us. Although we had enough space to put our children into two bedrooms, when we moved here we chose to have our then three children sharing one bedroom. This decision allowed us to have a spare room for family visitors, which was a big priority for us when we moved out of London. And because the bedroom became a dedicated place for sleeping, we created a separate playroom in a little side room downstairs.

In the first year they shared the room as a trio, I'd often find, in the middle of the night, they would have pushed all their beds together, having, in their sleep, abandoned the idea of their 'own' beds. Our priorities around sleeping arrangements changed after our fourth and final child was born, but at the time it was an arrangement that really worked for us all.

With social media full of imagery of sprawling individual bedrooms for each child, it would be easy to feel like we should have prioritised this for our own children, especially as we moved to a bigger home. But it's important to have the confidence to make your own decisions. No one else lives in your home but you!

Multigenerational living

Multiple generations living under one roof is nothing new and it is much more common outside of Europe. Inhabiting one home may be a mix of parents, grandparents, aunts and uncles, siblings and children of all ages – each individual with their own needs and desires for their environment. My maternal grandma lives in a cul-de-sac in West Yorkshire, an area that is densely populated by a well-established and thriving Pakistani community. With each passing school holiday, I'd make a new temporary best friend and be welcomed into their family for the next few weeks. We shared stories over shared meals – I saw nothing unique about the elderly matriarchs of the family preparing our meals because I was spending time with my own grandma who was doing the same. Unlike me, though, my friends wouldn't be returning home after the summer – their permanent home set-ups included three generations and it all seemed to work seamlessly.

Part of the reason we spent the six-week school holidays at my grandma's was to allow my mum the opportunity to work while we were off school. Throughout our childhood, she worked night shifts for UPS, ran a vintage stall on Portobello Road, sold wares at craft sales and worked as a childminder. Living 250 miles away from her parents and siblings meant that there wasn't the everyday backup she'd have had if she'd stayed local. One of the obvious appeals of multigenerational living is the care aspect, whether that's extra help with childcare or support for those who are ill, injured, elderly or living with a disability.

Multigenerational households present new challenges but also opportunities to build communities of care and understanding between generations. In these dwellings, each generation can find ways to support one another without compromising on the quality of life they seek. With thoughtful consideration, home (ideally) becomes a place where all are welcomed, valued and able to make meaningful connections with one another.

Again, this is a question of establishing priorities for each member of the household, and this can be particularly challenging if, for example, one member of the family is moving into an already established home. For everyone to feel comfortable and to have a sense of belonging, changes may need to be made. Similarly, there will likely need to be some terms agreed,

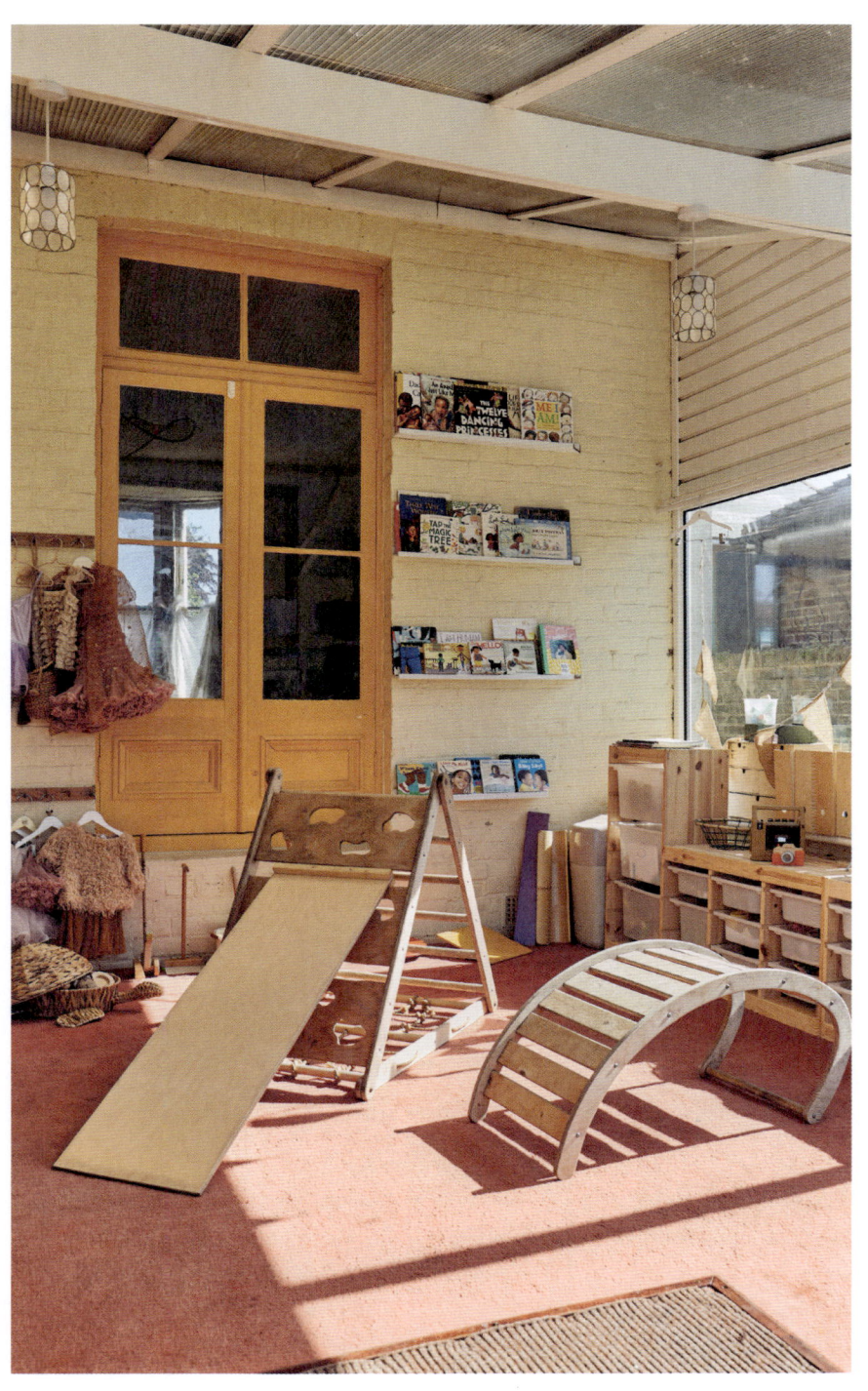

such as regarding privacy: are all parts of the home free-range for each family member? Agreeing on expectations and boundaries will be an important initial step towards harmonious living, and it will likely take a little while to get into a rhythm that works for all.

The kitchen is often a bone of contention in multigenerational homes, with very different ideas about when and how to cook and eat, so this can be a good place to start when it comes to establishing some shared ground rules. It can be helpful to remember that for older people, cooking may be how they demonstrate their love and their 'usefulness'. Finding opportunities for this cooking-as-love to be welcomed can be a joyful experience for all the generations.

Learning from the wisdom of those who have been around longer is a privilege that so many of us miss out on, particularly those of us living in economically wealthier countries where there has been a steady decline in multigenerational living. Though I am not fortunate enough to live with, or even near, my mother or grandmothers, their influence in my life is ever-present (primarily now, thanks to the joys of video calls!).

Communal living

When I first started thinking about communal living, I thought of flatshares, but that word tends to conjure up a very specific idea of young people who have only recently moved out of the family home. These days, though, it's not just young professionals at the start of their working lives who may find the prospect of renting a private flatshare appealing. In recent years, there's been a huge increase in people in their fifties and over doing the same, as well as an increase in shared living situations like 'mommunes' where single mothers and their children live together, pooling resources, time and childcare. In addition to the fact that living communally is much cheaper than living solo (with rent and bills split between co-residents), this set-up offers a unique opportunity to meet and collaborate with like-minded individuals from diverse backgrounds. Many people living in these types of accommodation have gone on to forge lasting bonds that will serve them for years to come and that type of camaraderie counts for a lot, especially for today's younger, more digitally inclined generation, many of whom have had

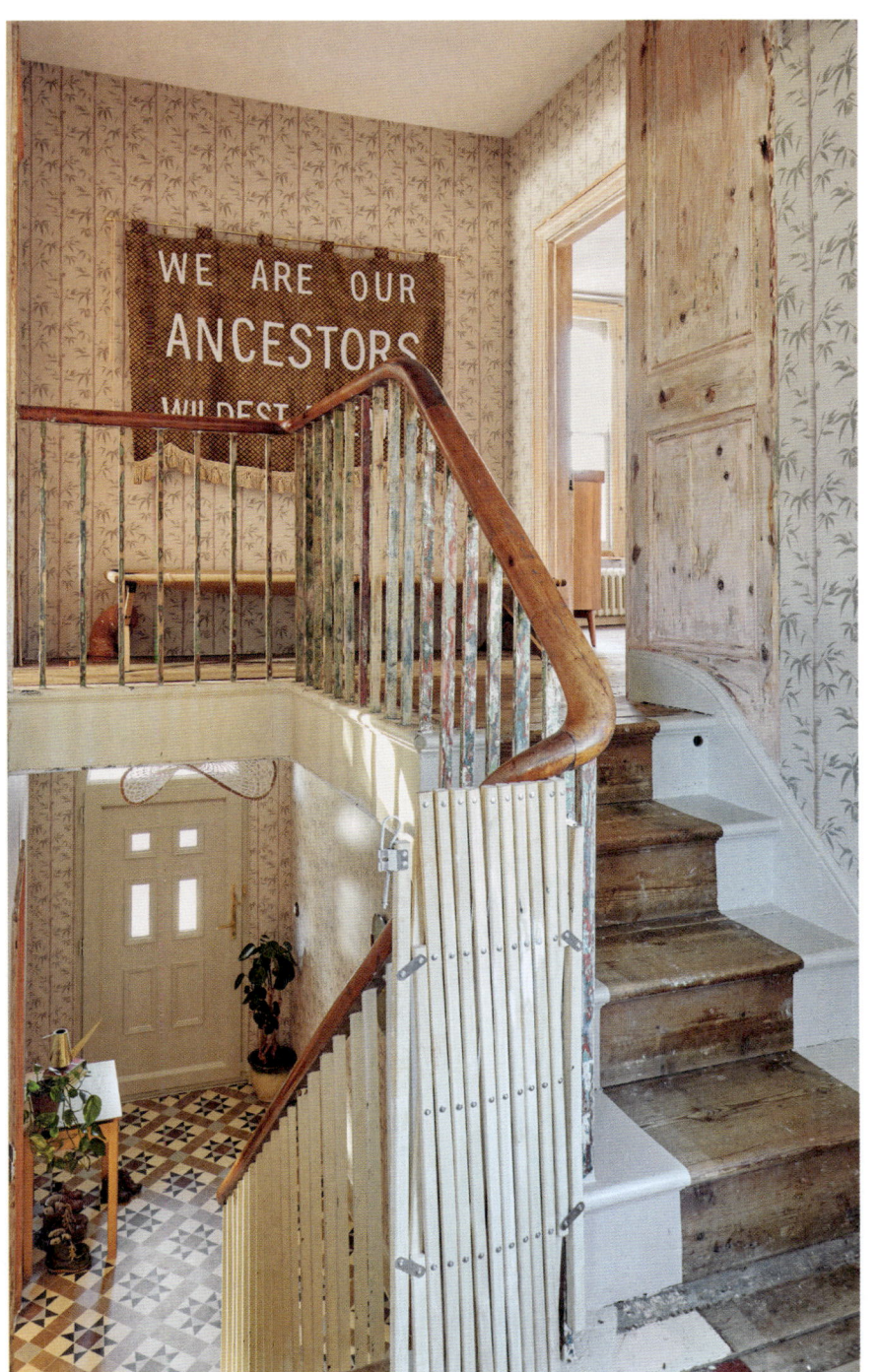

as much experience forging friendships online as they have in person.

On the face of it, flatshares provide a mutually beneficial habitat for adults trying to navigate life; suddenly they are no longer alone and isolated but instead part of a new-found community (if they're fortunate enough to find a harmonious flatshare). As chaotic as my four years living in a flatshare was, it provided me with an invaluable affordable opportunity to start life on my own terms. On a practical level, a flatshare can grant stability and support both financially and emotionally, as well as allowing flatmates to pool knowledge and resources, such as cooking skills or DIY techniques (if they're blessed with them!). Sharing with others from different walks of life with varying priorities taught me fierce negotiating skills. It taught me patience and, over time, restraint (sometimes!).

When it comes to negotiating in communal living, again it is a good idea to talk openly about priorities. Work out not just individual priorities but shared ones too, and don't be afraid to ask questions upfront. After all, there is no point in being upset that everyone in your new flatshare eats meat if living in a vegan household is a core value for you. Know yourself and be curious about understanding the priorities of those you live with.

Questions to ask yourself, and others, before you move into a shared living space:

- Is there/do you need a shared communal space or does everyone just have their own bedroom?
- What time do you get up most days?
- What time do you want to go to bed?
- Are you a light sleeper?
- Do you have/want pets?
- How are bills split and paid?
- What do you consider 'noisy' or 'quiet'? (It is surprising how much these definitions differ between individuals.)
- How tidy are you? And what does tidy mean to you?
- Can we afford a cleaner? (If you can, this is often a solution to any issues over who cleans what and how often.)
- What does privacy mean to you?

No matter how carefully you choose your flatshare, things can go wrong. From my own experience I know how emotionally turbulent life can be when you feel unsafe in your own home. Ultimately, knowing your priorities and trusting yourself means knowing when it is time to remove yourself from a situation that isn't likely to get better.

Living alone

Living alone can be a great privilege. It's increasingly expensive and challenging to have a place of your own as a single person and to manage everything by yourself, but when I chose to move into my one-bedroom flat I was very fortunate to have a slightly less-than-market-rate rent that, despite being a stretch, still allowed me to have a space that was mine alone.

You might think that making decisions about your living space is very easy if you don't have to consider anyone else's opinion, and I admit I loved the freedom when I had my own place. I've noted though that there can be a tendency for some people living alone to regard their space as temporary, or for them to think, 'It's only me so I can tolerate this wonky shelf/stained ceiling/broken door handle'. Even if you consider this solo arrangement to be temporary, your home is your home, and it should still be a place that brings you joy and security. It is emotionally draining to be in a home where you feel you're putting up with things you don't like – you deserve to be in a place that affirms you, no matter what.

In my own experience, I have found that very often we go for the cheap, quick, temporary fix – e.g. a flatpack bookshelf – for reasons of time and money, telling ourselves that at some point we'll upgrade to something better. And then ten or even twenty years later that flatpack bookshelf we never particularly liked is still there. As you'll see later in the book, it is worth taking the time and effort to source the things we truly love and will treasure for years to come.

For many of us, living alone happens due to a change of circumstance, perhaps a break-up, a fresh start after the children have left home or a move to a different city. And a change of circumstance might also mean a change of priorities. So, even when you don't have to consider other people's opinions about your living space, it's important to be clear on your personal priorities about your home – especially if they may have changed.

Consider some of the following questions:

- **What is the primary feeling you want to have in your home?** Would it be pristine and monastic/the party flat/a cosy sanctuary from the world?
- **How will you achieve this?** For example, if 'comfort' is your primary aim, that's about more than just cushions – really dig into what comfort means to you.
- **How long do you plan to live here?** E.g. are you going to really invest in this space, or will your amendments be things you can easily take with you to a new home?
- **Do you enjoy entertaining?** If so, how can you create a space to do that?
- **Will family/friends stay over, and if so, how will you accommodate them?** For instance, a sofa bed may be a good investment in a space with only one bedroom.
- **How can you make a temporary arrangement feel more like home?** If you're unable to change the landlord's furniture or the overall décor, think of the small, personal objects that remind you of who you are, those you love and what your values are.

Start where you are

Much of this book focuses on the practical ways we can invest in our spaces. I think that much of what holds people back from going ahead with the tweaks and changes that would help them really relish their homes is this notion that until we land 'the one', we shouldn't be investing in our spaces at all. Glossy interiors magazines and social media play a part in subliminally coaching us that if we don't yet have a kitchen island or a sleek boiling water tap then we haven't got our priorities right. Personally, I think that's an industry tactic used to hook the attention of those of us 'without'. Unattainable ambition and the despair it can breed are a somewhat deadly combo, and it's my mission to free us all from that feeling that 'home' is something in the future rather than the here and now.

Once again, every living arrangement is temporary. That is why it's so important for 'home' to be something we carry inside us wherever we are. It is never the boiling water tap or the kitchen island, and having those certainly doesn't guarantee happiness.

I want to encourage you to build a home you love right here, right now. Don't limit yourself because you're in a flatshare or social housing or certain that this isn't your 'forever home'. Approach each and every domestic set-up you occupy as one that you deserve to enjoy, one that should nourish you and build you up. No matter your living situation or your financial resources, it is possible to maximise your surroundings and create a home that provides understanding, security and comfort to everyone involved.

While your particular set-up may require a little more ingenuity than some others, and you might need to think outside of the box – you should be meeting every home exactly where you are and building on it. After all, home extends far beyond its physical boundaries – it's not just a building; it is a state of mind. Let's make sure we all have the opportunity to find our own version of joy and peace at home.

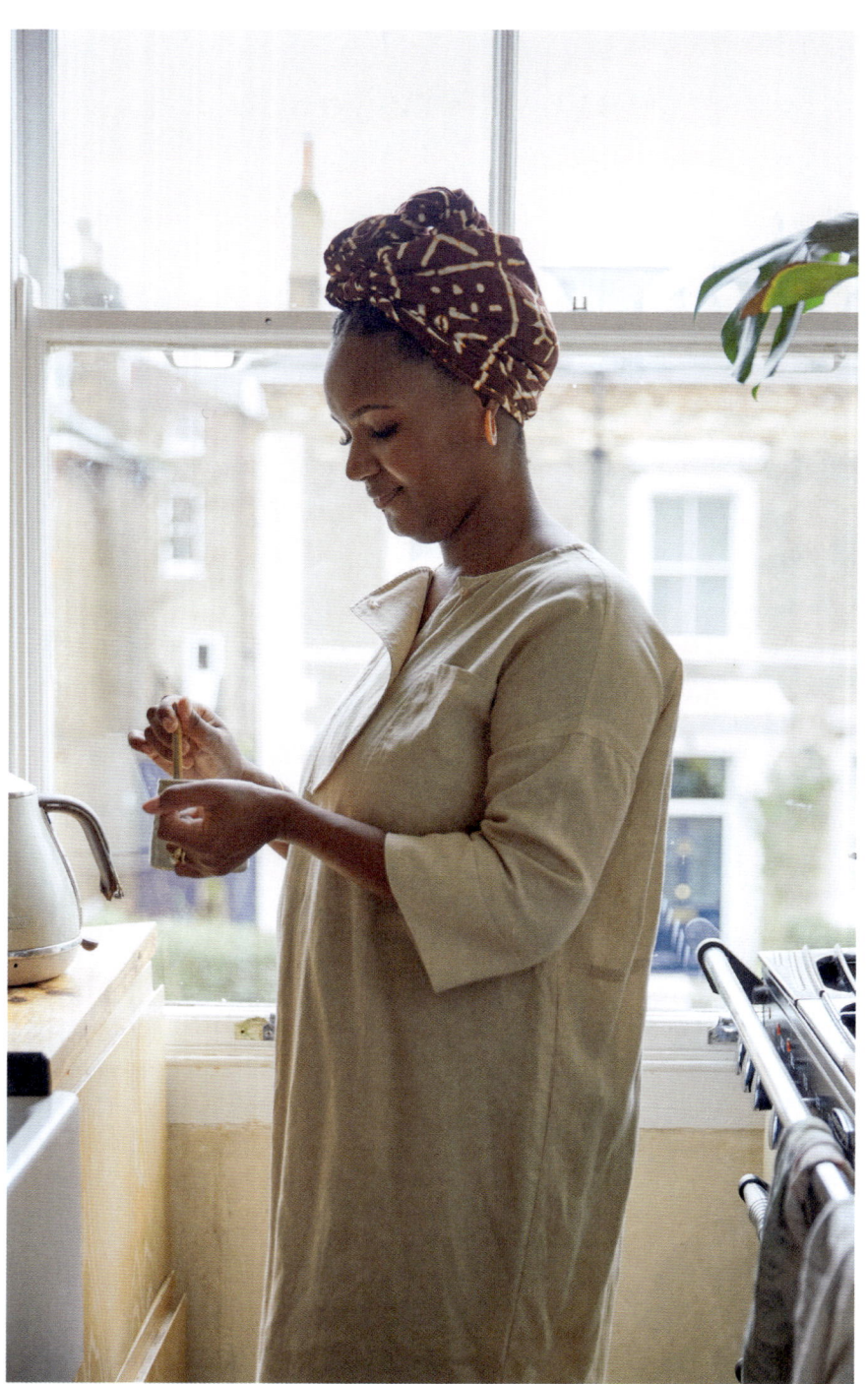

Rental renovations

In the UK, where my family lives, renting is often seen as inferior to owning a home and as a temporary arrangement that you will move on from as soon as possible. This is thankfully not the case everywhere. In many parts of Europe, for example, long-term or even lifelong rental is commonplace and the goal (or obsession) of home ownership doesn't exist in the same way as it does here. In countries where renting is more entrenched in the culture and isn't necessarily as linked to status or income as it can be in the UK, tenants enjoy better rights and protection under the law. This means that in some parts of the world, it is normal for renters to invest more in their spaces, to make them feel like home, sometimes even installing kitchens – a bit like J and I did in our maisonette.

Some people feel it is perverse to put in much effort unless you own the property, but I just can't get on board with this view. I watched my mother graft to transform near-derelict homes, restoring them to their former glory, and it was those transformations that inspired my husband and I to invest in our own rental spaces over the years and ensure they reached their full potential. As my social media platforms grew, we amassed a lot of criticism for investing in rental spaces as they didn't 'belong' to us – but the way that we saw it was, we didn't expect to ever live in a home that 'truly' belonged to us so why shouldn't we make the most of where we were?

I would encourage you, even as a renter, to consider how you might make a space feel more like your home. If you've established your priorities as we've detailed earlier in this chapter then it will hopefully be clearer to you what that home would feel like, whether it's more space for family gatherings, or more private space to be alone, or a bathroom that feels like a retreat from the world.

If you're renting from a private landlord in the UK, it's essential that you get their permission (in writing) before making any changes. Many contracts even ban you from putting up artwork on the walls, particularly if you're screwing in picture hooks or similar. I find this outrageous – that landlords are happy to take rental payments but unhappy that a tenant may be so bold as to make it feel like a proper home, complete with their favourite pictures on the walls and trinkets on shelves. That's not to say every landlord is of this opinion, of course, but always check first (and get their permission in writing, preferably). Similarly, if you are moving into a place that is rather worse for wear and you feel motivated to improve it (whether that's painting or sanding floors), it's always worth trying to negotiate lower costs with the landlord to compensate you for these improvements – it may not lead anywhere but it's worth a try. It's in everyone's interest – landlord's and tenant's – to create and maintain a lovely home.

Even though we have long since moved on, I'm really proud of the homes that we created in our rental spaces. In many ways, making those changes felt like a way of finally owning something and so we approached each restorative task with real vigour. From the warm and hearty micro-kitchen, reminiscent of a worn, well-loved Sicilian scullery, to the boldly serene bathroom that I designed to glamorise even the most mundane task of brushing our teeth, we created homes that were little slices of 'us' wherever we went. While they weren't technically ours, they were our homes, nonetheless. As we've settled into our newest home, I'm reminded of the beauty that can be found in any space, no matter how temporary or permanent it may be.

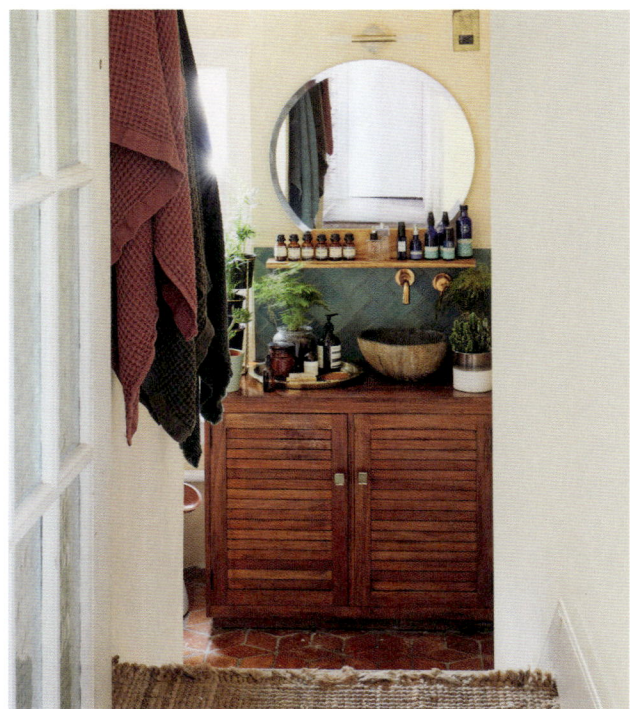

CHAPTER 3

WHO WORKS HERE?

If you're part of the many millions who work from home, either on a hybrid or daily basis, then welcome to the club. Even before the pandemic changed our working patterns, there had been a well-documented rise in the number of workers based at home for all or part of the week. Home was once the place we went to after work – separate and distinct from our offices, retail spaces and other workplaces. Now it is common for work to be something we do regularly from within the domestic space.

This has all meant that our homes have had to adapt accordingly, working harder than ever to accommodate living and working. This chapter is primarily for those of us who can work remotely fairly easily. I recognise that there are many millions of workers propping up economies worldwide, whether tradespeople, retail staff, hospitality workers, those in healthcare or education and many more, who likely do not have the luxury of this choice.

At the time of writing this book, my two younger children, aged three and one, are home with me while I work, and I'm looking forward to my three-year-old shortly starting pre-school. While I work during the day and attend online meetings, unfortunately it often isn't until the kids are in bed that I feel like my productive work truly starts. This adds a whole other stressor on our home, as it functions (not always harmoniously!) as a sort of co-working nursery space by day!

In our home set-up, we don't have a separate study or even a proper work desk. So, what I've done is think carefully about how I can make the space we do have work hard for our needs. Throughout this chapter, I'll be posing questions that encourage you to think about your daily requirements at a micro level, so that your space can best support your wellbeing and productivity, while still feeling like home.

A change in rhythm

I've been mostly working from home for several years now and it still feels like a luxury. The thought of not having to rush bleary-eyed each morning into one of my retail roles often makes me pinch myself – not because I didn't enjoy aspects of those jobs, but rather because of the immense strain that commuting put on our family dynamic. Before our big move to the coast, J and I both worked in retail with ever-changing schedules and salaries that were absorbed by day care and wraparound childcare costs. I'd find myself cycling one daughter between my workplace and the childminder or nursery (while also relying on my sisters for back-up care), while my husband dropped off another. No matter how much we tried to plan, it felt like we were always on the back foot.

Like many, for me, working from home was a much-needed change of pace. Of course, there's also a big appeal in saving time and money on a commute, especially for those at the mercy of traffic jams, train cancellations or the stress of trying to fit in pre-work commitments, like dropping off kids to nursery or school. For some, a new approach to working shone some unexpected benefits too. And it wasn't all about those basic joys, like skipping an early morning shower (farewell face-to-face meetings), squeezing in some exercise or catching forty winks over lunchtime; for those who find workplaces overwhelming or exhausting, carving out a space at home became a game changer. Many of us – and I'm one of them – carry out our best work, generate our most creative ideas and enter our uninterrupted flow state in the quiet of our own environment. Ask any work-from-home introvert if they miss in-person brainstorming sessions and you'll likely be met with an emphatic no! At last, an opportunity to work efficiently, stick to the allotted hours we're paid for and seek some balance between our work and our personal lives.

If your working pattern has changed in recent years, how have you adapted? Have you figured out which type of environment you are most fruitful in? For example, do you enjoy the camaraderie of people around, or music playing, or do you require silence? When creating a work-from-home environment, *how* you prefer to work is such an important consideration.

I've explored some of the positives that certain people (read: me) find when working in a more solitary environment, but what if you thrive on the buzz of a busy office, how can you bring some of this into your home working? It's not only some extroverts who struggle to work from home; many who thought they'd love it have found the day long, and sometimes felt confined or secluded, which is conducive to neither productivity nor wellbeing. There are many clever ways involving tech that help combat work isolation: some people log on to a team video call, not to hold a meeting, just simply to feel like they're working alongside colleagues. Others start the day doing something sociable like a group exercise or even a chatty online call with a friend or team member. I've heard of others working alongside family members, flatmates or friends who work in different jobs to facilitate some companionship.

I invite you to ask yourself two key questions:
How do you like to work?
How do you *need* to work?

So, how do you like to work, when you have the choice? Does the nature of your job allow you to share a space with other members of your home if needed, or ideally do you need total privacy? Does it allow a bit of both? And what is essential for your working set-up? Knowing your preferences and your needs, both in terms of what your job requires, but also how your personality is best supported, will help lay the groundwork for a more functional environment.

Africa WFH likes	Africa WFH needs
Roaming with laptop throughout the day	*Strong Wi-Fi and booster*
Working at home	*To commute to London 1 day a week*
Being adaptable around the children	*Some help with childcare*
Curating content	*An aesthetic background for video calls*

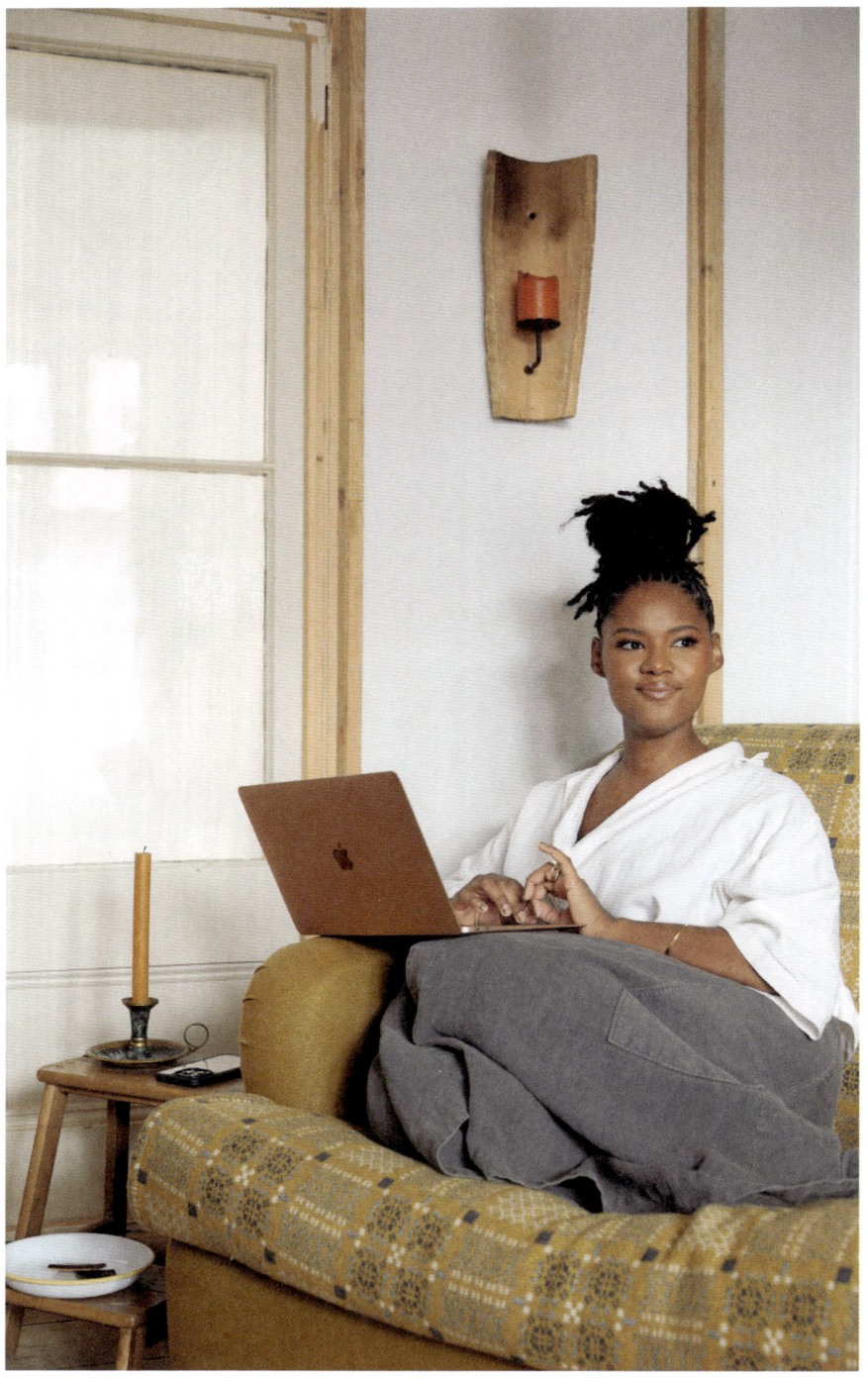

Your situation will be different to mine, but asking yourself these two questions – in as much detail as I have outlined here – will establish a starting point for making your own blend of work and home feel more unified.

Creating a multifunctional home

No doubt you've watched those viral videos of cute kids disturbing their parents' work video calls, or heard about disastrous times people have inadvertently left their computer cameras on, showing them in full PJ mode or worse! It's been a learning curve to say the least. As we've emerged from the eye of the pandemic, blinking into the light, many of us are re-evaluating our working habits yet again. Before you get started designing (or re-designing) your space to have a more productive and comfortable area to work from, consider these other key factors.

Home as meeting background

I've given a lot of advice so far on how much your home needs to reflect you and no one else, and I stand by this. However, our homes have never been so visible to our colleagues and peers as they are in the background of video calls. Even a few years ago, only your closest work friends would have been familiar with the layout of your living space. Now, it's common for your boss to know the colour of your sofa and the pattern on your curtains, all through online meetings. It's always possible to blur out your background on these calls but, in my experience, this can look like you're hiding something (e.g. you're secretly calling in to work from the Bahamas rather than your home).

Just as we dress up for interviews or key meetings, I think it's worth giving some thought to what our digital backgrounds might indicate to others, as well as how we like to present ourselves professionally. In one of my earliest meetings about this book, my agent and editor complimented the styling of the room they could see behind me. I ended up admitting that the room itself was full of plaster dust and decorating sheets, but because the meeting was about a book on creating a home you love, I had spent some time curating a corner of the room with a plant and a few key pieces of furniture to create a look I felt best represented me and the book I wanted to write.

It's obviously not practical to rearrange the furniture for every online meeting you have, so it can be worth thinking in advance about what message you want your home to convey for you in these situations. You might choose a blank wall if you prefer to give nothing away, though this can be quite stark. A bedroom is usually best avoided if possible. Greenery offers a softening effect to a background, and plants are easy to move if you want to make adjustments. A bookcase can be great, though do check titles to avoid the mistake of a friend of a friend who ran a whole meeting with a book called *Erotic Vagrancy* poised right above her head.

When it comes to my own background for work calls, I like to offer an encapsulation of my home (and by extension my Instagram feed), in one tiny frame. So, rather than finding a plain background, I'm trying to include signature colours, plants, a statement vintage piece and perhaps a piece of artwork too. Bear in mind that I am a creative, working alongside other creatives, and what you want to convey may be different.

Finally, when it comes to online meetings, don't neglect lighting. A ring light on a tripod is an inexpensive investment if you spend a lot of time meeting people on screen. If you'd prefer not to buy specific lighting equipment, I'd suggest avoiding harsh overhead lights (which make everyone look terrible), as well as sitting by a window which lets in some natural light.

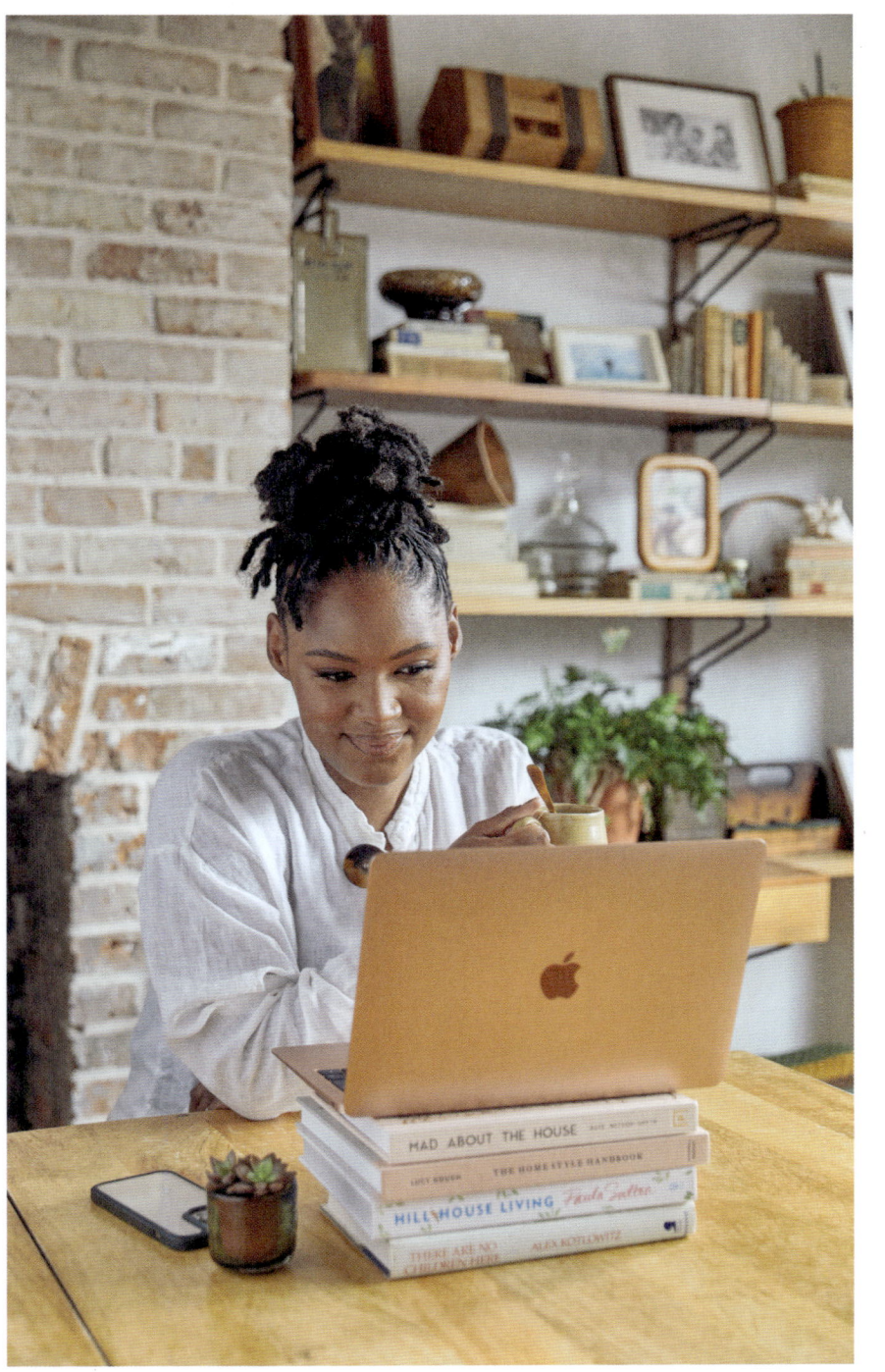

A functional space

Like anywhere in your home, creating a workspace is about setting out the environment(s) you want to be in, which allows you to focus and flourish. This will look different for everyone, and you will have to work with what you've got. Very few of us have the space for a home office that isn't also functioning as a spare room, a children's playroom, a clothes-drying space or similar.

If you're expecting me to say I have a pristine, calming separate home study or office pod complete with standing desk and a drinks fridge, close the book now! When my three- and one-year-olds aren't napping, I tend to nestle myself on an with my laptop propped precariously and that spot gives me a great vantage point of their play space, as we have a glazed door divider. As soon as they nap, I take my work to the dining table for a bit of productive distinction – making sure the TV and any other distractions are off. I personally enjoy the fluidity of having a somewhat roaming workspace as it works best for my neurodivergent mind. In the summer months, I might plonk myself in the garden, and from April onwards you will usually find me in the greenhouse at various points in the day – anything for an early boost of vitamin D!

While I have my wants and needs outlined above, I have also worked out my non-negotiables when it comes to working away from the office. These are much more basic than the likes and needs outlined above and serve as a reminder that it is still possible to work just fine in situations where I don't have my set-up exactly as I love it.

Non-negotiables for WFH

- Laptop
- Wi-Fi
- Comfortable chair
- Warmth (I can't work in a cold space!)
- Children occupied/distracted

Clear clutter

This is what makes the biggest difference to my state of mind when working from home, because spaces that are free of clutter allow more fluidity, especially if, like me, you like to feel untethered to one spot for the whole working day. It's not easy to feel productive or inspired when your desk is overlooking a pile of washing that needs putting away, so try to carve out a few minutes of clearing up before work starts, even if it's just your immediate surroundings. Some people find that their home is never cleaner than when they work from home because of all the domestic distractions – a small win, perhaps!

Get comfortable

You might balk at my confession of working from an armchair but because I move about so often supervising my little ones, I actually find it quite cosy and sustaining being there for a time. What's important is that you find what works for you. Think about what furniture or furnishings you'll need to support you while you work.

Here are some of the fundamentals:

- A properly supportive chair and footrest (if you work for a company or organisation, you may be able to bring your office chair home or request allocation in the budget to purchase a dedicated one).

- Consider a standing desk if you are trying to reduce the amount of time you spend sitting in a chair (again, some employers might sponsor or contribute to one of these). Similarly, some people find sitting on the floor a good option because it encourages movement – you will adjust your position more throughout the day than if you're on a chair. Try sitting crossed-legged or kneeling, or a combination of both (a cushion or yoga block can help make this comfier) for some of the day.

- Think about how your set-up will potentially support (or hinder) your comfort. For example, if working at a computer, do you have an effective monitor (rather than just a laptop screen) and separate mouse and keyboard? If you take a lot of calls, will a headset make this more convenient? I have a relatively inexpensive bendy contraption that raises my laptop to eye level that I highly recommend, particularly if you are working from a surface not quite at standard desk height. See modifications like these as investments in your wellbeing as well as your productivity.

Wall-mounted desk and vertical storage

When space is at a real premium in your home, having a desk you can fold away when you finish working can be helpful. You could mount it either at desk height or higher if a standing desk is your thing. Similarly, wall storage for materials or stationery will help keep your desk clear, aiding your focus. Which of these can be used as more than one thing, such as a side table becoming the desk. Consider what you already have too, e.g. a dining chair becoming a sewing chair.

Alcove/below-stairs desk

If space is at a premium in your home, it can help to think creatively about underused areas. Not to go all Harry Potter on you, but is there a workspace that can be carved out under the stairs? Or an alcove in which you might fit a small desk? A landing or cupboard, however small, which might allow you to create a workspace?

Supplies on the go

Do you need to bring things in and out of the office, like a laptop, paper documents or any other materials? How can you do that efficiently? For example, do you have a bag or basket (with straps) that your supplies can be stored in when work ends for the day (perhaps one that blends well with the décor of your home), that's also suitable for transporting into the office? Knowing where your charger is will mean you won't be scrambling round your home in a panic as you try to get out of the door on one of your office days. These little things that make life simpler can go a long way.

Soak up natural light

If your space allows, try to work beside a window or even outside. If not, or when it's gloomy outside, use lamps rather than overhead lights to give a warm, relaxed feel. There are an increasing number of portable battery-powered lamps available if your home suffers from a lack of sockets.

Incorporate greenery

Plants are a must for me when it comes to a workspace and I like to hang them in various corners. There have been several studies showing the benefits of greenery on your state of mind, in both your home and your work environment. I love rubber plants, monstera, pothos and succulents (you can get teeny succulents to sit next to your laptop if you are really tight on space).

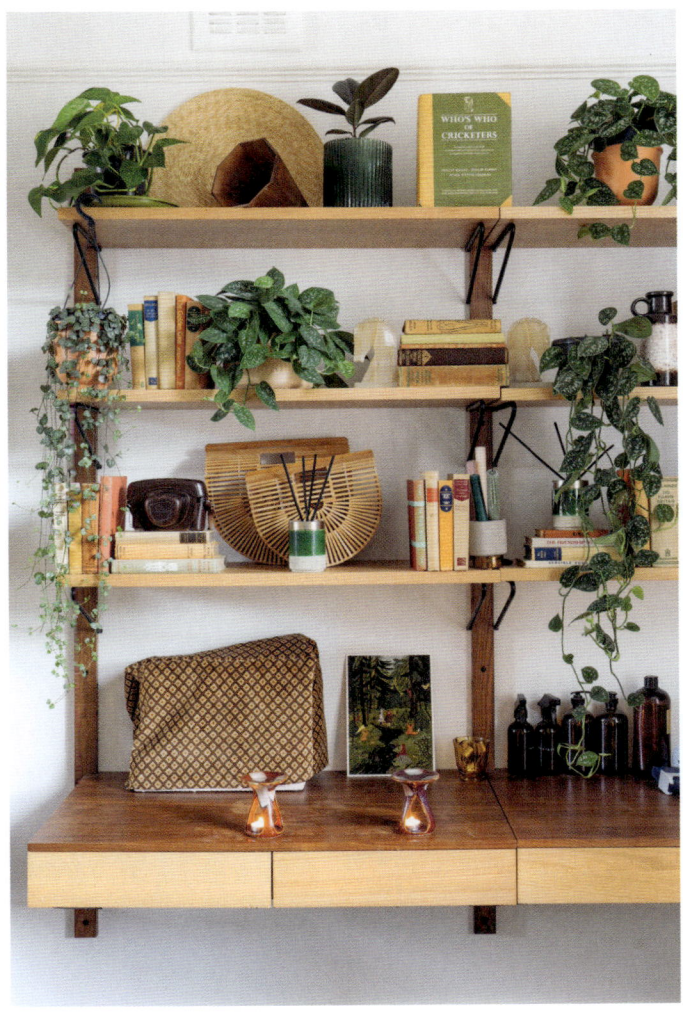

Ensuring home feels like home (even when you work there)

For many of us, work is not something we find easy to switch off from. It infiltrates our lives, much more than previous generations', in that we are always contactable, usually able (and often expected) to check in remotely and it can be hard to maintain boundaries – especially if you have a boss who likes to play fast and loose with them. Since most of us don't have the luxury of separate workspaces at home, we need to make a concerted effort to prioritise our sanctuary of home, first and foremost.

Cohesion

If you are creating a work-from-home area, I'd suggest, where possible, ensuring it blends in with the rest of your décor, so that any work set-up doesn't look too out of place. In our home, we tend to opt for natural materials, such as our lovely old mango wood dining table, which is durable enough for eating on and doubles as a WFH desk and a craft space for the kids.

Something that will naturally encourage cohesion is finding new uses for pieces already in your home: what furniture do you already have that can be integrated into your working set-up?

If you do need to bring in dedicated items, such as a sturdy office chair (let's face it, not the most beautiful of items, but very practical), think of how you might customise it to make it more 'you', such as draping some fabric over it, giving it a nice cover or even having a go at making one yourself.

Keep your physical workspace minimal

Unless you are happy being reminded of work out of hours (which for many triggers work anxiety), try to avoid having physical reminders, like wall charts or paperwork out all the time. Even the most disciplined and boundaried person finds their mind drawn back to work when they are surrounded by physical reminders.

Tidy up

Where possible, pack your work materials away, including a laptop if you have one, once work is complete (keeping a basket, shelf or drawer free for this exact purpose will make it easier to do). Other options might be to curtain-off your space or use room divider for a similar effect. And if you have small children or young pets, it's safest to keep important work materials well out of reach.

Have one space for work

This wouldn't work for me as I like to move around with my laptop, but some people find having one place at home that represents 'work' to them helps them get into that headspace faster when they sit down to start the day. If this works for you, a dedicated workspace can also help prevent that feeling of work creeping into every part of your home.

Maintain boundaries

Work can too easily become an identity-marker – a way that other people judge us and we judge ourselves. So many of us define ourselves through our work, linking our value to our job. When we become consumed by our work (even if it's the headspace it takes up rather than the hours we're actually working), it leaves less time in our lives for the people and things we love. So, maintaining boundaries at home, when we have actively brought our work into it, has never been more important.

For example, have an ironclad rule about when work is over, such as: the laptop goes away at 7pm, or, I don't look at my work phone between 9pm and 8am. Alternatively, if you, like me, enjoy working from different places in your home, try to have at least one place that you never work from, which represents total rest and a break from work – this could be your sofa, and it definitely should include your bedroom.

I also have separate laptops for work and personal use, and that distinction is very important for ensuring separation between the two.

You can also set yourself some habits to mark the distinction between home and work, such as going for a walk before your working day starts, or after it ends. If you have school-age children, this boundary is often created for you by having to pick them up from school.

CHAPTER 4

THE PERFECT HOME DOES NOT EXIST

Have we ever asked so much of our homes? With so many of us working from home for at least part of the week, and trying to squeeze in hobbies, raise children and host family members while tackling the daily grind of cooking, chores and keeping on top of life admin – it's quite the ask for *any* home to deliver what modern life demands. There's nothing like burning the homestead candle at both ends to bring the flaws of our home to light – like the ragged edge of a chipped doorway that snags on your clothes every time you pass it. When you spend a lot of time at home, these shortcomings are even harder to ignore.

Whatever your financial situation, there is always going to be some compromise with your home and/or its location. You might crave more space, a better layout, more natural light or a garden, and feel resentment for these perceived deficiencies. It can be a hard pill to swallow, particularly if you're paying handsomely to reside in a home or area which you feel misses the mark, working your fingers to the bone just to live in a home that you may not even like that much. There is so much inequality around housing, causing frustration for those who can't and may never get on the property ladder, and for those of us who are on it, rising mortgage rates and the rising cost of living threatens to keep us in compromising spaces and living situations for much longer than intended.

We are hardwired to look for faults in our surroundings, which means a tendency to focus on them over the positives. In practice, this means we might have a 'grass is always greener' mindset or hold on to the idea of a 'perfect' home, always striving for the next goal. In reality, there is no perfect home because there are always compromises, and further to this, what suits us now may not further down the line as our needs change.

The problem with striving for perfection when creating a home is that it will actually hold you back: an impossibly high standard will always make you feel lacking. This doesn't mean you can't be ambitious for yourself and your home – far from it – and I hope this book shows just that! But the quest for perfection is often fuelled by attempts to show others a version of ourselves that isn't authentic, and so it can get in the way of living in a home that nurtures and comforts us.

Perfectionism comes in many guises, and in this chapter, we will look at some of the ways it can insidiously creep into our everyday lives and erode our perception of our homes. Whether your current home is yours for a few weeks or years, I hope the advice here helps you keep perspective. Before you get stuck into the more practical advice in the rest of this book, I'd encourage you to be curious about your current mindset around your home and see if any of what's coming up resonates.

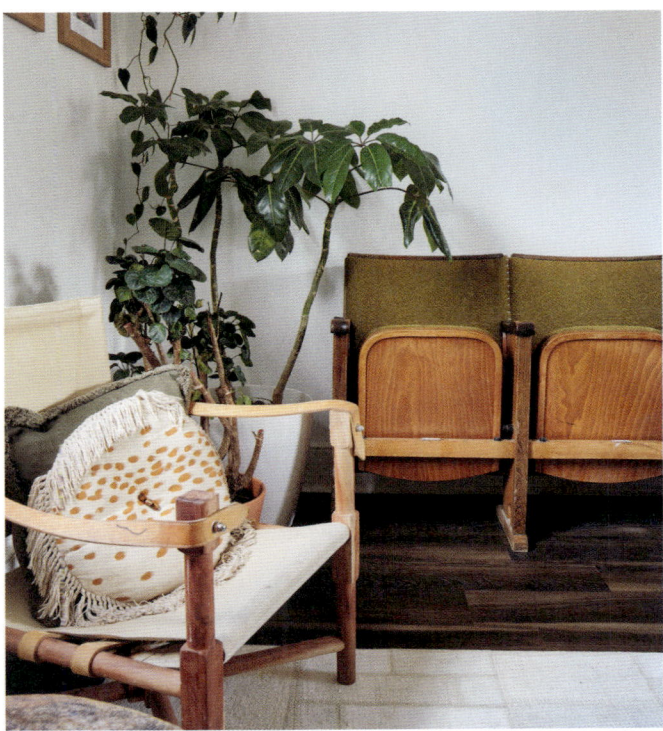

Values over perfection

Embracing your core values is something that comes up again and again throughout this book because I feel so strongly that to live in a home that's authentic to you, your environment should embody your personal values. You may be used to hearing schools, charities or businesses talk about their 'values' – essentially, ideals they promise to adhere to in their everyday dealings (some more successfully than others!). Such organisations typically advertise them on their website; traits like 'courage' or 'reliability' might adorn posters on their walls, no doubt fading into the background after a while. I'm conscious not to come across as too 'out there' but I've found it really helpful when creating homes to think about the values I hold as an individual, those that we as a family want to live by and in turn how these values manifest in our home.

For example, J and I talk to our children a lot about kindness, confidence and integrity – three values that are important to us and which we want to instil in our children and see reflected in our home. Here's how we've put these values into practice in our home.

Kindness

We model to our kids that respecting our surroundings is akin to kindness. We take pride in our family belongings and the four walls that protect them. That means each doing our (age-appropriate) part to keep our home and everything in it in working order. Obviously as the parents of young children we've had the inevitable stage of them drawing on the walls, etc. Kindness goes both ways, and those crayon-meets-wall scenarios were often an indication that our art materials weren't as accessible as they perhaps could have been, which is easy to fix.

Confidence

We try to embody this value by learning new DIY and gardening skills; giving something a go, learning on the job and knowing that the result won't be perfect but that doesn't matter. This means our home is always a work in progress but it gives us and our children the confidence to believe we can take action and make a difference (both in the home and outside).

Integrity

Upholding integrity for us means being conscious when sourcing items for our home, looking at where each object has come from, evaluating the ethical and environmental footprint and, where those fall short, making sure the intended lifespan of the product goes some way to mitigate that. In our home this looks like buying a lot of our furniture second-hand and prioritising independent makers and small brands rather than big businesses. It also means taking our time over choices, and giving careful consideration to everything that we bring into our family home.

I find that focusing on values rather than striving for perfection really helps ground me to what's truly important in my home.

What values are essential to you – at home and beyond? How might you take steps to incorporate your own values into your living space? Being honest with yourself is key here – I've included my values not to say that you should have the same ones, but so you can see how we try to embody ours at home.

My values are	I embody them at home by

Striving for better, not 'perfect'

In the four years that I lived in my turbulent flatshare, I worked my way through nine different jobs (probably the best indication of my mental health at the time). The most random of these was managing a luxury kaftan boutique in the outlet mall of Bicester Village, Oxfordshire. The round trip to this job was just shy of five hours a day, which took its toll, but while working there, I felt a world away from my London life. I would spend my lunch breaks flitting through the various boutiques, assuming different lifestyles in my mind while I tried on dresses that exceeded my monthly rent.

As payday loomed each month, I would allow myself one indulgence, and take myself off to the Le Creuset boutique to purchase a new pot, each in a rich teal hue. I'd daydream my commute away thinking of more peaceful times in my imagined future, when I'd be living the type of life where my Le Creuset pots would line the shelves of my non-communal kitchen, rather than being stored in their boxes in my bedroom. My colleagues – no strangers to my living conditions – all thought I was mad, but those large yet controlled purchases gave me a sense of hope and purpose.

Both sets of grandparents had raised me serving meals from bright orange cast-iron casserole dishes. There was something about the lifetime guarantee of the Le Creusets that just felt so comforting to me. It transcended my current scenario and allowed me to hope for better times. By the time I moved into my second home aged twenty-one, I had four casseroles, a cast-iron kettle, and enough mugs to host all of my friends. My maternal grandma, who'd been keeping tabs on my purchases, always encouraged me, 'One day, home will look very different for you, Africa, and you'll have all these wonderful pieces to remind you of your journey.'

It can be hard to strike the balance between living in the moment while also planning for the future. Was I wrong to delay gratification by not opening those boxes of pans and cooking with my Le Creusets in the grubby flatshare kitchen? Was I focusing too much on having the 'perfect' space in which to crack them out? Or was the sheer sight of the pristine packaging enough to incentivise me through those gruelling, long workdays towards the better home that I longed for? I wasn't fixating on attaining my 'perfect' home, just a 'better' one. I needed a glimmer of hope to help me graft my way towards a different future. I recognised the positives of my home life at that stage – the craving for freedom that had motivated me to leave my family home – but my pan collection let me believe a better time was coming.

How far do you look into the future, and does it take away or add to the enjoyment of living for now? I don't have all the answers, but I believe that acknowledging our desire for better and being realistic is personal growth in itself. Aspiring is a natural human condition, but aspiring for perfection will always lead to disappointment because it's unattainable.

What hopes and aspirations do you have for your home, or your future home? And which parts of them might you be able to bring into your current living situation?

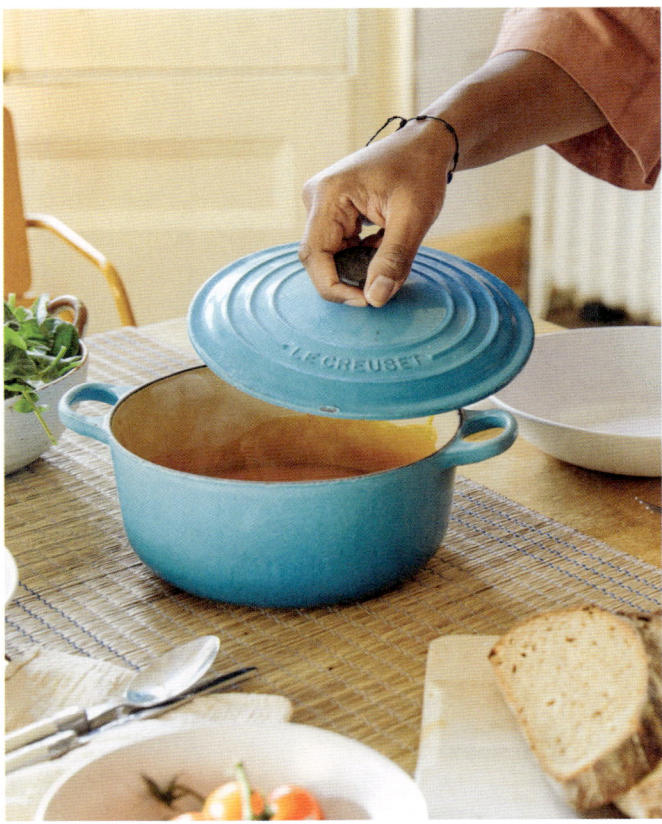

Accepting what we can do, letting go of 'can't'

Some of us are more affected by our surroundings than others. For me, my environment has a huge impact on my wellbeing and sense of self. I've lived in homes that were beyond inadequate and I know the toll that can take. I also know that while you won't ever make your space perfect, there are plenty of measures you can take to enhance it. An inviting, clutter-free hallway with somewhere to store coats and keys, a calming bedroom with good-quality bedsheets, a curtain hung up to keep out a draught or a little window box by the front door with a few inexpensive plants – these solutions can have a positive effect on your mood. In fact, I believe there is a 'marginal gains' effect with them – that is, the cumulative impact of lots of small tweaks can make a surprisingly big difference to daily life.

When you look around your space, what are the small improvements that feel affordable and achievable? I find it can be helpful to start with the little irritations, such as finding somewhere for kids to leave their shoes so you're not constantly tripping over them. Or clearing out the drawer of 'useful' stuff which is so crammed you can never find anything in it. Smoothing these out takes away some minor stresses from daily life and allows home to feel more restorative.

You'll likely have some grievances that remain out of your control, such as noise pollution, accessibility woes or an out-of-the-way location, which you can't do much about. Maddening as these are (and, trust me, some homes have very nearly pushed me to insanity), it can help to find day-to-day coping strategies so these annoyances don't drive you too far round the bend.

Our great neighbours have always outnumbered the inevitable rogue ones, but dealing with a difficult neighbour can be all-encompassing as it's literally happening on your doorstep. We have lived in places where neighbours really overstepped boundaries, both literal and figuratively. One incident regarding shared access left us feeling so worn down and vulnerable that I obsessed about our safety almost to breaking point. I found I could only relax once we reclaimed some agency in the situation and resolved to respectfully but firmly put a plan into action. In the end, I find that putting my energy into what I can change is much more satisfying than obsessing over what I can't (some days I'm better at this than others).

Humans are predisposed to focus on the bad stuff as an early survival instinct, so it takes effort to retrain the neural pathways in your brain to start seeing more of the positives (there are *always* some). This doesn't mean you're trying to trick yourself into feeling content in your surroundings when you're clearly not. It's completely normal to hold opposing views at the same time, so we might feel grateful we have a roof over our heads but frustrated that it's not a larger space. Practising – yep, I'm going to say it – gratitude for what you have is scientifically proven to have positive effects on your overall wellbeing as it gets you into the habit of focusing more on the good than the bad, which in turn has a positive impact on your mental health as a whole. There's nothing new in this advice but I'll say it anyway, because I have found it really grounding to say four things to myself that I'm grateful for, especially when I feel weary about my household to-do list.

For example:

- Having outside space
- Adequate space for a dining table
- Having a children's playroom
- The abundance of natural light in our home

What are four things you're grateful for in your current home?

1. ....

2. ....

3. ....

4. ....

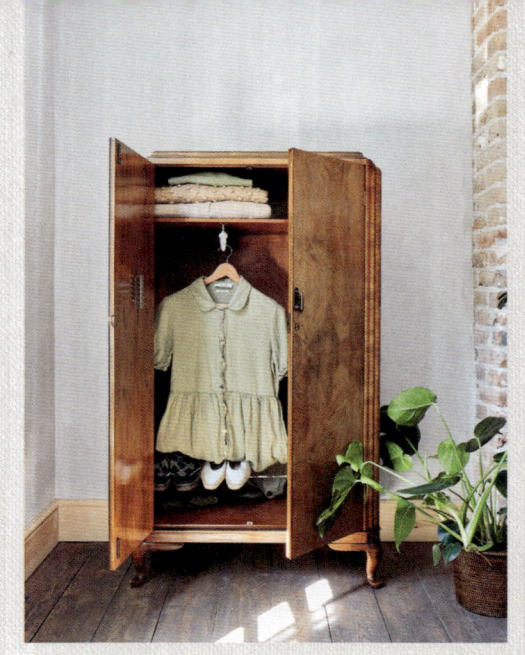
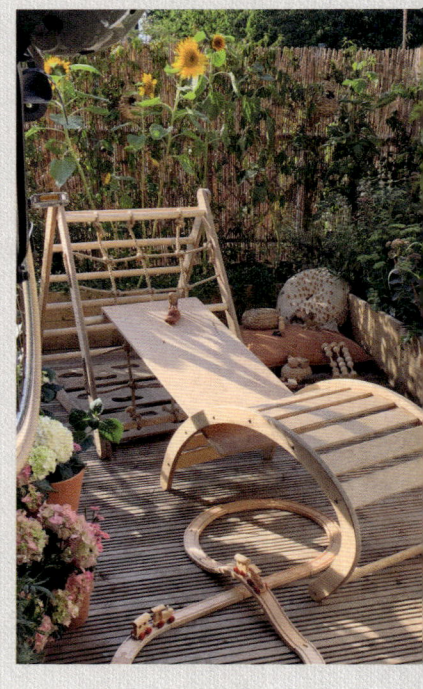
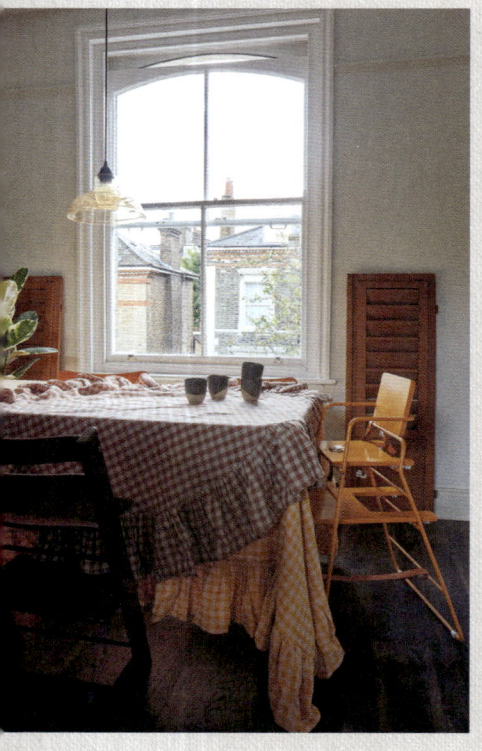
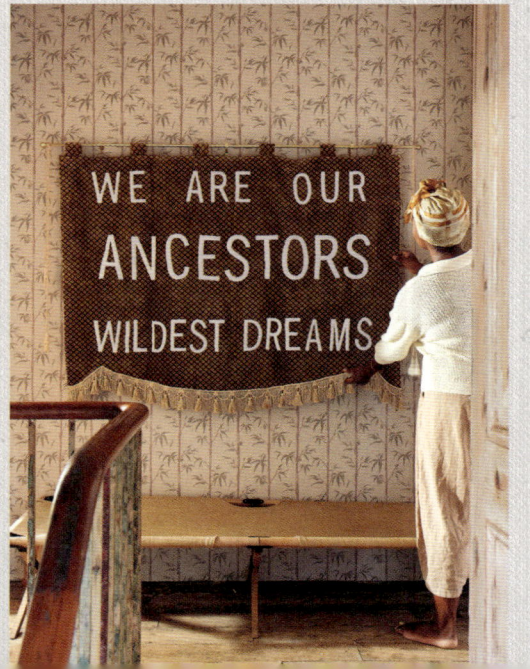

There's a beautiful saying that goes, 'Remember when you prayed for the things you have today.' You don't need to be religious to see the wisdom in taking stock of your journey and pausing to be thankful for any perceived growth when it comes to building a home. That can be tough when it hasn't been a straightforward journey, but downsizing after a divorce, for instance, can still lead you to appreciate your newfound financial freedom, and a new flatshare post-breakup can still be hailed for the opportunities it might bring.

You can't spend your way to perfection

There's a multibillion-pound industry trying to convince us that we need things we don't. It's so easy to fall prey to our culture of consumerism, what with the quick thrill of the 'click to buy' button. This ease of purchasing, the increasing availability of 'pay later' schemes along with our culture of celebrating pristine show homes rather than real-life works-in-progress has led to a perfect storm of buy-buy-buy. Striving for perfection can leave us blinkered, losing sight of what's important to us in the homes we're creating and instead confusing 'want' with 'need'.

I wonder how much our expectations have been affected by the advent of social media and the inundation of 'perfect' home imagery. On the one hand, platforms like Instagram and Pinterest can be invaluable at providing inspiration, as well as giving confidence to your decision-making if you're having a wobble. On the other hand, they can give us such unrealistic expectations that when we try to hold our homes up to these standards, they fall way off the mark. Beautiful rooms in every style under the sun adorn these sites, calling out to us – *A marble sink? Of course, I simply must have one! A dining set that's worth two months' rent? Wonderful idea!*

I have made an effort to become more discerning with the accounts I follow for this reason, particularly enjoying those that focus on the realities of creating a home, warts and all. That means I'm more drawn to progress pictures and accounts that give guidance on specific DIY jobs or advice on planning and budgeting, than finished rooms. At the time of writing, I particularly like @townleyterrace, @whathavewedunoon and @bricks.and.disorder. In the spirit of this, in recent years, I have made changes to the way I post in a bid to capture the reality of doing up an old home over time as our budget allows. I'm conscious that my own contribution to social media may add to the noise of perceived perfection and that's one of the reasons I've been transparent right from the start about the reasons we were able to rent in a desirable part of London and that for us achieving home ownership literally took a shift in the world (the pandemic) and a seventy-mile move to allow us a mortgage on our three-bed fixer-upper.

 Like many of us, I have previously fallen down the rabbit hole exploring dream homes, doing deep dives into huge kitchen extensions, transparent drinks fridges and luxe bifold doors. In a positive frame of mind, I might pick up some ideas, but if not, they'll likely give me a niggling feeling that there's something I *should* have but don't. Comparison will not only stifle your homemaking creativity, it can also leave you feeling inadequate and questioning every decision or change you've already made. Every beautiful photograph can mentally move you towards losing sight of not just the beauty you've already created but also your own needs, not to mention budget; seeing these 'perfect' visions can make it so easy to want to overspend.

 I am very much a layperson when it comes to the psychology of shopping or acquiring, but I have found it fascinating reading up on theories around this behaviour. When we strive for a 'perfect' home or 'perfect' aesthetic, we do so because of the feeling we think it will spark when we get it. You might covet an acquaintance's new four poster bed, subconsciously thinking that if you forked out a small fortune for the same one, you'd be as happy and stylish as their online persona. I've fallen for this myself – creating a longing is why advertising is so effective after all – but after years of trial and error, I've come to realise that blindly following our 'wants' in the hope of attaining that 'perfect' space, rather than focusing on the true *feelings* we're searching for, is one of the biggest pitfalls in creating a home that's authentic to you.

 What about turning this concept on its head to create a valuable opportunity? In future, what if every decision we make regarding our homes, stems from a conscious questioning of the feeling we're striving for? This ethos has become central to my approach when creating any space I've lived in over the years, whether rented or owned. It's what I believe makes a house a home rather than some false ideal of the 'perfect' space. You might like to keep this at the forefront of your mind too. Whether sourcing a small item of furniture or decorating a large home, what feeling are you trying to create? Will your purchase fulfil a real need or is it just a distraction from some uncomfortable feelings?

I invite you to go back to the lists you've already created about what makes a house feel like home to you, and what values you want to embody in your living space.

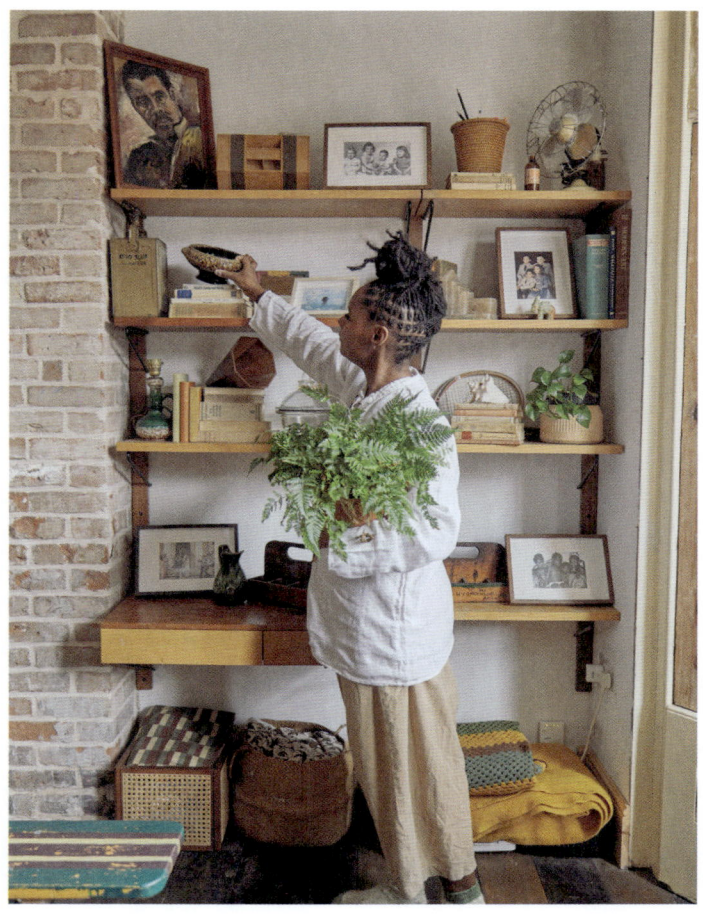

Practically (im)perfect in every way

If you've seen some of the pictures of my home online and you're wondering if it looks like that every day, let me reassure you it very much does not. A lot of those snaps are taken professionally (by Kasia Fiszer who manages to capture everything so beautifully) and I'll have cleaned, tidied, primped and plumped, you name it, often for hours before she arrives. I wish I could tell you it was a one-woman job, but I'd be remiss if I didn't acknowledge my sister who always comes to my aid and assists me with a deep clean pre-shoot. Even in our last, more modest two-bed home, it was a full-blown operation to get our living space photo ready.

I like looking after my home and of course on those (increasingly rare!) days when it's all ship shape, I enjoy the tidiness and order, but the rest of the time I try not to get hung up on mess. Part of having an online presence in my industry, though, means that my home is my creative backdrop and very much my CV for securing work. I often think I've made a rod for my own back in not being able to show my home in its more lived-in state, but that's why I'm such an avid 'story sharer' and I keep the reality posts tucked away in stories or on my dedicated home renovation account for balance.

We make a point of discussing with our children our expectation that every family member helps keep our home a nice space to live in. I remind myself that as a family of six, the house will sometimes (read: almost always) be in disarray – as it should be in a home where we want people to relax and enjoy themselves. While we encourage the children to put away their toys, I don't want to be hovering round them as they play, commenting on every stray Duplo that doesn't make it back into its box. I've found that if everything has a home and we all know where it needs to go then the mess doesn't bother me, as I understand that it's temporary. Assigning everything a home also makes the cleaning process much less daunting and makes it easier for children to help put things away.

I find something a bit off-kilter about a fastidiously neat space, and I think rooms look far more inviting when you see signs of actual life, such as toys on the floor or stacks of books in a 'to-read' pile beside a cold mug of tea. Or perhaps rather less contrived and more realistic are pieces of clothing strewn around (do anyone else's kids just strip off as they move from room to room, leaving a sartorial trail in their wake?), recycling stacked by the back door or piles of dishes in the sink.

I'm the first to admit that my husband and I often get caught up in the never-ending to-do list, barely coming up for air before fixating on the next job that needs doing, whether that's a DIY project or even a domestic task like cleaning the bathroom or putting on a wash. And then there are times when I just lean into the chaos; my energy levels on any given day will dictate how motivated I am. Letting go of needing things to be a particular way can be a gift.

Onwards

I hope there has been some food for thought in this section that will help you explore your feelings around the idea of home and become curious about them. The rest of the book aims to show you why not being in a 'perfect' space need not be a barrier to creating a unique, authentic home that you love. It can be so freeing to develop a mindset that embraces what you have, rather than obsessing over what you don't. This does not mean you won't choose to strive for better in the future or that it will limit your ambitions for your home, just that you can create a base now that will enable you to grow in the right direction. It might feel like the odds are stacked against you, but I'll guide you through ways to make your space work better for you.

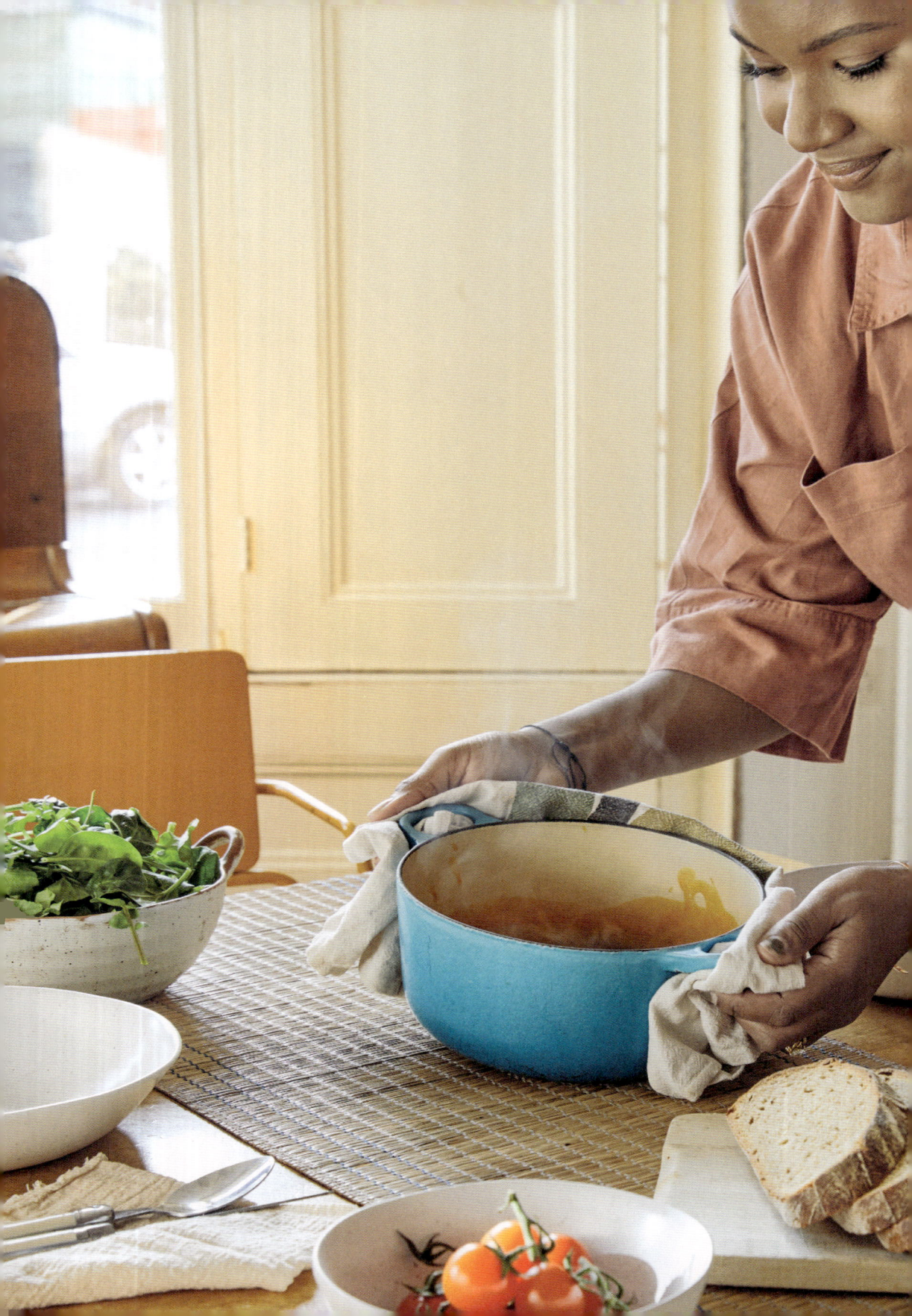

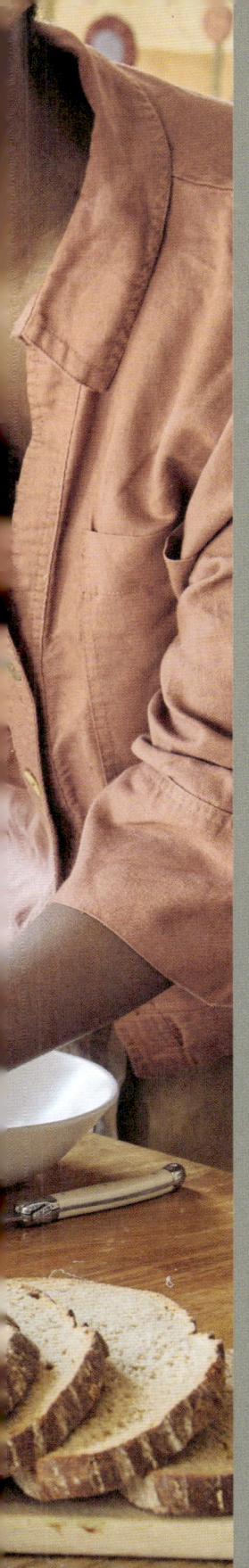

EMBRACE

When it comes to your home, do the words 'blank canvas' fill you with excitement or dread? If the latter, I'm very much hoping that this part of the book will change your mind and help you see opportunity over anxiety. Here, we'll be looking at the bigger picture of your home as well as smaller opportunities for improvement, and I'll walk you through some of the enhancements I've made in my homes, past and present, that have brought about positive change for the whole family. If you feel like you don't know where to start, don't worry. I'll be sharing some prompts to encourage you to think about your space, whether it's working for you and find new ways to inject your personality into it.

I won't be telling you what shade of greige you must paint your walls, nor will I make you reduce your possessions by half (though I do love a clear-out)! My advice is all about individuality rather than the 'current' colour or object. Embracing your home and everything you bring into it allows you to create a space that truly reflects you, and that is timeless. When you live somewhere that really feels like home, you'll not only have a place you love, but you'll also absorb the many benefits that come with it.

Remember who you're doing it for

When I was growing up, even as a young child, I recognised that my papa's home in London was not remotely *him*. He worked long days and nights for his family, which by then included a new partner and her four children, along with the three children they had had together (and the four he had had with my mother). His home, an ex-council flat that he had purchased for his girlfriend, was renovated quickly but poorly and I don't think there was a single design choice in that home that reflected either of them. Instead, every décor decision was based on what would have impressed his parents, despite the fact they had been estranged for decades.

Thousands of hard-to-come-by pounds were poured into converting perfectly functional windows into uPVC ones with faux-lead effects. Impractical lacquered faux-yew planks were laid on every floor surface. There always seemed to be an aim of creating the type of home that would finally elicit praise from his parents. It was a home that was designed for their approval rather than one that worked for him and his family. Even at a young age, that felt notably sad to me.

When you think of your home, it's one thing to be inspired by your family heritage (as I was with my grandmother's range cooker) but quite another to be restricted by ideas of what will impress others. Observing my dad's earnest but misguided approach to creating a home made me more determined than ever to create homes that would meet *our* needs and reflect *our* tastes.

Consider your own choices at home, and who you are making those choices for. Do you feel things have to be a certain way because you fear disapproval? Don't be afraid to make different choices for yourself and your family.

Don't rush the process

When we moved to our home on the Kent coast, a few items had been left behind by the previous owners, including a lovely little wooden chair. We weren't short of seating, but there was something special about this one, which made it hard to let go of. Amid the chaos of moving boxes, it took on many roles from tool holder to ladder and even a miniature table for the many pizza takeaways in those early days – a trusted friend in no time at all. Of course, it had to stay, and it still makes me smile to look at it, remembering those late nights in our new home, stripping wallpaper into the early hours. My grandparents taught me to have a 'lifetime approach' to curating one's home and the treasures inside. For them, 'curation' was less of a deliberate process and more of a gradual acquisition of pieces as they could afford them, knowing that they would last a lifetime.

I have sometimes struggled to find the right balance between living in the here and now but also planning for the future. In the past, there were times when I had jobs that saw me working seven days a week, particularly when J and I were saving up for something, like our wedding. My role models growing up were real grafters, so this level of intense working didn't seem at all strange to me, since during my childhood I'd see my dad work sixteen-hour days and my mum up before the birds to sell her vintage finds at one stall or another.

I still have that mentality and frequently have to remind myself of the joy of slowing down a bit, being in the now rather than careering towards yet another goal. Slowing down doesn't just allow us to be kinder to ourselves but I promise your homes will look and feel better for it. Whether a trinket from a seaside holiday, a postcard from a friend, a tactile cushion cover you stumbled upon at a car-boot sale or a favourite side table passed to you from your childhood home, worn with a lifetime of mug rings – these layers of your history will work together to create a feeling of home. And they are far more meaningful than any 'statement' lamp or showy sofa. These are the ways to bring love into your home.

CHAPTER 5

FINDING YOUR OWN TASTE AND STYLE

In Nora Ephron's playful essay 'Serial Monogamy: A Memoir', she writes about how, on visiting her friend's ridiculously stylish New York apartment, she felt immediate regret for every interior design decision she had ever made. Such is the great taste of this person that Ephron's perception of her own home is completely altered, and she is filled with an urgent need to change every single thing about it and emulate her friend's beige-toned apartment, from the sofa to the plates. How many of us can relate to that? There's nothing like seeing someone else's beautiful space to make you question how you should, or, even worse, *already have* decorated your space. But stay strong! Because if you are tapping into your own tastes and creating a style that's authentic to you, you'll be able to resist the green-eyed monster and even the most tempting of trends.

Your taste (no one else's)

There's no such thing as 'good' (or 'bad') taste – there, I've said it, and it's true! If this is news to you, I hope it's freeing because the more we hold up our design decisions to the taste police, the more we stifle our creativity and take away personality from our homes. What one person loves, another will not, and our homes are all the richer for these differences. In fact, I've found that overly tasteful and curated spaces, without the movement of everyday life, can lack character and intrigue. My family members (particularly older generations) are frequently confounded by the choices J and I have made in our décor. I had to laugh when my dad first visited our current home in its semi-unpacked state and, pointing to our much-loved theatre chairs and well-worn leather sofa, asked us if the previous owners had left behind all this 'old stuff'! 'No, Papa', I told him, 'we have been lovingly building up this collection of characterful pieces over the past few years!'

Narrowing down what you do and don't like can be such an overwhelming task, given that we are inundated with inspiration on social media and elsewhere. The fact that at the touch of a button we can see hundreds of images of whatever we want to search for – 'bohemian bedrooms', 'pastel kitchens' or 'terrazzo floors' – is both a blessing and a curse. When we're inundated with images of other people's beautiful spaces, or when the algorithm starts its assault, it can be hard to tap into what we actually like. So, it's important to find the sweet spot – of course be inspired by others, but don't be derivative. When you copy a style or someone else's home down to the last cushion cover, it will never feel quite right as it won't be authentic to you. You probably won't feel so at home if, due to lack of confidence or any other reason, your home reflects someone else's tastes. Making your home individual to you doesn't mean you have to throw away your IKEA sofa, because that too, can be part of your story.

I also encourage you to find inspiration away from accounts on Instagram and Pinterest, which can often lead us to feeling like there is some kind of 'must-have' item or décor decision. I love to find inspiration in unexpected places, from interesting colour combos worn by people on the street to old tiling at a train station or artful shop signage. My phone is full of slightly random photos of these scenes, which I often upload to my work-in-progress mood boards, either with a dedicated project in mind or as an archive for future inspiration.

Keeping your eyes open in your day-to-day life will draw in ideas that never would have occurred to you otherwise.

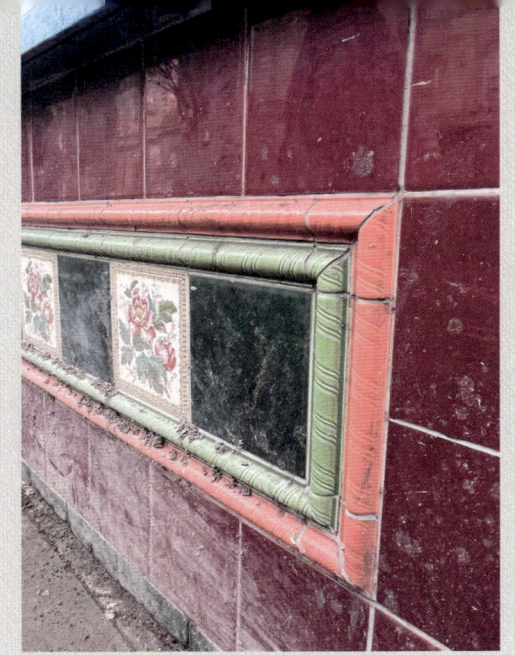
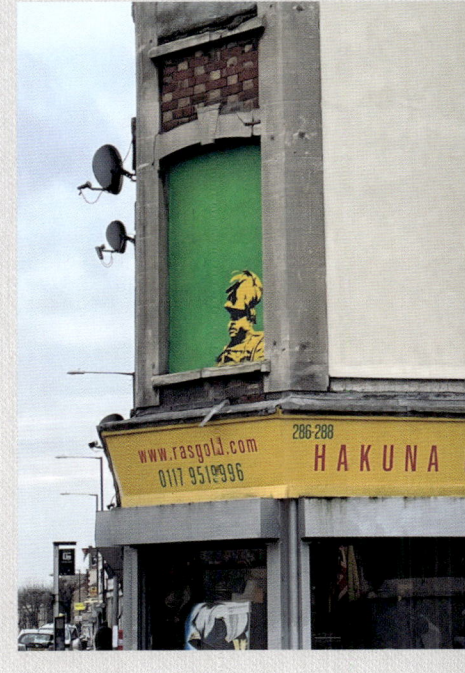
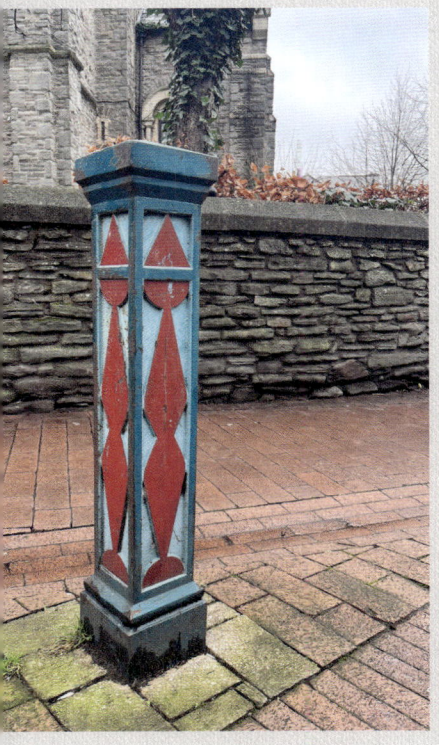
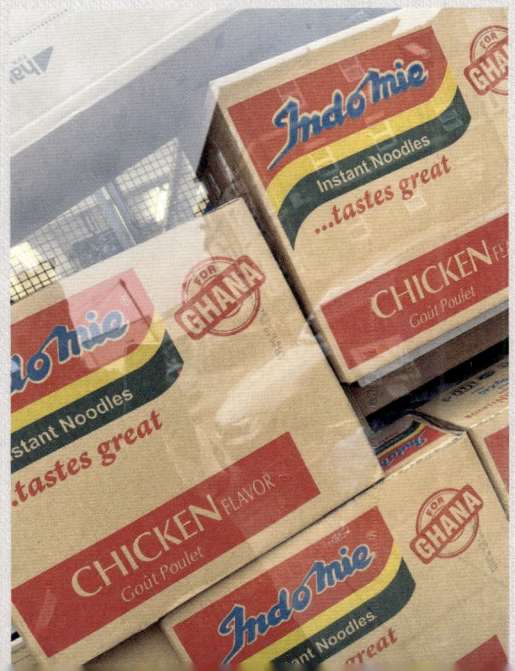

Being mindful of trends

Of course, we're going to be influenced by trends, that's how life goes. And it's not necessarily a bad thing, despite the word 'trend' having developed negative connotations over the years – often being used derisively, like the word 'fad'. If you love something, it doesn't matter if it's part of a current trend or a previous one, but, before committing to it, ask yourself how you'd feel if next season or next year your choice was no longer featured on 'hot right now' lists or their equivalents. If that doesn't faze you (and it wouldn't me), then go for it. With this approach, you'll be much more likely to still love the things that make up your home long after they are hailed as this season's must-have in an interior's magazine.

There's a difference though between being inspired by trends and the wider world around us (including culture, arts and real-world events) and being unduly influenced by them in a way that blindly leads us away from our true tastes. If, like me, you've ever fallen for one of life's more ridiculous trends (hello charcoal toothpaste), don't judge yourself too harshly, we are all at the mercy of the multibillion-pound consumer industry that strives to inspire profit-making FOMO. Companies work hard to stay ahead of trends in order to sell us products that go hand in hand with said trend when it reaches the mainstream. It's a cynical, contrived business model – a sophisticated, often subtle machine that drives longings so deep within us, playing on our inherent desire to keep up with the pack, it's easy to mindlessly spend on any old thing we're being flogged that week. OK, anti-capitalist rant over. But I have found that just being aware of the selling machine out there helps me to be more considerate of every purchase I make, because before I hand over my bank card I ask myself, 'Am I blindly buying into a trend? Does this piece truly reflect my taste? Will I love it just as much in three months from now? Will I still love it if everyone I know gets one, too?'

EMBRACE

Finding inspiration and forming your own aesthetic

The first step in discovering your own taste is to put away your phone! There is a world out there ready to inspire you. If you can, visit galleries or museums (many are free), flick through some art books at your local library, go to the cinema, peruse shop windows, take walks in the great outdoors, have a doodle on some paper. Inspiration will strike, consciously or otherwise, often in unexpected ways. Immersing ourselves in a variety of media will also help us tune into our unique aesthetic, which you can, in time, inject into your home.

Forming your own aesthetic doesn't necessarily mean limiting yourself to one 'look' and not deviating from it (in fact, I think that can make a space look a bit flat). Working out what you're drawn to becomes easier over time, and more instinctive. For example, I would say I love the era classed as 'mid-century modern', the period in furniture-making, architecture and design that was prevalent for around two decades after the Second World War. I've always been drawn to furniture from this time; sleek, unfussy and in natural materials like teak, with its rich, deep brown hues. It tends to be reasonably priced too. However, I didn't set out to follow this style or become a dedicated disciple of it. In fact, I was working at the interior design showroom when I first realised that I kept being drawn to particular reproductions and that they were all of this style. I soon learnt that nothing contemporary even came close to those original pieces.

You might look at a room (or a photograph of one), a piece of furniture or an item of clothing and have an immediate reaction to it, whether you like it or dislike it. Other times, however, it isn't obvious what you do or don't like. When looking for inspiration, whether you're in a space or scrolling through Pinterest, rather than obsessing about every single detail and working out how to copy it, down to the particular shade on the wall, think about what it is you like about the room. What's the feeling you're getting? Let that be your guide. If you're looking online and pinning images to a digital board, when you look back on them as a whole, you will likely notice a similarity of style, showing you a natural inclination towards a certain aesthetic. Does it feel comfortable and lived in? Or are you drawn to it because its vibe is uplifting and imaginative? Examining the overall feelings you are left with will help you identify the aesthetic you are seeking.

Self-belief is important here and when you let go of the idea of creating the perfect end result, you will be freer to be open-minded in forming your aesthetic. You don't need to overthink it or let it all start weighing you down like a chore. Homes should come together organically and over time. Furnishings will naturally move around and come and go as your space evolves, along with your changing needs. Trial and error are a huge part of creating a space you love. Even when designers use programs that map out their clients' floor plans and furnishing placements, those tools can only guide them so much and still can't predict the feeling that will be created in a space.

The three-word pitch

Our homes are multifaceted (just as we are) and I don't believe they can really be appraised in a few words or a catchphrase; however, the marketeer in me wants to put this thought experiment out there! It's a bit tongue-in-cheek but worth having a go if you're at a bit of a loss as to where to start with tuning into your aesthetic. Apparently, fashion stylists use a similar system when creating looks for clients, so let's apply it to making choices for our homes here.

Two questions:

- What three words do you think someone else would use to describe your home?
- What three words would you like your home to embody?

For me:

- I think someone else would describe our home as: warm, relaxed, family-friendly
- I want our home to embody: inspiration, creativity, welcome

Other examples might be:

- Calming, understated, elegant
- Colourful, eclectic, fun
- Moody, dramatic, glamorous

If you're feeling brave, you could always actually ask close friends the three words they'd use to describe your home.

When you are looking to make any improvement to your home, be it a decorative one or sourcing furnishings, keep in mind the three words that describe what you'd like to achieve. Does the lamp you're eyeing up fit your three guiding words? Will that fabric you're considering align with your vision?

Be mindful that this isn't a failsafe method – even if you have nailed the atmosphere you're seeking through the three-word pitch, not every single item in your home will align with it (which is a good thing, as homes that are overly polished can feel a bit staid), and furnishings can fit multiple categorisations in different contexts. I wouldn't want you to use this strategy in a way that limits you or stifles your creativity (especially because homes that mix lots of styles can look wonderful); it's more of an aid for when you're struggling to stay focused, or if you are suffering from decision fatigue.

A rule of thumb that adds flexibility is that if an item/improvement fulfils two out of three of your key words, it's a good fit. If it only delivers on one, it may be too far removed from your overall vision.

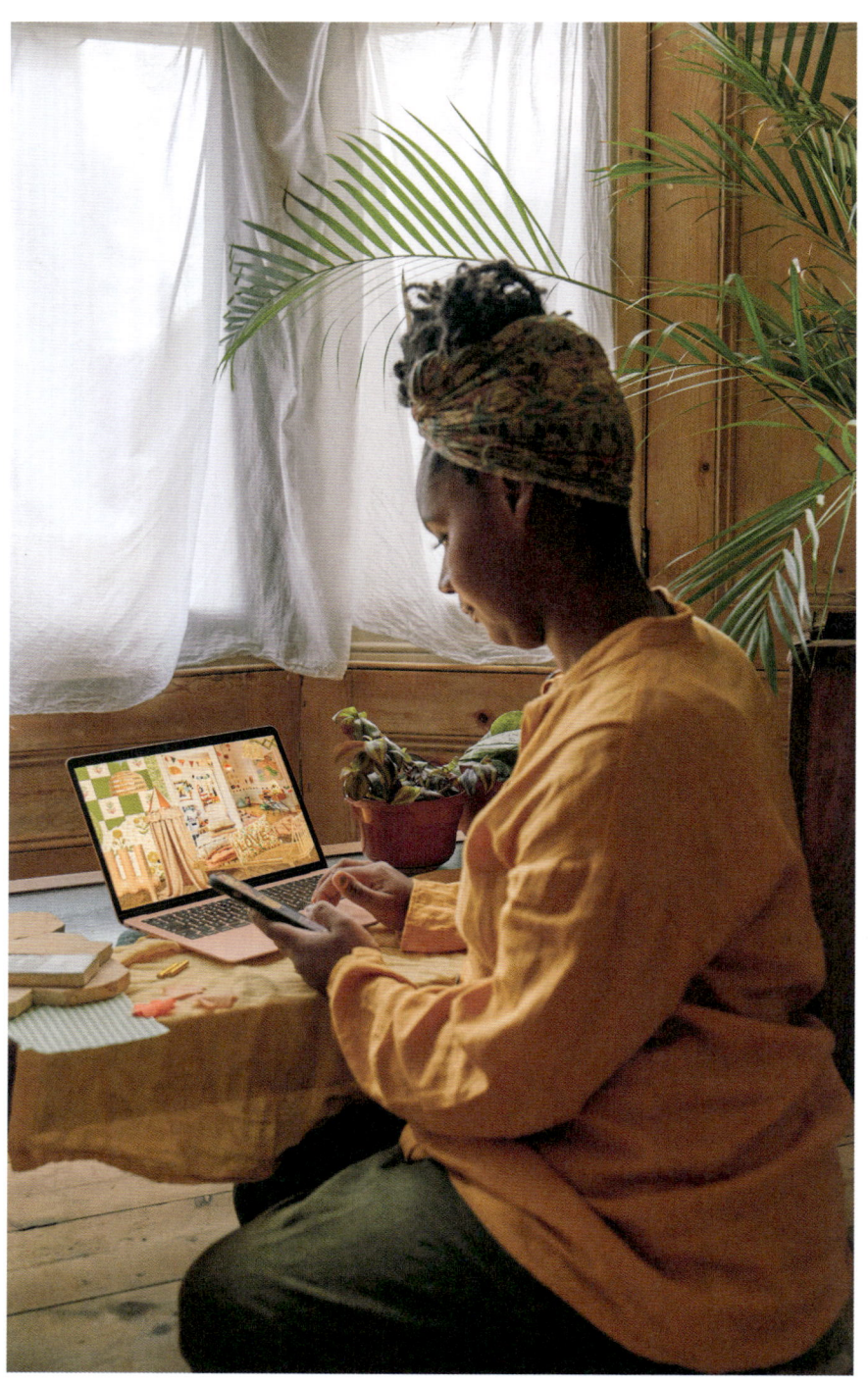

The art of the mood board

I love mood boards, and, judging from how much feedback I get on the ones I have shared online in the past, it's likely you do too! I love how analogue you can make these in our screen-centred world. If you can, I'd encourage you to make a real-life hard copy mood board, as well as, or instead of, a digital one.

Mood boards have been used in various formats for years, both by individuals developing personal projects and in workplaces where designs or concepts need to be communicated to colleagues or clients. Not limited to interior design, people use them for all sorts of schemes, to help break down the components of a project and ensure each element is working together in the right way. They offer an immediate visual proposal and are often the clearest way of bringing the different elements of an idea to the fore. I particularly like that they're less focused on a precise end result and revolve around the various elements that will work together. I find them especially unifying when I'm trying to visualise all the different aspects of a room, like how the paint colour or wallpaper will attune with the flooring, furniture and soft furnishings. They stop my thoughts from meandering too much and keep them all in one place. A mood board will motivate me if I need to get started on a project, help me problem solve if I am wavering about something, or highlight an aspect that isn't working, which I hadn't even thought about. As a project develops, it feels really rewarding to see some or all the constituent parts of a mood board come together.

My approach to creating a mood board

The very first thing I'd suggest before you get started on your board is to determine your brief for the space. Depending on the size of your room (or even a corner of a room), the brief could be large and comprehensive or small and straightforward. For example, if you're creating a mood board for a kitchen/living space that's open-plan, its brief will be cooking and dining, but it will probably also need to function as a place to watch TV, or to work from home, or for children to play in (the list may go on). List every single purpose that the room will serve and go from there.

Remember that mood boards do not need to be one hundred per cent reflective of your finished space. If you subscribe to the view that our homes evolve with us as our needs change, then you'll know that the fluidity of our requirements can't fully be captured by a mood board anyway. Instead, see a mood board as a visual cue to help with the overall feel you are after, rather than a rigid design prescription to follow to the letter.

Physical mood board

The joy of a physical mood board is its tactility – the ability to touch fabric samples or assess the exact sheen of a tile sample is a very pleasing thing. Paint and wallpaper companies, fabric brands and tile stores will all send samples (which are often free or just postage charged). Gather any objects you can that will go into the space, such as a paint swatch (some paint companies now sell painted stickers rather than tester pots), a flooring sample and any soft furnishing swatches, as well as larger pieces such as a door handle or artwork. Layer in any small objects you have that will be incorporated into the room once finished, such as a plant, candle, or any trinkets. You can then play about swapping elements in and out. Depending on how many samples and materials you're incorporating, a large tray, box lid or similar will be useful, or just lay it all out on the floor.

Once you're finished (though it may keep evolving!), you might like to take a picture of your board so that you can easily look at it, or previous versions, when out and about.

Digital mood board

I have a really visual mind that perhaps stems from my love of reading as a child. I can walk into any space, regardless of the scale of project, and immediately, my brain starts whirring with ideas to bring out its full potential. My husband on the other hand, well, let's just say he often needs a little more convincing – leaving me only too happy to whip up a mood board to share my vision.

I'm not the most tech-savvy person, and years ago, I'd see elaborate, CAD-designed room mock-ups and feel very out of my depth. Since then, I've found a simple method and a platform that works for me, and I make a point of putting together simple but visually effective mood boards for my family whenever I have an idea about creating a space.

The platform I use (for pretty much all my freelance projects too) is Canva. I have the Pro plan and for me it is money well spent. I tend to go for a landscape document: 1920 × 1080px, the same size as my phone screen rotated. I like to start with a flooring option for the bottom of my mood board. So that it doesn't feel too static, I'll usually lift an 'in-situ' image taken from a distance and then start layering photos on top. Canva has a brilliant feature whereby you can remove the background of an image with just the touch of a button. It's easy to crop images and adjust the colour tones too. Once flooring and wall textures have been added (different textures add dimension), I just start to overlay items and materials in larger blocks. The last things I add are fittings such as taps or light switches and I make sure to remove any background on these. And there you have it, a quick way to create an effective mood board to convince yourself . . . or those you live with!

Telling a story

As you become more attuned to your own aesthetic, you'll likely want to have objects in your home that reflect your style (and by extension, you). Pieces that have a history – that are personal to your journey – will immediately make your space feel more like your home, whether it's a holiday postcard from your best friend, a favourite printed fabric from a local craft fair or a much-loved ornament passed down from a grandparent no longer with you. These sentimental objects can be a great enhancement to a recently decorated room, or a newer-build home, adding extra character to an otherwise generic space.

In the Source section, we will look at process and provenance, as these aren't just about filling your home with random 'stuff'. The good feeling of 'home' comes from warmth and cosiness, being surrounded by things that are personal to you, that evoke happy memories or nostalgia. I'm not suggesting that your tin opener is going to make your heart do cartwheels every time you open a can of tomatoes, but if it doesn't fall into William Morris's famous edict of, 'Have nothing in your house that you do not know to be useful, or believe to be beautiful', consider whether it's worth the space it takes up in your home.

Keep the things you love on display and ensure that every member of your household is represented, including any children who live there. Beautiful china tea sets, studio pottery, shells from a beach trip, chipped tiles, certificates, photographs, anything goes – let whatever you love surround you. Using older pieces with a past life will give a lived-in feel, which can be especially valuable in a room that doesn't have lots of built-in character, and if they're part of your own history more's the better. Scuffs, dents, patina are all part of its journey (and now a part of your story) and add beauty.

This extends far beyond beautiful ornaments or decorative objects. In our smaller homes over the years, one of the bigger challenges I faced was hiding those large but necessary cleaning objects in plain sight. For me, that was as simple as going for an attractive green enamel mop bucket and wooden handle mop combo, crudely recovering my ironing board with some sample fabric and a staple gun and switching out my constantly breaking wire clothes dryers with well-made wooden ones instead. The objects you use every day should also bring you joy.

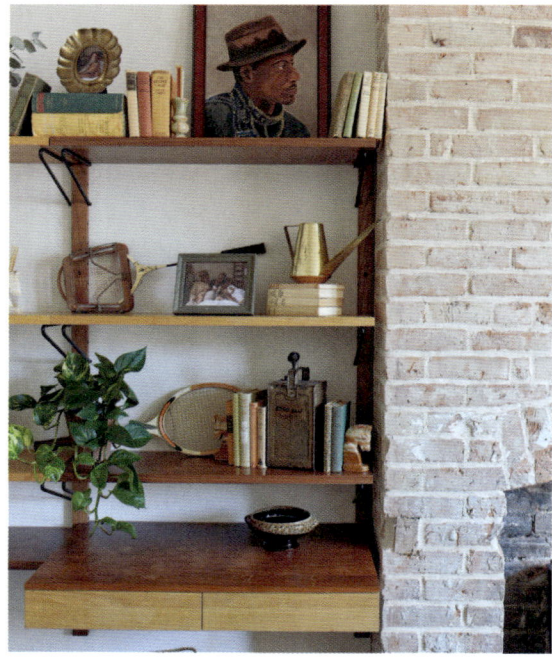

EMBRACE

Honouring your heritage

For me, it's important that my heritage plays out in my style. In every home we've lived in, we have weaved our heritage throughout, incorporating nods to our loved ones and to our history. We particularly love how photographs on shelves and artworks that evoke our ancestry spark conversations with our children. As if by osmosis, they absorb what's around them. The visual depictions of those no longer with us means they continue to be spoken of fondly and regularly.

After packing up our flat in London for our big move to the seaside, a lot of our heritage treasures sat in boxes for a long while before we had the chance to unpack them in our new home. In the end, it took us over a year to get these little gems out and up and we weren't quite expecting the impact they'd have on us all. It was amazing how impactful it was to reunite with these pieces again, to hold pictures and objects, appreciate their tactility and to feel a jolt of connection to our past. It was like the essence of 'home' was right there inside them.

I started thinking about whether we needed these objects – prints, black and white portraits of my grandparents, ornaments collected from market stalls locally and abroad, trinkets from Carriacou that we'd stuffed into suitcases – to really feel settled in our new house. It wasn't as if, over the first year in situ, we'd struggled to feel at home, but there was something so special about unpacking those boxes, finding these visual connections to our heritage, and then surrounding ourselves with them. It can be strange seeing your things in a new environment, removed from their previous home and suddenly seeming out of context in a new place. But the pieces we uncovered immediately seemed to fit. We excitedly got to work finding new nooks for everything, and with every treasure handled with love, I was surprised to breathe a sigh of relief as each item slotted into its new place.

For us, the Cann Hall Road sign represents more than the physical home we enjoyed there; it also evokes the journey and sacrifice of its owner to attain it, and the warmth, love and security provided within its walls over decades. It symbolises the extent of the journey that my husband's grandmother, Joyce, went on. A Windrush descendent, hailing from Jamaica, Grandma Joyce had a brief stint in Scotland (that proved too cold to bear) before moving south to spend her life in service of others, working first for the NHS (as many of the Windrush generation did) and then for the postal service. At one point she had her own corner shop, and finally, needing a slower pace of life, she became a lollipop lady for a local school. Her nonstop approach to work allowed her, later in life, to purchase a modest but beautiful home in Leytonstone. A home where she raised her kids and where my husband was also able to live for a short while as a young teenager. Grandma Joyce has been a huge inspiration to us. When I was newly dating J, he brought me home for her seal of approval. With my own grandma holding such an influence over many of my personal life decisions, I loved that he held his grandma's opinions so dearly. I had the street sign commissioned for one of my husband's milestone birthdays (I was a bit anxious about its impact, as by that time Grandma Joyce was no longer with us, but it was received graciously) and even now, every time we pass it, it inspires a moment of gratitude and reflection.

You're allowed to change your mind

In fact, I'd encourage you to change your mind as much as you like when it comes to your home. For me, change is a key element of an evolving home, a joyful thing in itself to avoid stagnation. Reshuffling objects, big and small, can also be a surprisingly effective way to trick your brain into thinking you've bought something new (I honestly think a rearrangement delivers a similar dopamine hit).

Some 'improvements' end up not improving things, though, it has to be said. Some changes you make or adjustments to a room just look weird – an annoying truth (that I have faced on more than one occasion!) and every professional interior designer or stylist will have experienced this. Sometimes, it's obvious why an update isn't working (the wrong paint colour on the walls, a rug everyone trips over, a piece of furniture that's too big for the space), and sometimes you'll just get a feeling that 'it's just not right'. Trust your gut. Even if you feel like you have to keep something because it was expensive, if it feels wrong every time you see it, that purchase wasn't worth it.

You're not going to get it spot on all the time and its normal to experience

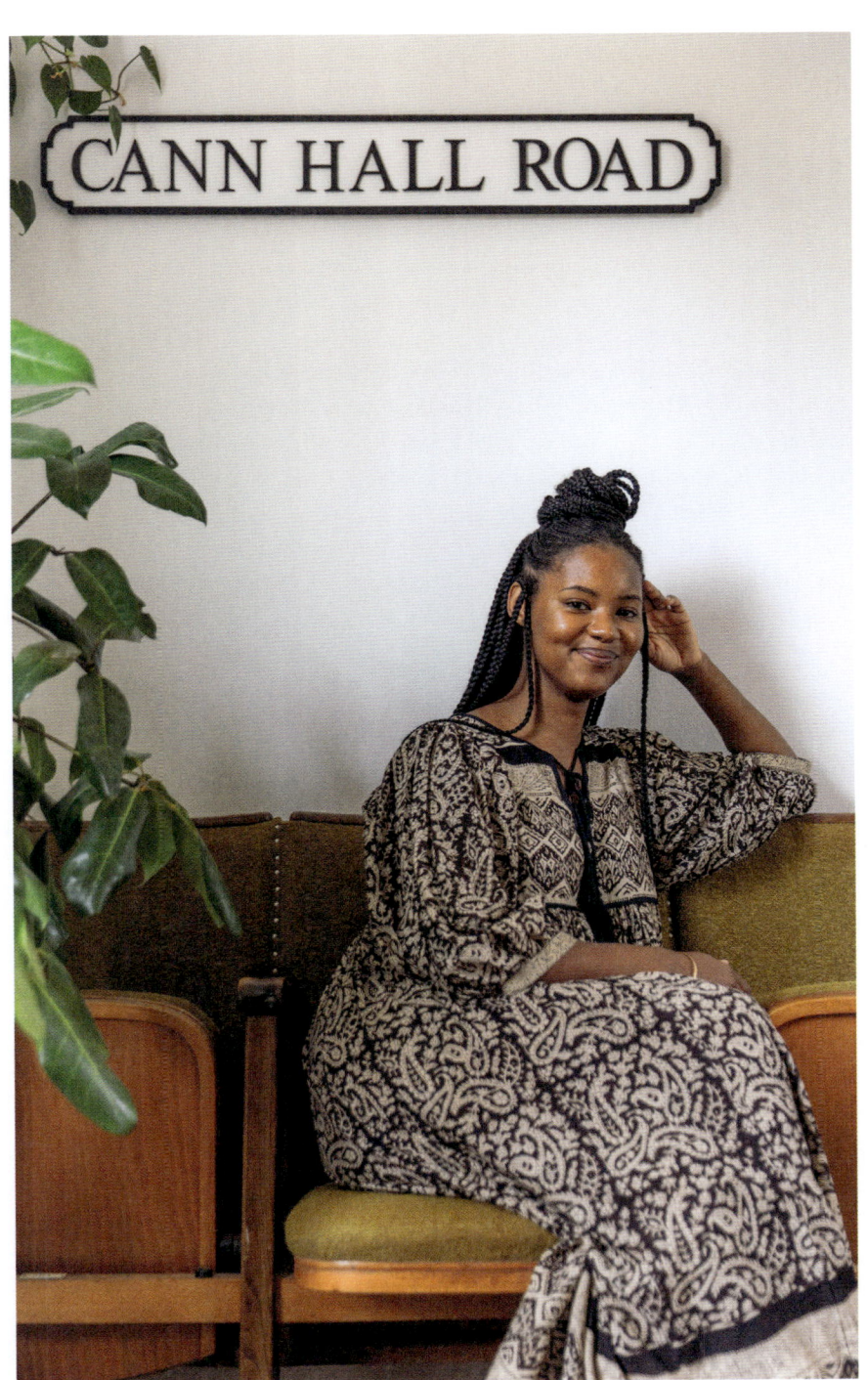

regret or buyer's remorse from time to time. It can be really easy to admonish ourselves for making a mistake – buying a piece of art that looks different once hung at home, or, my all-time favourite, mismeasuring a bit of furniture when getting carried away on eBay, but if you are pushing yourself creatively (as we should all have a go at doing), there will be a few clangers. Another reason I love to buy vintage is that if you have bought something that isn't working in your home, you'll likely be able to sell it on for a similar price so you needn't hang onto it.

I would advise you to wait a while, though, after the offending 'improvement', because I have found that changes in my home often do feel a little 'off' at the beginning but then they settle in and become part of the background (in a good way). It's kind of like a new pair of shoes – you have to break things in a bit and see if they become comfortable. So, give your changes a chance and see how it feels to get out of your comfort zone. But if it's still not working for you after a while, don't panic – embrace changing things again to get the feeling you want for your home.

Take your time

Taking time over my home decisions doesn't always come naturally to me. I am a dive-in-with-both-feet kind of person, but I love the idea of an evolving home, ever changing to meet the needs of its occupants, continuously adapting to the ebb and flow of life within its four walls. Although the thought of our home never being finished would have made me lose my mind when our builders were doing major structural work, I've come round to the idea (although I still don't miss the house's lath and plaster carcass!). At the start of any revamp, I tend to have an idea of how a room will look but I try not to become too focused on the end result, instead enjoying the process, knowing that there are many ways a room can come together. And if you are a committed faffer (like myself), there is a joy to wandering around a room, fiddling with furnishings and knowing that nothing stands still for long.

EMBRACE

Start with the corners

I know from experience just how overwhelming it can be to approach a new space. Even when armed with a mood board and a sense of personal style, the overwhelming task of transforming a room into a cohesive haven looms large. One of the more useful pieces of advice I have shared over the years is to start with the corners of a room, and let the design naturally unfold. It never fails to create a harmonious, three-dimensional space.

Picture our former living room, a large open-plan dining/living space that had the potential to feel somewhat soulless and disjointed. The process began with a decision to dedicate a corner to the memory of J's Grandma Joyce. In this corner, a set of vintage theatre chairs not only addressed our spatial constraints but also introduced an element of timeless charm. These chairs, meticulously chosen, were not just a practical seating solution but an anchor for the room's character.

The top left corner became a canvas for creativity. Here, I introduced a hanging pothos plant, its verdant tendrils cascading gracefully down and caressing the theatre chairs. The juxtaposition of nature against the vintage backdrop created a harmonious blend of the old and the organic. It was more than just décor; it was a living, breathing testament to the interconnectedness of design elements.

As the room expanded outward from this initial corner, we didn't merely add pieces; we chose to weave a narrative. The Cann Hall Road sign, placed with intention, became a poignant addition to Grandma Joyce's memorial. This corner, once an isolated space, now held the soul of the room – a small sanctuary where we could sit and reflect on moments shared with a beloved (great-)grandparent.

Starting with the corners allowed for a gradual, thoughtful progression. Each addition was a deliberate brushstroke on the canvas, contributing to the overall composition. This method isn't about randomly filling spaces; it's a strategic and mindful approach. By addressing smaller sections first, we avoided the trap of disjointed walls, and instead witnessed the seamless blending of intentional elements.

So, if the prospect of tackling a blank canvas overwhelms you, embrace the corners as your starting point. This method also allows me to embrace negative space where necessary – not striving to fill every part of a wall for the sake of it. Instead, allowing those corners to be the anchor that grounds my creativity, allowing the room to evolve organically. In these smaller spaces, you'll find the opportunity to infuse personality and purpose, creating a harmonious, three-dimensional space that beckons with warmth and charm.

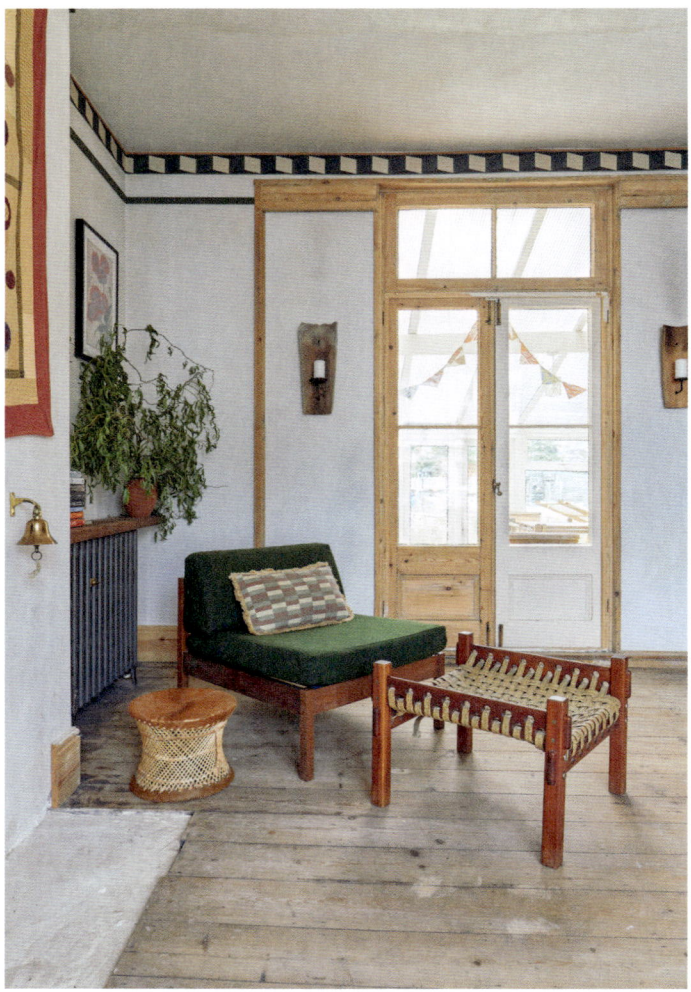

CHAPTER 6

YOUR HOME AS A WHOLE

I've found that we often become preoccupied by the smaller aspects of our home, especially ones that annoy us every day (mine are a leaking tap, a dodgy washing machine dispenser and a bathroom door lock that even Burglar Bill would struggle to open). Sometimes, these become distractions that take our focus away from making more fundamental improvements to our space. But when you take a step back to look at the bigger picture of your home instead of the micro niggles, you'll start to recognise how well it functions day to day or how it might be lacking. Many of the changes I've made to my homes over the years, big or small, have gone against popular advice; some worked out and some didn't. But the main thing I've learnt is that we should work with our homes, quirks and all, not against them. In turn, they will far better support us.

Tapping into your needs

It's so easy to be lured towards an aspirational life that you know in your heart of hearts won't meet your daily needs. What's the point of a beautiful but unyielding low back sofa if you love to lounge? It might look pleasing, but when all you crave at the end of the day is the soft, marshmallow cushions of a corner sofa, then what? Why bother with the time and expense of lusting after or even creating a minimalist kitchen if, like me, you're a chaotic cook that needs to have all their utensils on display? Similarly, if you're not fussed about a garden and have a wonderful park across the road, maybe private outdoor space doesn't need to be on your must-have list (despite people or social media telling you otherwise!).

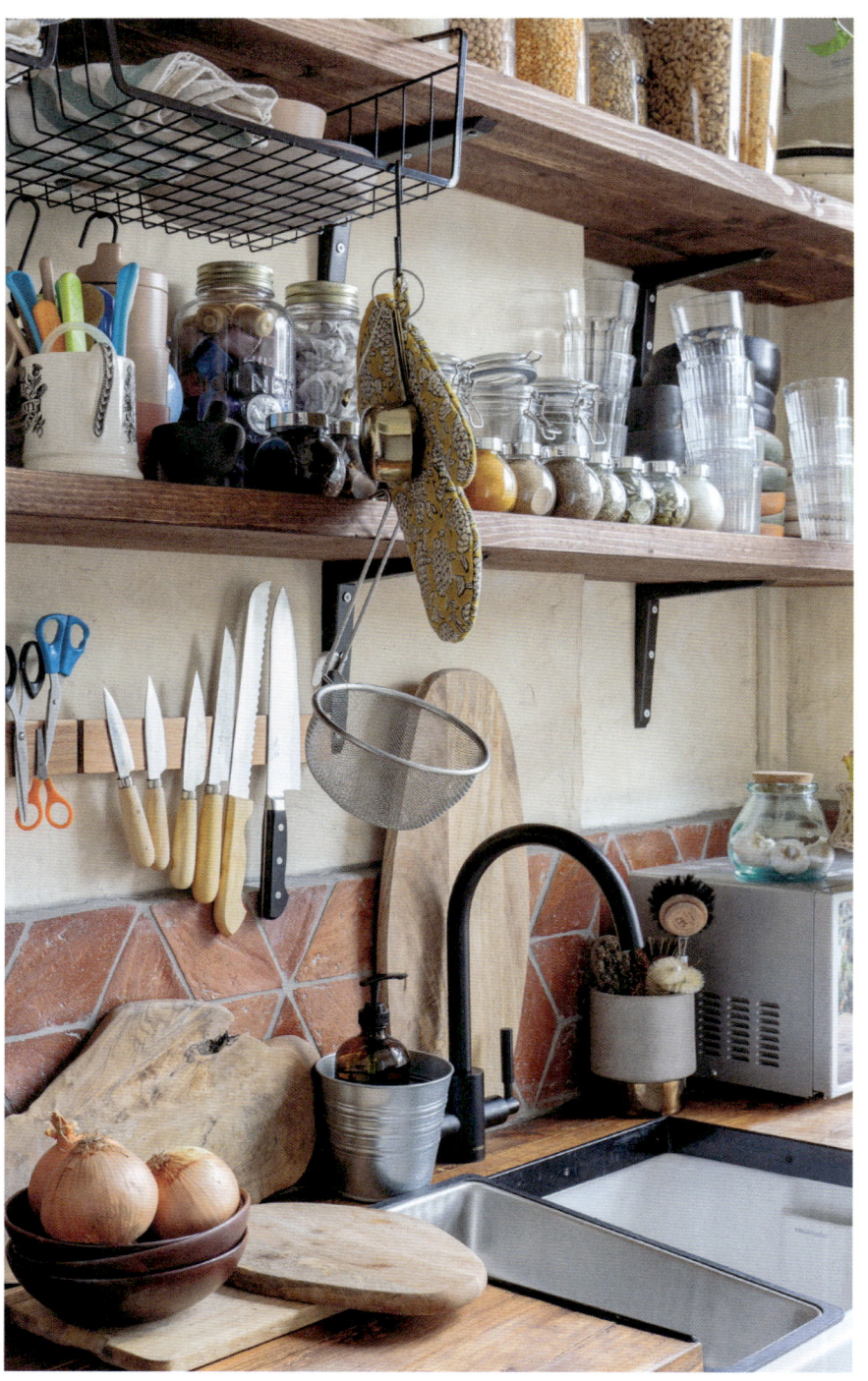

Getting real about your needs and wants may mean letting go of (or putting on hold for the future) the fantasy home life we all have a habit of inhabiting. Fantasy home lives may include things like owning a bike or other sports equipment that you never use (despite being super outdoorsy in your alternate reality!) or wanting to be the type of family that doesn't own a TV, when the reality is that you all love a bit of telly downtime. The problem is that unless you have lots of storage for these fantasy interests, they will likely be impinging on your enjoyment of the now, while you live in a space that isn't truly reflective of who you are. In the past, when I unconsciously prioritised a fictional life that didn't represent my everyday experience, I not only drove myself to distraction, but was left feeling inadequate because I wasn't living up to the (impossible) standards I was setting myself. It's like hanging onto clothes that haven't fit for years or those more out-there pieces that no longer align with your current life.

When you come to see that a home can be set up in any number of ways to meet the unique needs of its inhabitants, it is really freeing because it helps remove perceived limits you may be harbouring. For example, the people who lived in my house before us did not have the same family make-up as ours and were at another stage of life to us. So (unsurprisingly), they used the house in a very different way to how we do now. Both homes were well-loved and beautifully decorated, but very different all the same. Similarly, if we were to move on, I would fully expect the house's new inhabitants to make changes to the configuration, flow and furniture placement to suit their needs. In a couple of years from now when our youngest is close to school age, I can well imagine us changing up the layout of our home once again. And when they're all grown up and have moved out, it just might become that B & B/farm that J and I so often joke about!

Discerning your priorities

In the same way that only you can establish your needs, similarly your priorities are for you to determine, based on your unique circumstances and preferences. For J and I, the kids having a dedicated space to play was a vital part of our wish list when we were leaving our flat in London – at that point we had three children sharing a bedroom. We had configured a triple-storey bunkbed to fulfil our most basic requirements for the room, and the rest of their modestly sized bedroom worked overtime as a playroom with clever toy displays and storage. Every hidden nook and cranny of the room was used, but, through no fault of our own, I now know just how over-stimulating that was for our children.

As I said earlier in the book, ensuring we had a playroom for the children would, of course, mean a compromise too – them all continuing to share a bedroom, at least for a time. A lot of people have questioned our sanity around that choice (given that their bedroom resembled a cute dorm room of sorts for a year!) but we stand by the decision.

Another priority was to have a dedicated guest bedroom for our loved ones when they come to stay, especially because they'll have travelled for hours by the time they reach us. For me, just the idea of a spare room represents so much more than the physical space it occupies, it represents assurance that we can welcome our wider family and friends and be surrounded in familiarity in an area that's still relatively new to us. My warmest memories as a child stem from the openness with which my grandma welcomed me into her home over the years. Often I'd turn up unannounced, having spent the four-hour train journey contemplating my life choices, and I just knew I'd have my pick of one of three already made-up guest rooms to rest my head on for as long as I needed. To be able to do the same for not just my grandma but also the next generation of family members who might need a brief sanctuary is huge to us. The guest room also became crucial over the preceding year when ill health meant we had to rely on family more.

We considered priorities around home as a whole earlier in the book, and here I'd like to suggest you think about those priorities in terms of the separate spaces in your home.

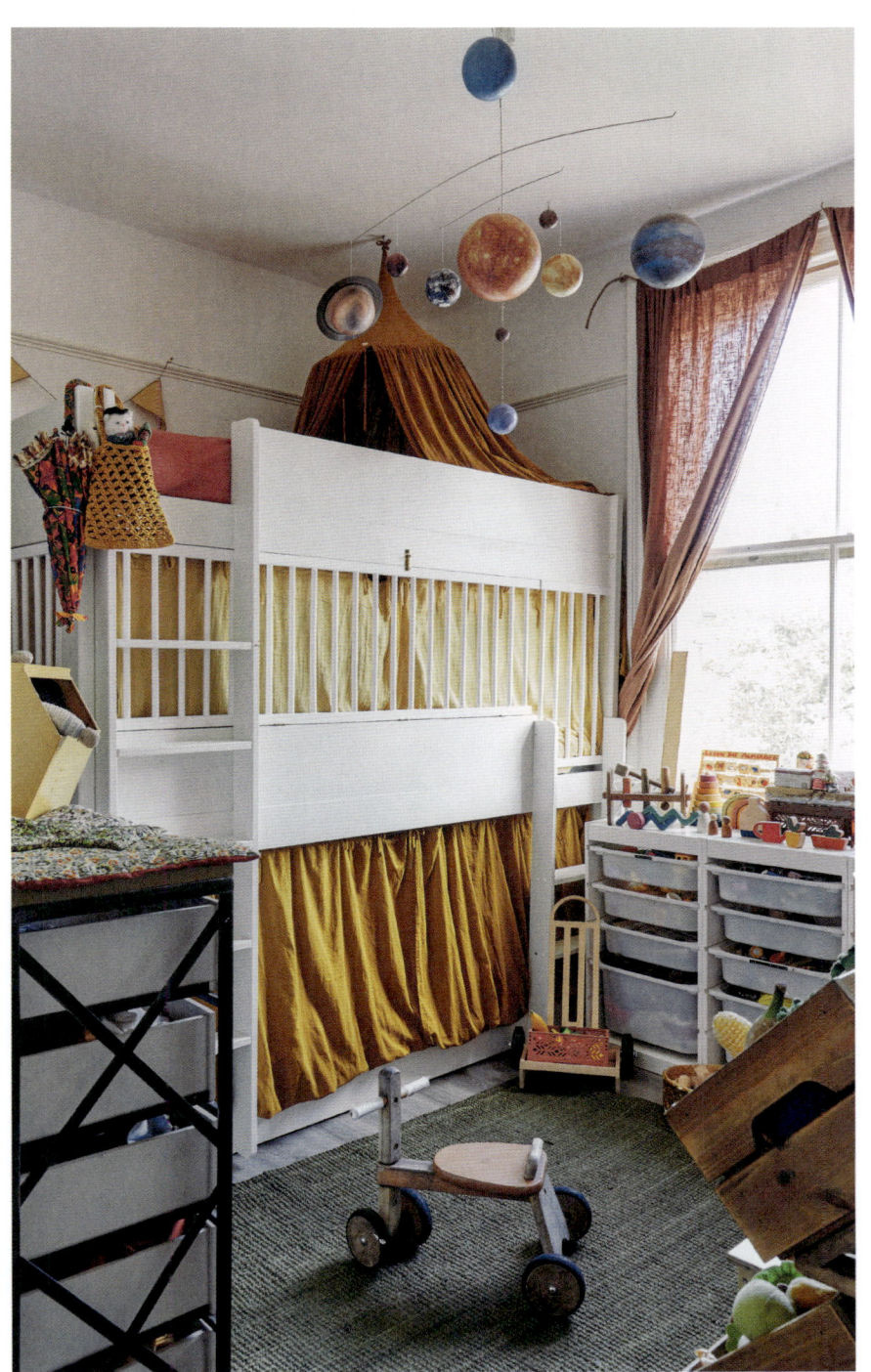

Here is a quick checklist that might help focus your priorities:

- What will I use this space for? If it's more than one thing (such as a dining table that also needs to function as a WFH desk and/or a craft or homework table for children), list each function in order of priority.
- Aside from me, who will use this space?
- Are there any non-negotiables for this space? (For example, our small patio had to accommodate a barbecue for my husband, a miniature shed for me and a little water play station for the kids.)
- What will I be giving up in changing this space? Will prioritising in this way be worth any compromise that might result?

Remember to prioritise the small details too

Envision a day in the life of your future self, starting from the moment you wake up. For example, if you like to get up and make a hot drink before slinking back into bed to drink it (oh yeah), what might help to support this little ritual? A soft rug for the feet to step onto? A bedside table or shelf to safely place the cup? A lamp you can reach from the bed (if you don't have a socket, a battery-powered light could be used)? I'm a big believer in carving out smaller joys, looking after ourselves and keeping our cups full – think of little ways that your home can help you do this throughout the day.

The importance of design

The way in which our homes are designed can be life changing. This might sound like an overblown claim but each and every one of us has a physiological response to our environment that affects how we feel, which goes on to impact (for better or worse) our relationships, our work and of course our overall wellbeing. It's the reason why in recent years there has been a bigger focus on the impact of architecture and design on a building's occupants and calls for a more sympathetic approach that optimises our health. This more considerate design has been at the forefront of many architects' minds when designing new public buildings, such as hospitals and schools, where studies have shown that patients and students fare better in calming spaces that let in natural light, are temperate, easier to clean and have good acoustics. In simple terms, when our bodies experience comfort in a space our minds correspond, and we tend to feel less stressed and more at ease.

Good design in your homes will not only help you feel encased in safety: the way your home functions, from its layout to the arrangement of furniture, will hugely affect how you live. I find this fact so overlooked in our lives, especially given that there are many things we can do to optimise it.

'Good design' may sound very vague as a concept – like I'm talking about a particular style of decoration – but what we're looking for here is a way to consciously coordinate the space we live in to enhance our wellbeing. And there are some very simple ways to do this. The rest of this chapter looks at ways to incorporate good design into our home (even when our space is not naturally blessed with it).

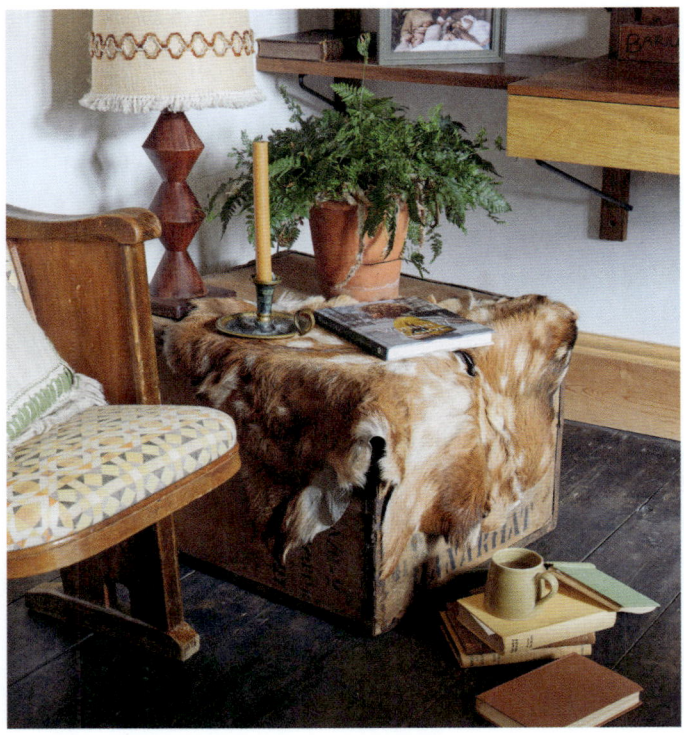

Flow and cohesion

The term 'flow' is bandied about a lot but it can sound quite vague, can't it? In basic terms, it just means how you organise your space to make moving through it a pleasing rather than irritating experience. You might think that if you have a small room you'll just have to put up with a certain amount of tripping over things in a way that you wouldn't with a larger space, but that doesn't have to be the case.

We knew quite early on that our small kitchen in our Islington maisonette would need re-evaluating from scratch. The kitchen that had been fitted was a mass-produced, one-size-fits-all style that didn't take into account the practicalities of the very small room (for example, there was no space to open one of the cupboard doors while also standing in the kitchen!). If you are about to move into a new room or new home, or even if you have lived there a while, I recommend drawing out a floorplan to help you work out how it will function and where best to place furniture, lighting and soft furnishings such as rugs. A floor plan, with all the furniture marked on it roughly to scale, will help you get to grips with a room, showing any flaws in flow before you find out the hard way and have to lug your sofa across the room in the hope of finding a more advantageous spot.

In the first instance, you can do this simply by using pencil and paper and not worrying too much about scale (or if you are more tech-savvy by all means do this on screen – there are lots of free programs online that help with space planning). Looking at your space from a bird's-eye view can help you see how you will have to move around furniture and show you bottlenecks. It'll also help you work out where you might incorporate some storage opportunities (essential unless you want to be tripping over books, toys, shoes or any other essential life detritus). You will also see the most commonly used pathways, such as the route from the doorway to the sofa or the fridge to the hob. Don't be afraid to change things up, like the furniture placement, especially if you've lived in a space for a while and/or if your needs have changed – for example, you have an extra flatmate or find yourself working from home more.

Easy ways to improve flow

Seeing where your home works well and where it could be working harder for you will sync up with your priorities, as we saw earlier in this chapter. Here are some tricks to help boost a feeling of spaciousness even if square footage is tight.

Map things out on the floor

Before hiking furniture about and hoping it works in a new corner, mark out the space with masking tape and you'll get a better sense of how it will feel in the room (more so than with measuring tape alone).

Choose materials wisely

Children's author Judith Kerr, who often drew her real home into her illustrations, said in an interview that she never had anything in her home she minded getting damaged. There's a certain relaxed wisdom to this. I wouldn't go so far as to say there's nothing in my home that I wouldn't mind being damaged, but choosing materials and furnishings that realistically meet the demands of traffic in your home will help its longevity. That cream bouclé sofa may be the one of your dreams, but is it the practical choice for a home with children and/or pets?

Consider shape and size

A sofa or two armchairs? A round/oval dining table or a square/rectangular one? If you've worked to create a space but it's just not coming together and you don't know why, consider the shape of your pieces. I'm not suggesting you go out on a spending spree; you might be able to improvise with what you already have (at least in the short-term) to see if it's worth finding a more permanent piece. I always check local stores, charity shops and neighbourhood sale or swap groups for things like tables, seating and lamps, and I often seem to stumble upon something suitable and inexpensive.

Embrace seasonality

Experiment by moving things around as the seasons change, for example, in summer you can place a sofa or armchair in front of a radiator (which would otherwise block the heat in winter) and have a different view of the room while sitting there. As the weather warms up, pack away any heavier blankets,

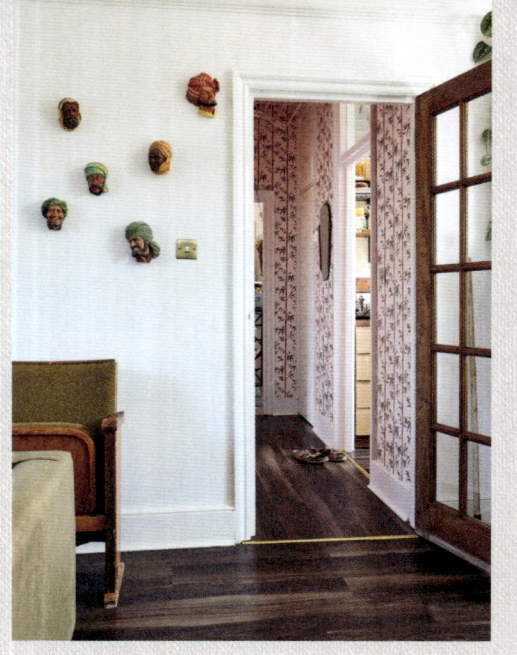
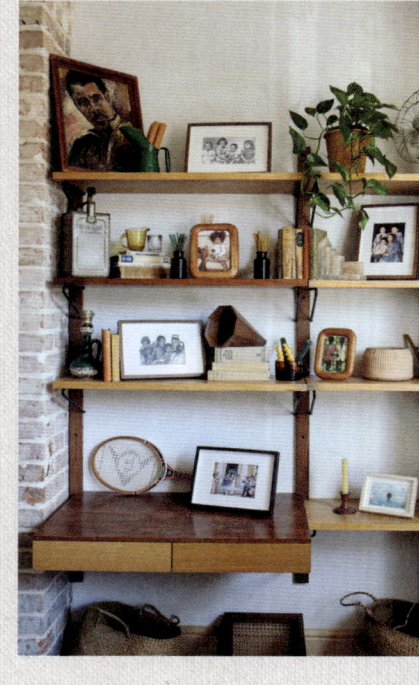
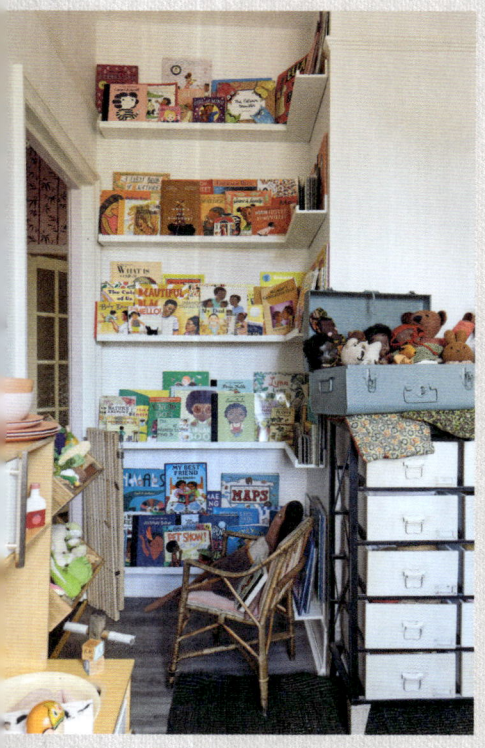
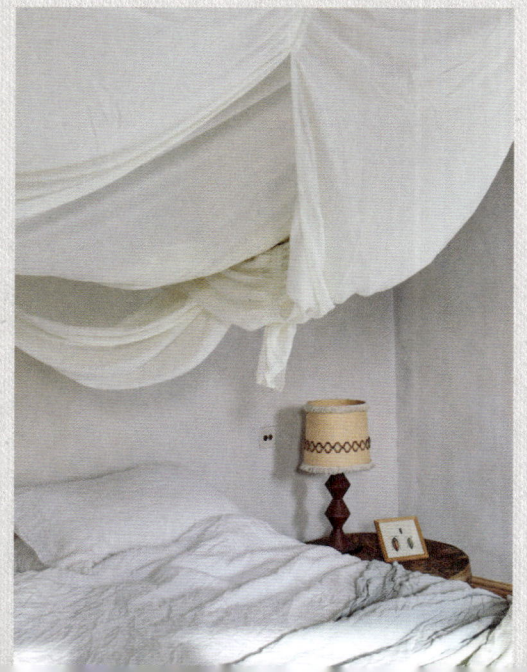

bringing them out again as autumn arrives. Moving artworks around your walls can also help you notice them again if they've been fading into the background.

Vertical storage

Moving things off the floor and onto the walls can be so advantageous, especially in smaller spaces. Shelving, free-standing wall cabinets, coat hooks, stationery organisers, wall-mounted side tables and desks that can be folded down when not in use, and plant pots on shelves or suspended from the ceilings will all help with that. One of the biggest wins in our previous flat was removing the children's bedroom door entirely and mounting a floor-to-ceiling bookcase in the dead space behind it. It was a triumph and I've loved seeing it replicated when I've been tagged in pictures from my Instagram followers over the years since.

Negative space

Not filling every inch of space can really add a feeling of spaciousness, particularly in high-traffic areas. I'm a magpie at heart but sometimes a big clear-out reminds me that (a little bit) less is (sometimes) more! There can be a certain beauty in empty space, a sense of openness. Maximalists among you, feel free to disagree!

Cohesion and colour

Many interior designers advocate cohesion throughout our homes through use of colour, often choosing a palette that seamlessly allows one space to flow organically to the next. I am naturally drawn to a palette of earthy tones like olive greens, burnt orange, mustard yellow, mahogany brown and warm neutrals like creams and whites. These colours wind through my home in the paint on the walls, in fabrics, furnishings and artworks. However, I don't believe you have to stick to a set palette to create a wonderful home with a cohesive feel (although you may like to do so, if that's to your taste). I have seen homes rich in contrasting elements – patterned wallpaper, paint all colours of the rainbow, clashing prints and patterns on fabrics, a juxtaposition of textures – and somehow it all works. Sometimes throwing the rulebook out the window and tapping into your gut feeling really pays dividends.

I think colour is one area of the home where it's best to go for your tried-and-tested favourites, because these are often quite intrinsic to you already. For example, what sort of colours do you gravitate towards in your wardrobe, or in the furniture and objects you already own? If you go very off-piste with a paint colour, will you need to buy all new furniture to go with it? I'm not saying be boring with your choices or stick to plain white or anything like that, but ensuring that the colours in your home are ones you already love will help make the place feel like it's yours.

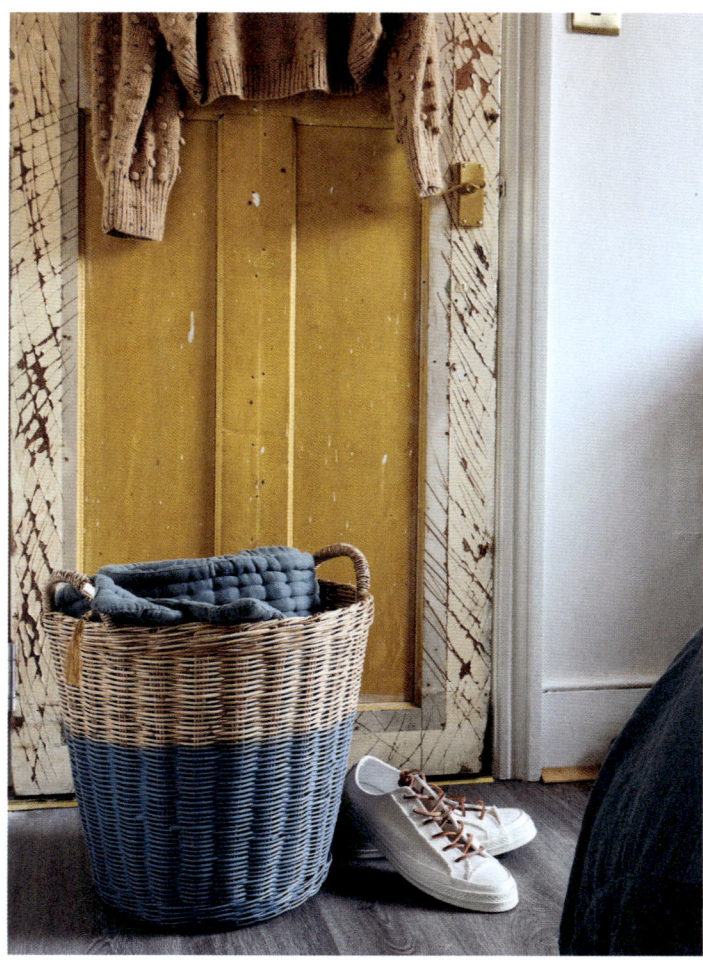

Open-plan versus broken-plan

For a long time, we've been sold the renovation idea, 'If in doubt, knock it out', meaning knocking down walls to create a bigger space from two or more smaller rooms. It can seem like a great idea, but sometimes when you consider what you'll have to lose to make it work, you may decide otherwise. Ideally, our homes will have one larger room, usually the kitchen, to act as a convivial space that can comfortably accommodate every member of the home (hopefully with space for visitors too), in addition to another living space that you can cosy up in and enjoy a bit of peace and quiet. However, I accept that this much space is a huge luxury and probably not the reality for most.

Older houses, like the ones built in the Victorian or Edwardian periods, which make up a large portion of the housing stock in the UK, often feature narrow galley kitchens, that tend not to be big enough to fit a dining table, while homes built in more recent decades have often been designed to have one bigger kitchen/dining/living space. These bigger open plan rooms can feel really sociable and spacious, but if they're the only space you have in the home to 'live' in, and there isn't a separate room that can be used as a study, playroom or TV room, that open-plan kitchen has to work hard to fulfil everyone's needs.

This is something that came to light for many of us in lockdown during the pandemic. Though a huge privilege to be able to stay safe at home, the reality of a whole household using one room for all their competing needs – Zoom meetings, homework, downtime in front of the TV, making meals and tidying up – highlighted what is lost when too much of our square footage is given to open-plan living.

Breaking up open-plan spaces

A large, ill-used area can feel smaller, and by token a smaller space can feel much more the sum of its parts if used well. Breaking up a space according to its function (aka zoning) means you can take advantage of every part of it, compartmentalising to meet your needs.

Furniture placement

Using a sofa or table to create 'boundaries' within a room rather than placing it up against a wall can be an effective way to mark zones.

Open shelving

This can be a really good way of separating two high-functioning spaces and gaining storage in the process, while still allowing light to shine through.

Different décor

Mixing up the styling, whether through the paint colour, flooring or soft furnishings, will create a deliberately segregated look in an open-plan space.

Rugs

Try a rug. Try two rugs! Textiles are a brilliant way to demarcate one area from another and add warmth and noise absorption in the process.

Plants

Divide spaces with greenery in the form of large potted plants on the floor and smaller ones on open shelves or in baskets hung from the ceiling.

The joy of a nook

I read somewhere that as mammals, we are programmed to seek out small, cosy spaces to relax in. It might be a quiet corner with a comfy chair to read a magazine in, or a makeshift tent behind the sofa that kids create as a private den (no adults allowed!). I like to think of these tendencies as how a small forest animal will burrow underground seeking warmth and shelter. When we don't have the luxury of a room of one's own, the best we can aim for is a cosy corner.

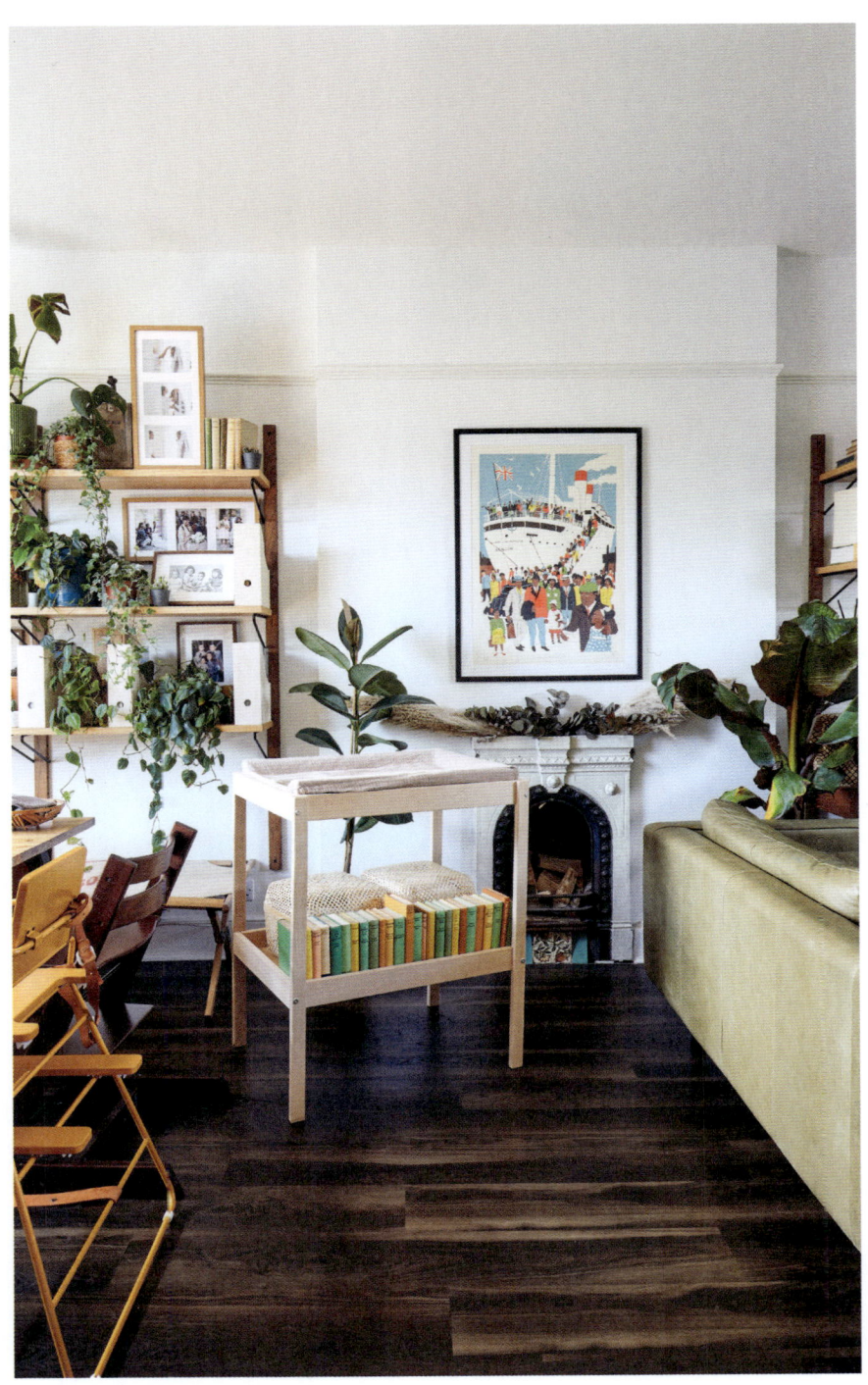

Storage

It seems like the world (or my small corner of it) has become slightly obsessed with the need for storage and having more of it. So, my deep dive begins here by looking at different types of shelving and how to incorporate easy storage fixes in the next chapter. You've no doubt been inundated with images of pristine pantries or freakishly tidy toy cupboards, all adorned with clear boxes (often colour-coded!). I love a storage basket as much as the next person and there's something deeply satisfying about an organised cupboard of bed linens, but I can't help but wonder if we've slightly fetishised all our 'stuff'.

Ode to a well-placed shelf

Shelves add immediate character to homes of any period or layout and can be very versatile if done right. In our new home, there were several alcoves calling out for some shelving, and we kept an eye out for discarded wood we could use. Buying new timber can be incredibly expensive, and prices have risen in recent years. (We've been known to drag good pieces of solid wood we've found on the street home to turn into shelves!) Whether they're floating shelves (i.e. the fixtures are hidden) or held up by lovely brackets (which you can always find second-hand on websites like eBay), I'd almost go so far as to say you can't have too many shelves, especially if you're endowed with lots of books, art or objects close to your heart that you want to display. Furthermore, shelves can hide all the ugly essentials of life when you stack them with attractive boxes or baskets – who needs to know your lovely bolga basket is home to all the chargers for the household electronics? Below are a few ways you can sneak in some extra shelves at home without sacrificing space.

Shelf over a radiator

Placed at least 5cm over your radiator, these small shelves are useful, particularly in lieu of a side table if you have a chair or sofa close by (and it saves on floor space too). They're low enough for children to reach and so they're a nice way for them to display their treasures. Some people swear a shelf above the radiator makes a space warmer too, as apparently they direct more of the radiator's rising heat into the room.

A single high shelf

I don't know why these look so good, but they do. Placed at around 35cm from the ceiling (if using as a bookshelf), or around 25cm for smaller trinkets, they make good use of otherwise forgotten space and draw the eye upwards, which gives your room a sense of extra height. Admittedly, these shelves are not the most accessible, so you're unlikely to store your everyday items here, but they make a happy home for a collection of beloved objects (books will look particularly good up here).

Alcove shelving

Why mess with a classic solution! Installed floor-to-ceiling and used for books and ornaments, these can make a big statement in a room. Two to three shelves can also look striking when placed above furniture, i.e. a chest of drawers or another form of free-standing or built-in storage. Another option would be to have two to three shelves lower down for books, trinkets, toys or storage baskets, and to keep the space above shelf-free. If you have two alcoves either side of a chimney breast or similar, consider whether you want to keep the traditional look by maintaining symmetry or throw the cat among the pigeons by mixing it up a bit.

Floating bedside shelf

If space is too tight for a bedside table, a floating shelf can be a great solution. You can easily buy floating shelves or cabinets specifically designed to be bedside tables but I have found that they're often overpriced for what they are, and they're quite easily home-made if you have the inclination. If you're really tight on space, a bedside shelf can be very narrow, just enough space to rest a cup or similar. If you float two parallel shelves (one above the other horizontally), you can place a basket in between as a makeshift drawer (just measure up in advance to get the depth right. If there's a socket near your bed, you'll find that a hole drilled into a bedside shelf can be very handy for feeding a charging cable through, or the cable of a wall- or headboard-mounted lamp.

Shelf or picture rail above a bed

A shallow shelf or picture shelf above your bed will allow for the perfect focal point for your favourite artworks (and an easy platform for rotation). Just ensure that when you're measuring for it, you sit up in bed to ensure it's placed with plenty of room above your head (or the head of the tallest bed inhabitant!).

I hope this chapter has helped you see how we can find solace in prioritising genuine needs over aspirational aesthetics, viewing our homes as dynamic entities shaped by personal experiences. Discerning our own priorities is crucial, as is using wisdom to design spaces that evolve with our changing lives.

Flow, cohesion and colour intertwine in this design symphony, offering avenues for both rebellion and conformity. Open-plan and broken-plan living have merit as we navigate breaking up spaces for versatile use. The well-placed shelf becomes a poetic blend of practicality and visual appeal, while storage permits an artful curation of one's possessions. In this design narrative, broader strokes paint a harmonious picture, reflecting who we are and nurturing our daily lives within our homes' grand tapestry. In the next chapter, we will be exploring beginner-friendly updates with impactful results.

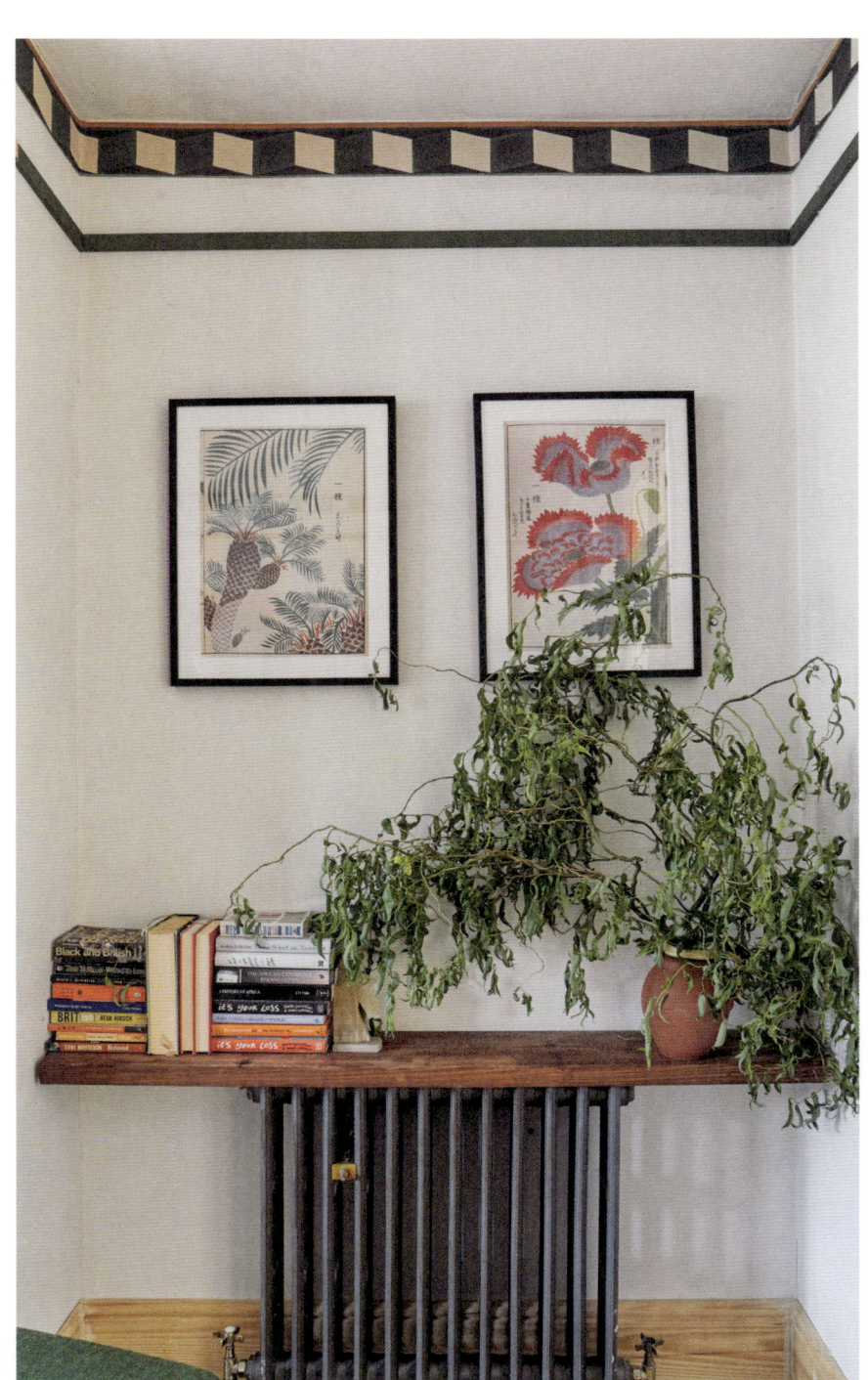

CHAPTER 7

EASY UPDATES

As a child, I watched my mum, a savvy, free-thinking creative, work magic in every space we ever lived in. A camcorder recording captures her elegantly cradling my newborn sister as she tells her brother behind the camera about all the grand plans she has for transforming our little rented flat in Camden. A mosaic here, a dado rail there. Growing up, there never seemed to be any tangible barriers between my mum's visions for our home and her executing them, and that can-do influence has never left me. It was the 1990s then, and Camden Town was a hub of creativity. My mum would scour skips in affluent areas and lug prized pieces of furniture home, with four young kids in tow. And if she couldn't find the dream piece of furniture within her budget, you'd better believe she would make it! Her ingenuity knew no bounds, and as a newcomer to London, she made the most of every opportunity the capital had to offer.

I've never forgotten my mum's confidence when it came to transforming our homes and making them feel like ours, even though she didn't own them. This chapter explores some of the ways in which J and I have harnessed my mum's energy, putting our stamp on our homes while avoiding alterations that were too labour-intensive. When you don't have the time, budget or inclination to go all-out on a revamp, a succession of small wins become more than the sum of their parts. I hope you find some inspiration here that allows you to invest in your space, even if you don't own it or won't be there permanently. There's plenty you can do on a shoestring to breathe new life into a tired home. Let these ideas inspire you to think of more.

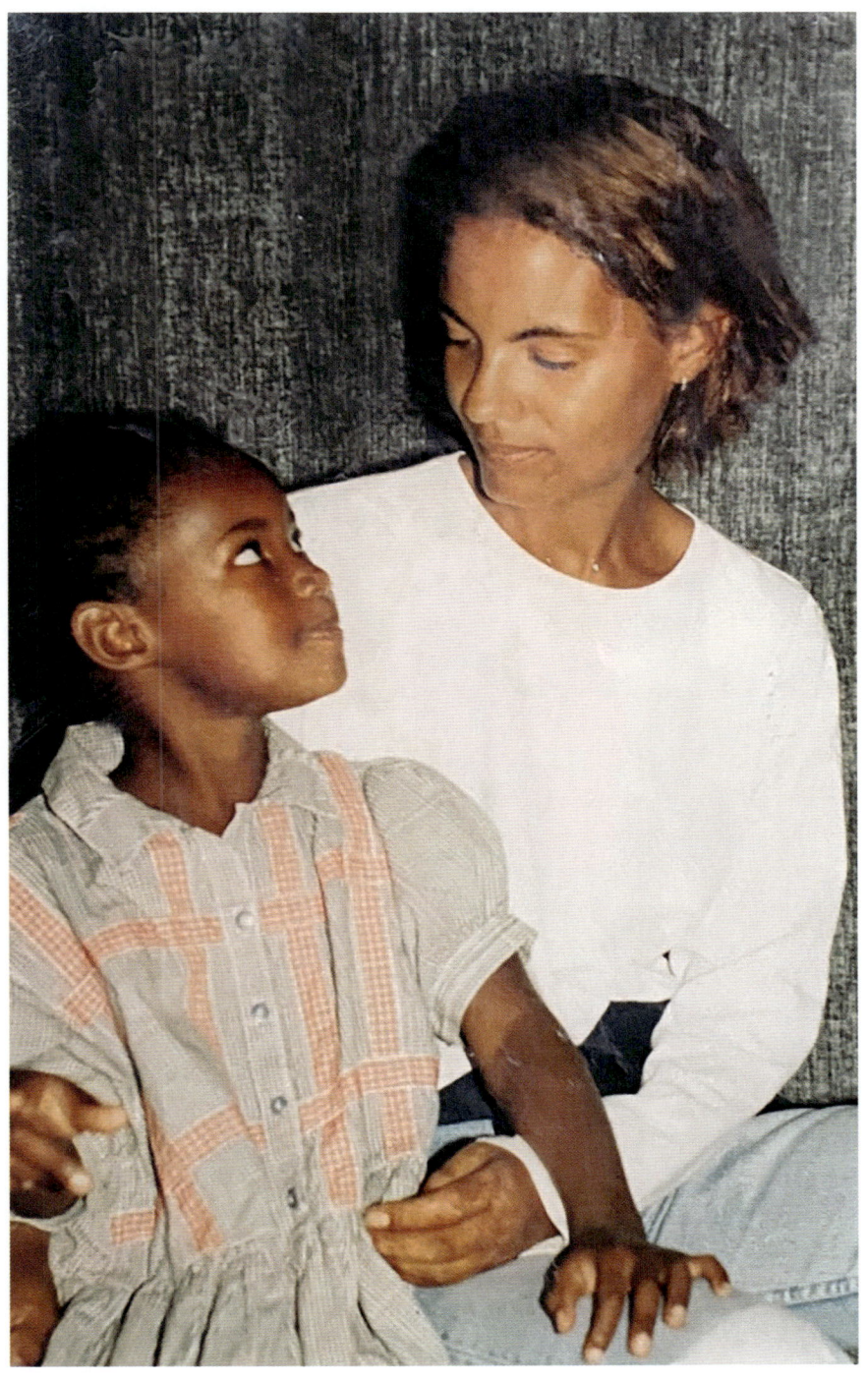

Pick up a paintbrush

One of the most radical changes you can make to a space, and for relatively little money (especially if you're willing to stick on your favourite music and do it yourself), is painting. OK, I realise there's a bit of subjectivity as to whether painting a room falls under the 'easy' aspect of this chapter, but I'm going with it! A weekend with a bucket of paint and some good podcasts is time well spent in my opinion.

For me, if my home were looking worse-for-wear, even in a temporary space and especially if it was covered in that landlord favourite, magnolia, I would take the time to give it a once over with a paintbrush. I never achieve the most professional job, but I've always found that painting, like cutting the grass in an overgrown garden, makes a bigger difference than you think it will, given that it can be done fairly quickly. In our current kitchen – an extremely tired room in desperate need of a revamp – we have painted the cabinets and replaced the handles as a short-medium fix while we save up over the next few years to bring it more in line with our tastes and needs. It's far from perfect but just that little update has made it a more liveable space for now.

Over the years, I've often been asked if I have noticed the difference between cheaper and more expensive paints, and the answer is that I have used both and would say there is a difference, which is, perhaps surprisingly, more noticeable when you use neutral shades like whites and creams. That said, it hasn't prevented me from colour-matching cheaper paints for more short-term projects to great effect, so don't feel like you have to shell out on expensive paints if they're not within your budget – we're all doing what we can with what we've got.

Getting started

There has been a big increase in paint suppliers in recent years, so there's never been more choice. Other than narrowing down by colour, there are a few other things to consider, such as the finish (see below for a breakdown of these), and the environmental and in-home air-quality impact of a paint (I advise ensuring it is breathable and has low VOC levels).

Much of the labour involved in painting is in the preparation, from clearing a room (or moving all the furniture to the centre of the room and covering it with protective sheets) to cleaning the walls of any marks or dust (using warm water, in addition to mild soap for more stubborn marks), and filling and sanding down any uneven patches (YouTube has lots of videos showing pre-painting repairs).

Depending on what you're painting, you'll likely need some or all of the following basic kit:

- Foam rollers and brushes (check what sizes you need), and a paint tray. Angled brushes are useful for 'cutting in' tricky areas that a roller won't reach, such as between the ceiling and wall or the corners.
- A sponge, warm water and gentle soap or washing-up liquid.
- Filler or sealer for any noticeable imperfections.
- A primer or undercoat, suitable for the paint you're using.
- Frog tape (don't skimp with cheap tape, it's not worth it) to protect other parts of the room such as woodwork and ceiling – or you can do without this if you have a very steady hand and feel confident!
- If going the whole hog and painting every surface in the room, follow this order: ceilings, walls, then woodwork. You will likely need at least two top coats depending on the colour and finish of what you're painting over.

Preparation

With a bit of luck, all you'll need to do before starting is give the walls a thorough dusting and a wipe down with warm water mixed with a little washing-up liquid. If you have plaster coming away from the walls or lots of bumps (quite common in older houses), attaching wallpaper lining paper before painting can be cheaper than hiring a plasterer to skim walls and easier than replastering yourself (a skilled job, not for the faint-hearted). Even if you don't manage to get your surface perfectly prepped, it's likely that painting will still improve the room overall, so have a go.

Paint finishes

Consider the type of finish you'd like.

- **Matt (also called 'flat'):** these finishes come in a spectrum but tend to show wear and tear more easily than emulsion or high-sheen paint.
- **Emulsion:** a water-based paint, often the go-to for interiors as it's faster drying than an oil-based paint. Not a great deal of texture to the finish, but it gets the job done.
- **Eggshell:** a smoother, move velvety finish which is more durable than matt, so it's very good for high-traffic areas.
- **Gloss:** I don't think anyone should ever use gloss! It's an oil-based paint, very shiny and super resistant to marks, but once you've painted something with gloss it's so hard to remove that there's no going back (at least not without considerable effort).

For areas with a lot of traffic or children frequently running around, I would highly recommend using a paint you can wipe clean and easily touch up without leaving a mark. We used a very porous limestone paint in our main bedroom, which looked amazing at first but rubs off when touched – not very practical with four little people scrambling into our bed each morning.

You can mix and match finishes throughout your home to deliberately add texture and intrigue, which I explain further below.

Samples

Try to get paint samples before committing to a colour. I'm terrible for skipping this one (remember my nauseating green bedroom wall?) but it always surprises me how deceptive colours appear onscreen or in a paint shop. Colours can look very different depending on the time of day or amount of light. Rather than test your colour directly on the wall, I suggest you paint it onto several medium-large pieces of paper and stick these up around the room, including beside any windows, and observe how the colour changes in different lights over the course of a few days. Think about what times of day you use the room – if you live in an open-plan space, you'll likely be in there throughout the day but if it's a lesser-used room like a bedroom, you might prioritise a shade that looks loveliest in morning or evening light.

Re-use

In many areas, there are paint 'banks', where people donate their leftover paint (usually adhering to a decent minimum quantity), which you can then buy for a significantly reduced price. This is a great scheme that cuts down on waste and some of these paint banks are charitable enterprises that distribute the earnings from discounted paint to local charities or initiatives. Similarly, local neighbourhood groups often have paint giveaways or swaps, which can be especially good if you only have a small area to paint and you're open to colour options.

Palettes

In the previous chapter, we looked at how palettes can create cohesion in a home, and some people like to create a natural flow by using complementary shades throughout their home, sometimes deliberately repeating shades to amplify connection. I promised in the introduction to this book that I wasn't going to tell you what colour to slap on your walls and I am sticking to that! However, if you're at a complete loss at where to start, colour experts often recommend starting with neutrals (generally speaking, think softer shades like whites, creams, greys or beiges). From here, if you'd like to, you can add similar shades or different colours entirely through the furniture or furnishings.

Creating a mood board (see page 97) that shows all the colours used in your home or all the colours you want to use will give you an immediate sense of the overall palette.

Stand out or blend in

Painting can have an almost magical quality in the way it highlights or hides features in our homes, depending on what you're aiming for. It's pretty simple:

- If you want to make something stand out, paint it a different colour to your walls.
- If you want it to blend in, paint it the same colour.
- For a tonal look, use slightly different shades of the same family of paints to add layers to your room.

For example, if you are fortunate to have a lovely feature such as beautiful architrave or coving, show it off by painting it a different colour to the walls or ceiling. For details you're less keen on, such as dining chairs that have seen better days or cheap doors that are a bit battered (but not in a good way), paint them the same colour as their surroundings. This approach can also work well for older, yellowing, unattractive radiators, so they don't stand out like a sore thumb against a new paint job (just remember to use specialist radiator paint that tolerates heat). Think about contrasts. For a subtle contrast, choose shades just one or two away from each other for the woodwork, walls, ceilings and any features (lots of paint brands have collections that highlight these). For an understated, floating feel, paint shelves (and wooden brackets, if using) the same colour as the walls. On the other hand, paint shelves a contrasting colour to the walls to make them stand out. Both will look great, so it's just a matter of your personal taste.

And always remember, you can just paint them back if you feel you've made a mistake.

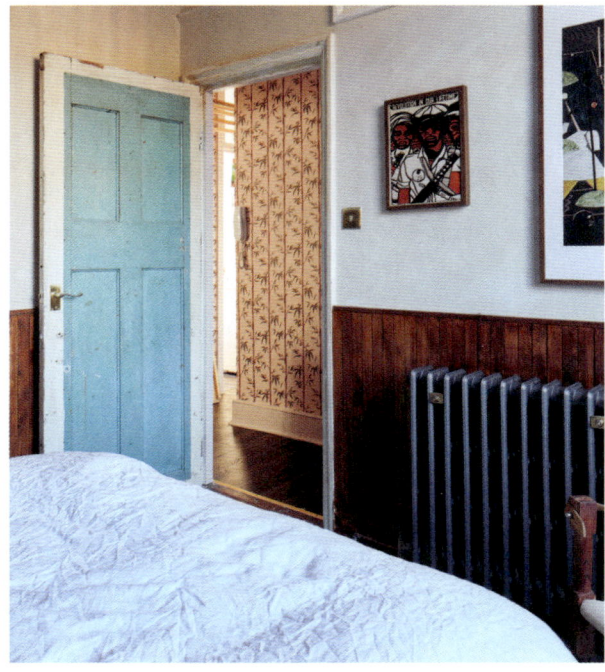

It's all about the details

Here are a few paint tricks to keep in mind for different effects in your home (some are counterintuitive):

Go small

If you don't want or need to paint the entire room, you can make a big impact by just painting smaller aspects, such as a door or skirtings. These will particularly stand out if you're using a contrasting shade. In our previous home in Islington, our bedroom was a display of landlord-selected 'sad beige' but we had a wonderful pop of colour in a turquoise and yellow reclaimed Victorian door.

Ceilings don't have to be white

Try painting your ceiling with colour – it can look really dramatic when you stray from what's expected, and it'll add a bit of intrigue to your space. You can use different colours for contrast, or, particularly if your room is in the attic or has sloped or vaulted ceilings, consider painting the walls and ceiling the same colour for a cocooning feel.

Wild woodwork

As per the previous point, woodwork, such as skirtings, architraves, doors, shutters, stairs and wooden fire surrounds, don't have to be white. I love when these are sanded down and left bare (or protected with a low-sheen oil), painted the same shade as the walls for a minimalist feel (known as colour drenching) or painted one shade darker for a subtle contrast.

uPVC

Plastic uPVC frames can be wonderful at keeping out draughts and noise while staying weatherproof, but they can often stand out unattractively, particularly if they've been added to an older building to replace original timber frames. Painting over the glaring white of uPVC window or door frames, using paint designed for that purpose, can be a game changer.

Picture rail

If you're lucky enough to have a picture rail in the room you're painting, you might be tempted to only paint your wall colour up to the rail, and have the wall above it match the ceiling. Just be aware that doing this can make the ceiling feel lower – which is fine in a room with high ceilings, but otherwise, you may want to reconsider.

Add an element of surprise

It's become clear that the advice of old to never paint a small space a dark colour is now outdated. Tiny spaces like cloakrooms, children's nooks and cupboards are often crying out for a rich, dark shade. Using a dark colour adds curiosity and charm to a room with a contrasting lighter shade on the walls. A small space is also easy to experiment with, as you can easily change it if you feel it hasn't worked as you'd hoped.

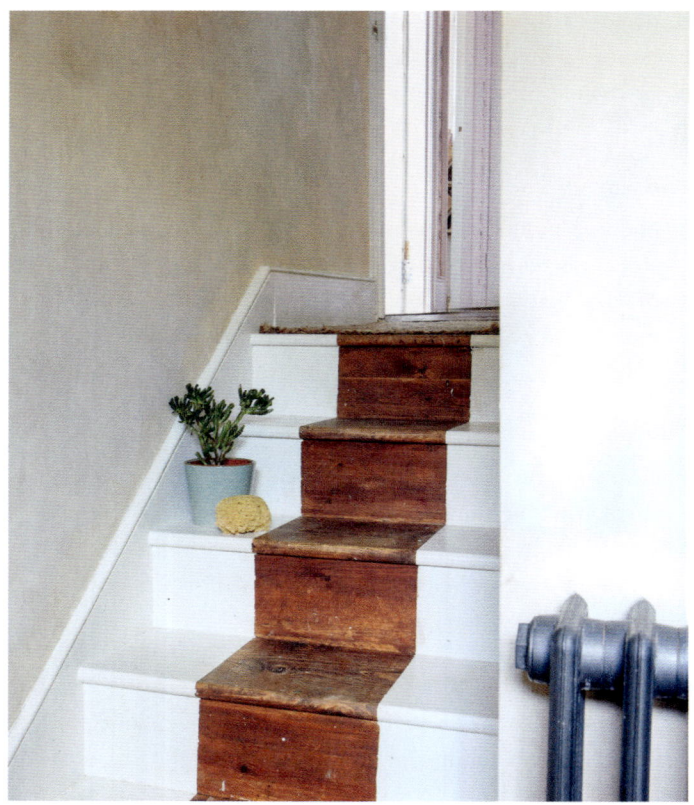

Wood stain

I love how some simple wood stain can transform a tired wooden floor, window frames, shelving or furniture. It can bring so much character and patina in just one coat and, depending on the colour and how many coats you use, you can create a variety of aesthetics, from Georgian library vibes to whitewashed Scandinavian minimalism. In our previous kitchen in London, we used a dark water-based stain on our shelves, transforming what was originally a light oak into a rich walnut hue. Using stains can be a clever way of revamping a more affordable type of wood, such as pine, to take on the appearance of another that might be out of your budget. Don't be afraid of mixing different woods in a room – a light ash stool will look beautiful against a darker glazed teak cabinet for example. Prepare your wood surface for staining by sanding down or vacuuming over it thoroughly. We used Kling-Strip paint remover on the spindles of our staircase bannisters, which is a useful shortcut if you need to dissolve layers of paint, particularly in hard-to-reach areas. Use stain samples on a patch of your wood to test what the outcome will be. Make sure it dries fully before casting your votes, and if you are undecided between shades, use a variety of samples. Use a brush, roller or lint-free cloth to apply.

Storing paint and stain

I really resent the precious cupboard space lost to leftover paint and stain pots; it's enough to make me want to paint every room the same colour to avoid it. Paint manufacturers usually advise not to use their products beyond six months of opening (though perhaps they have a vested interest in saying that!), so it's often not worth keeping large pots for long. My strategy is to decant enough from my pots into smaller jars for touching up wall scuffs and marks (leftover jam jars are handy). I label them (adding the finish, the room they've been used in, and the date) and then place them as compactly as possible in a plastic box with a clip lock lid. You can buy specific small pots for this purpose with clip lock containers but I have found reusing jars with screw top lids just as good, as long as they're placed in a box that isn't moved around often. I then donate any larger pots to a paint bank or a local giveaway website.

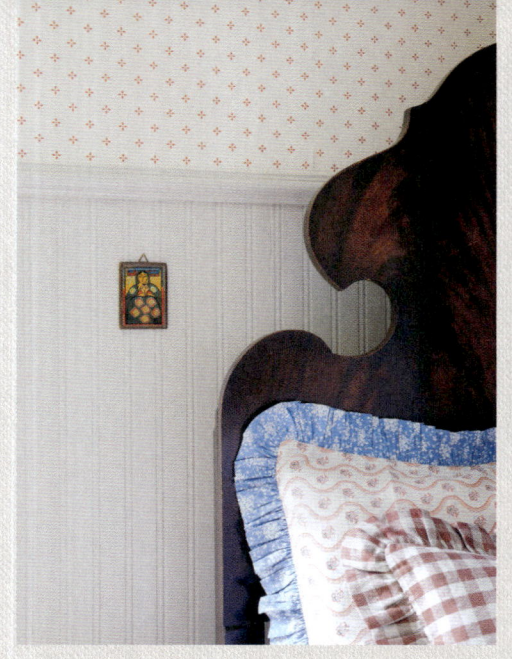
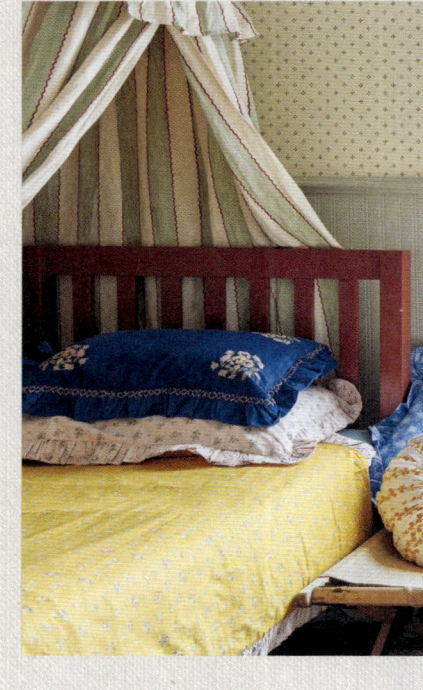
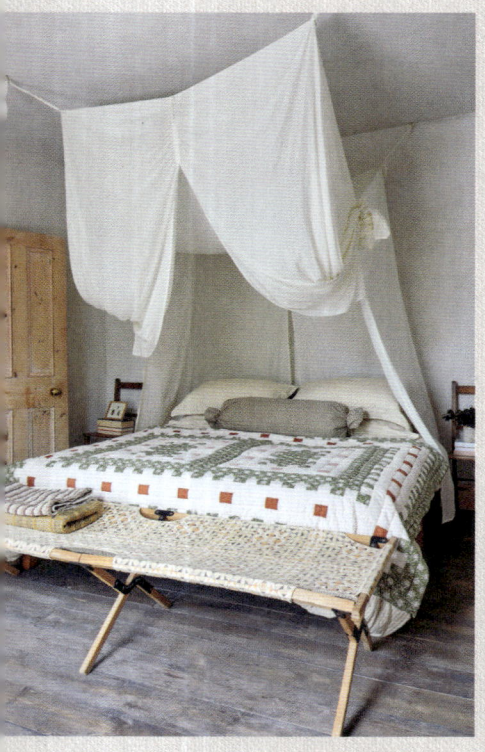
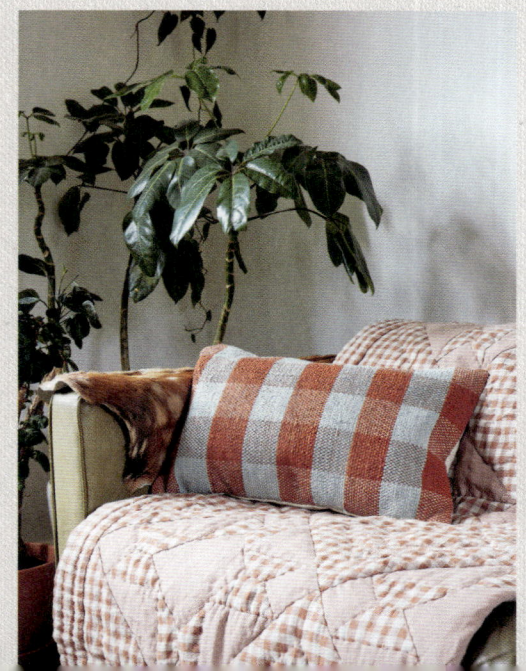

Fabric is your friend

If you don't wish to or aren't permitted to paint your space, there are many other things you can do to refresh it. Whether textiles on floors and walls; curtains on windows or in front of aspects you wish to conceal; or bedspreads, throws and cushions; fabrics immediately uplift a space. Of course, an added bonus is that you can take any fabrics with you if you leave and repurpose them in a new space.

Danish *hygge* and happiness expert Meik Wiking has written about the necessity for soft surfaces in our homes in order to feel secure, and I have found that texture is an essential (and often overlooked) component of a restful and restorative home. Just as with paint, think about the effect of contrast – a fluffy rug on a wooden floor, a cosy blanket on a leather sofa, a velvet curtain against a flat wall. Consider how texture can add more contrast, and more comfort, to your space.

Here are some ways to incorporate more soft furnishings into your space:

Curtains in place of doors

Chintz, stripe, geometric or pleasingly plain, using fabrics in your home will add warmth and personality. I love how curtains can be used to hide a multitude of sins rather than adding a door (usually much more expensive). Washing machines, door-free cupboards, the space under the stairs and a wardrobe rail within a recess are just some of the places crying out for a fabric front. Hung on a tension wire, these are easy to fit and move later on.

Shower curtains

Curtains rather than glass doors in the shower get a bad rap but they can work so much better in a smaller space, and if you are careful to pull the curtain across the rail after a shower, it will dry out more easily and prevent mould building up. There are lots of retailers and smaller manufacturers on websites like Etsy who will make beautiful (washing machine-friendly) linen or cotton shower curtains (with waterproof lining) cut to any size and with slots to hang from hooks of your choice.

Curtains and café curtains

Even if you are a sewing novice, you might be surprised at how easy it is to rustle up some very simple curtains. Fabrics such as muslin cotton or linen have a naturally relaxed feel, so it doesn't matter if they don't look perfect (personally I like the rough-edged look). Adhesive strips can be used easily to tailor fabric or ready-made curtains to the size you need, without a needle and thread in sight. There are also clever ways to create thicker, more plush curtains without the price tag, by joining together two lighter fabrics. YouTube has lots of tutorials for how to do this with or without a sewing machine.

Rugs

A rug can do a great job of hiding stains, absorbing noise, and can be laid over any type of floor to immediately transform a room. Your choice of fabric and weave will depend on your priorities – whether it's a high-traffic space like a hallway or a rarely used area like your bedside. You can buy some amazing vintage rugs online with a bit of searching, and if you're after a bargain, carpet shops often sell offcuts with sealed edges. I agree with the interior design advice that you should go for the most generously sized rug in a space – a little rug island in a bigger room somehow looks a bit measly. If you need rugs to add warmth or texture or to hide undesirable flooring in a bathroom, wet room, utility room (lucky you) or near the kitchen sink, you can source beautiful waterproof ones, many of which are made from recycled materials.

Sofas and armchairs

Embrace some lovely fabrics to give tired seating a second act. First, give your furniture a good vacuum and then start layering in your favourite fabrics (something for the seating base, back and arms, if there are any). The throws you use can be of the same fabric or all different textures (as well as shades and patterns) – whatever you prefer or have to hand. If you want to buy fabric, one surprisingly affordable way can be to source materials such as cotton or linen (or a mix of the two) by the metre and then either hem the edges yourself using a sewing machine (or by hand if you have the patience and you'd likely need to double up the thread) or send it to a tailor (often found in a dry cleaners).

If you have the budget, reupholstering a sofa or armchair can make it feel like new and saves you from sending a beloved piece of furniture to a landfill.

Cushions

I know I'm not reinventing the wheel here, but cushions are such a simple way to bring comfort to a home, and to yourself. Choose (or make) cushion covers that are very slightly smaller than your pads and they'll look extra inviting by fitting snugly around the filling.

Headboards

Hanging fabric on the wall behind your bed immediately injects a bit of drama into a room. The fabric can also be extended up to the ceiling and billowed out like sails on a ship.

Going a step further, you could have a go at reupholstering an existing fabric headboard – as upholstery goes, this is surprisingly straightforward, provided the headboard is a simple rectangular shape (YouTube has lots of step-by-step videos).

Bedding

I have never regretted saving up for good-quality bedding, as it feels like a solid investment in my wellbeing. For me, good-quality bedding means an initial investment in a good-quality mattress, and it's worth spending on a decent duvet and pillows too (for me that's always feathers, but I appreciate that's not for everyone). If your budget allows, a mattress topper is a game changer. Considering the cost per use, the soft and crumply linen sheets I've bought over the years have proven to be good purchases – they are lasting incredibly well and even seem to get better with washing. You may prefer cotton to linen, but, either way, I would always advise sticking to one hundred per cent natural fabrics rather than synthetic blends.

Easy updates for common problems

Bare walls

To me, there is something that feels very transient and unloved about a space with nothing on the walls, and adding artwork that reflects the occupant's identity is an easy fix. If you do not have permission to hammer in nails in a rented home, or you don't have the tools to do so, there are some simple solutions. Remember, anything can be art, from photos and postcards to fabric and DIY-dried foliage, or even a tree branch. You probably already have some suitable pieces that can be repurposed.

Velcro adhesive strips

These made a gallery wall possible in the first, uninviting new build flat that I shared with my husband. So impressive was their grip that my party-trick became shouting 'Look, no nails!' to unaware guests at any given opportunity!

Wall adhesive stickers

Also called wall decals, these can look like very convincing murals (some more than others!) and are a low-effort way to liven up a space – particularly in a nursery or playroom. Removable wallpaper is another option along the same lines.

Magnetic frames

These come in standard sizes and attach with magnetic strips to the top and bottom of a poster or print. They tend to be light enough to allow you to attach onto a sticker wall hook.

Propping up pictures

If you can't hang pictures on the wall, they can also look great propped up on a shelf or mantelpiece, or even kitchen shelves. And of course, they're super easy to rearrange at any point.

Lack of storage

In the previous chapter we looked at fixed storage options, but if you're looking for a less permanent solution – whether you prefer that style, are not permitted to drill into the walls or won't be in your current home for long – here are some more fluid options.

Modular storage

Shelving is obviously a great way to incorporate storage into your home as well as adding personality, using it to show off the objects you love. The modular Ladderax-inspired shelving we bought for our last home in London was a big financial investment, one we prioritised and saved up for because we knew that it would not only be invaluable for toys, books, plants, photographs and treasured keepsakes, but that it would also be simple enough to put up and take down. Crucially, it could also come with us to any future home and could be adapted to different spaces.

Any shelves placed on tracks (a bit like you often see in shops) offer great flexibility because you can easily move them up and down to accommodate all the objects you're storing. Modular storage can be added to or divided up if need be, so for that reason it can be a great option for either temporary or more permanent homes.

Free-standing storage

While bespoke storage is brilliant for maximising space, I've found that an old cabinet, bookcase or gentleman's wardrobe can steal the show in a room, becoming a more commanding focal point than something sleeker and built in. Older furniture that has already survived generations tends to be much more durable than many modern options, including flatpack (which often doesn't travel well if you're moving). Not only that but vintage furniture can often be reasonably priced and is easy to adapt to different functions around the home. Chapter 9 includes more info on sourcing second-hand pieces.

Everyday organising

I'm wary of sliding into home organiser mode as I am very much learning on the go when it comes to storage and organisation at home. But with four children and a job that sees me working from home a lot, some kind of system has become a necessity. Here are some basic ways to utilise the nooks and crannies in your home without overwhelming it.

Hooks

Add a hook to the back of every door, both higher up for coats, towels, aprons or dressing gowns, and lower down if you have children so they can hang their coat independently. Magnetic wall hooks and over-the-door hooks will leave no trace once removed. Keep an eye out in any skips you pass for lovely old hardware such as hooks or handles still attached to discarded doors (for this reason my handbag is just as likely to carry a screwdriver and measuring tape as it is to contain baby wipes and boxes of raisins!).

Vacuum storage bags

These are great for storing blankets and seasonal clothing, as well as protecting fabrics from moths. They slide easily under beds and sofas, saving you space in cupboards and wardrobes.

Dual function tables

Choose side tables or bedside tables that double as storage. For example, you can get lovely baskets with flat tops that allow you to store clothes, toys, blankets, whatever, that also serve as a surface for you to perch your coffee cup. Or a kitchen table with drawers to store cutlery and napkins, or a coffee table with a glass top and a shelf below which can display objects and ornaments.

Hangers

If you're short on hanging space (and who isn't?), you can get handy little plastic connector hooks that you simply slide onto your regular hangers to allow you to clip in another hanger underneath. Trouser hangers and scarf hangers also boost space in small wardrobes.

Lazy Susans

These are spinning trays, particularly good for bottles of cooking oil or similar, that you can put in your hard-to-reach cupboard corners or fridge, spinning the plate towards you to retrieve a bottle with ease (rather than knocking everything over). They also have a pleasing retro vibe to them.

Lath pullies

This space-saving clothes dryer, which can be pulled down from the ceiling, helped us make the best use of our very narrow but high-ceilinged hallway in our old flat, making light work of drying our many bedsheets. When lowered, the drapes also made for the best games of hide and seek with our littlies!

I hope that the insights shared here have inspired you to invest in and rejuvenate your living space, even if your time there is temporary. These micro tasks, weekend DIY projects or 'naptime jobs', as a friend of mine lovingly calls them (to be done while the baby sleeps), offer a manageable approach to breathing new life into tired homes. Instead of overwhelming large-scale endeavours, consider embracing these ideas incrementally, allowing them to stimulate further innovations according to your space's needs, your time constraints and your budget.

Draw inspiration from my grandma's steadfast approach to home transformation – focused on practical upgrades like regrouting, repainting, replacing tired textiles and repairing worn areas. The cumulative impact of these small victories unfolds into a vibrant tapestry that revitalises homes and makes them feel alive.

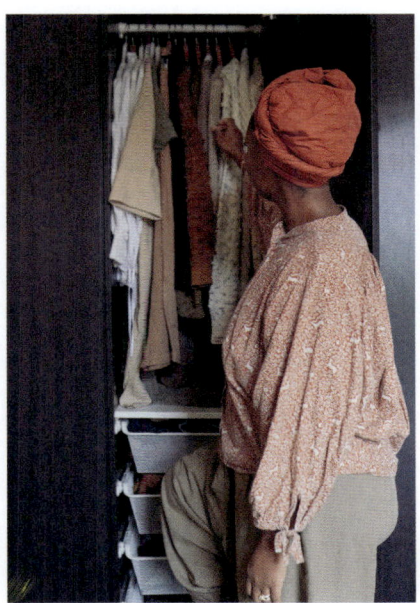
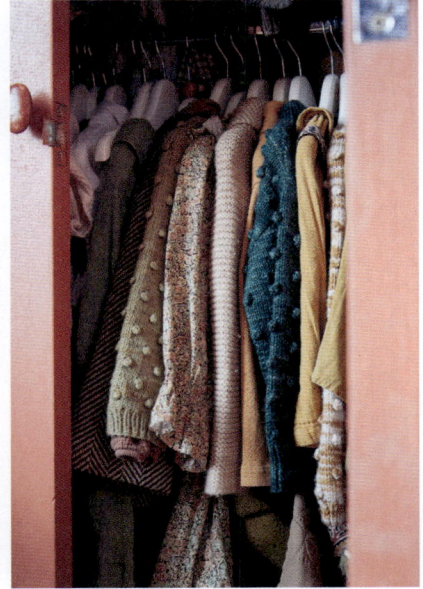

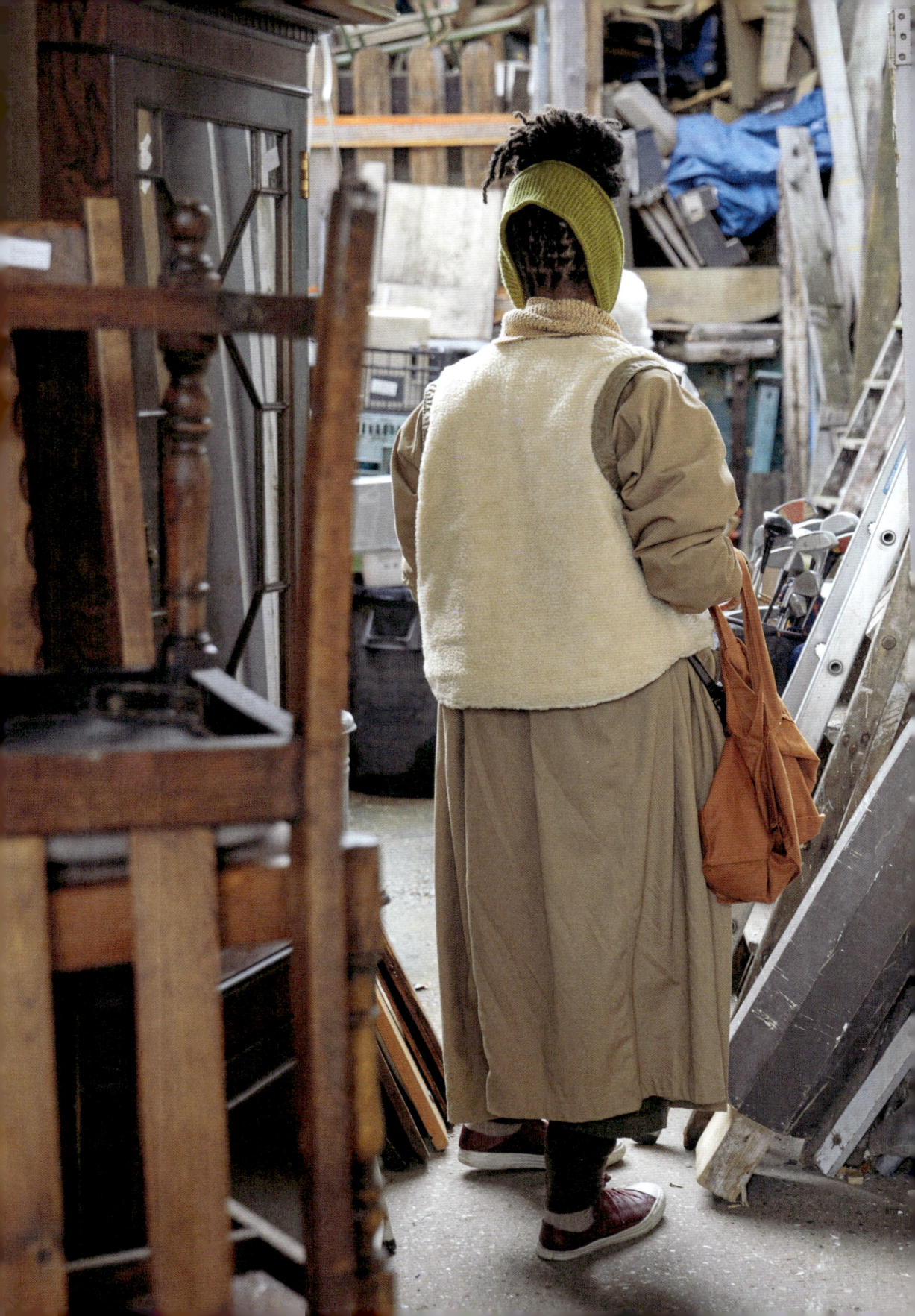

SOURCE

Growing up, I didn't really get to spend any real time with my three Grenadian grandparents. My dad had a strained relationship with his parents, meaning that I didn't see them after the age of about five, and my maternal grandfather passed away when I was very young. It wasn't until I went to secondary school in Carriacou that my paternal grandfather and I established a relationship, sat together on his veranda where he would recount stories of their arrival to the UK in the late 1950s and their quest to establish roots there, while also recounting tales of their homeland, pre-voyage. Old home and new home, old life and new life.

My grandparents' homes, and the precious belongings inside them, fascinated me as a child and helped me connect to the Grenadian part of my heritage. For many of us, our ancestors weren't able to save and pass down items to us. At times, it can feel like all the heirloom-filled homes belong to the select few who have unruptured lineages and generational wealth. Because of the nature of my ancestors' histories, the number of children they had and their financial circumstances throughout that time, it's unlikely that there will be any memorabilia passed down to us at any point.

But that doesn't mean I don't want to celebrate my heritage in my home.

Online vintage marketplaces have really bridged the inheritance gap for me and become the next best thing for sourcing pieces that speak to my history. I save online searches for all kinds of relics relating to my ancestry – sometimes similar to pieces that I recall from my childhood, other times, items that I have researched that are of significance. I check these periodically and if something tugs at my heartstrings and feels like it would be right for our home (and budget), I snap it up. Recently I lost out on a gorgeous, small steelpan drum with 'Grenada' hand-lettered along the edging. It would have hung beautifully on our walls. Still, now that I know it exists, I can set up and save an even more specific search for the right one in the future.

In our current home, I love that my children get to witness first-hand how much my keepsakes reflecting both my English and Caribbean heritage mean to me. These objects prompt questions and stories about their past and ours. They become bridges between the past, present and future, connecting us all through stories passed down the generations. Long after we're gone, I hope these pieces will remain to tell a tale of resilience, courage and pride – one that weaves us all together. I hope the tales my children hear allow them to continue the traditions, adapting them to their own lives in the future.

In this section, we explore why the items we choose to bring into our homes should reflect who we are and who we strive to be. In order to do this, we need to go back to the start of the manufacturing process, to think carefully about where our homewares and clothing have been made and by whom, and to ensure these origins reflect the values we want to uphold. I believe something has gone badly wrong in our retail industry, where a hyper-focus on profits has led to a system that actively undermines authenticity. This focus on profits over provenance has led to staff being exploited and, frequently, a greenwashed approach to sustainability (if corporations address it at all). The good news is that we can choose to create fabulous, authentic spaces unique to us while being socially conscious, and we will look at how to do so in the upcoming chapters.

The first step we can take is to become more mindful of respecting the provenance of our homewares, and I include a short guide to how we can remain vigilant in our pursuit of genuine cultural appreciation over appropriation. Many of us live in places where previous governments have colluded in and current governments uphold the theft of art and artefacts from other nations, so it's no surprise that there has been a trickle-down effect into consumers' homes. Stolen relics and other misappropriated artefacts should remind us of the responsibilities that come with celebrating cultural diversity. By embracing cultural appreciation over appropriation, we contribute to a more harmonious and equitable world – one where every culture's unique beauty is celebrated in its entirety. A major part of this is ensuring that we source considerately and with respect for the maker. We should adopt good purchasing habits where, for example, if we want a striking piece of 'Black art' depicting Black portraiture, it shouldn't be inconceivable to first seek out Black artists, acknowledging the many barriers they will have likely faced in the traditional routes to market. If we want a book on authentic Peruvian history, we must ensure that the author isn't just a purveyor of the culture, but someone with lived experience that qualifies them to share such things. For far too long, our cultural diet in the Western world has been diluted by a negligent, whitewashed lens.

Finding pieces that reflect their makers' heritage, philosophies and/or concerns (which you might discover if buying directly from them) makes bringing such objects into your home all the more special. This is why I love chancing upon markets, whether locally or abroad, and seeing all the one-off pieces that craftspeople have made. When I'm buying something, I always ask for details of the process – how a wooden bowl, a ceramic cup, a little watercolour was made; does the maker have a studio; what inspired them. I am yet to meet an artist who doesn't love talking about their creative process. If you're buying online from sites that represent artisanal makers, there is usually similar information to be found.

How we set up our homes and the materials we source will have an impact on how we live and feel. I am a firm believer in the old adage, 'Buy cheap, buy twice', and I keep this in mind whenever I'm tempted to cave in for a cheaper, short-term alternative that doesn't quite tick all my boxes. As alluring as it is to get the endorphin rush from the 'Add to basket' button, I know it's better to invest in well-made materials, second-hand where possible, and this often means waiting. Buying with intent slows down the sourcing process, which is usually no bad thing.

We are products of our environment and how we choose to live now is often a reaction to our own upbringing. The legacy of our earliest experiences of home can be so strong. In my childhood there was a distinct lack of both substance and security, which has left me with a lingering scarcity mindset. As a result, substance and security remain two things that my husband and I really strive to obtain for our family. I'll be encouraging you to think about how your early experiences have shaped how you do (and don't) wish to set down roots.

There's something wonderfully familiar and grounding about homeware that has travelled to different homes with you; it's testament to the ways in which you have honed in on a style that is all your own.

I like to view myself as a custodian of the pieces I find, sourcing quality heirloom furnishings that may come and go from my home as our needs change. Approaching second-hand sourcing in this way will open up opportunities for creating a unique and authentic home. I hope that you come away from this section empowered with hands-on tips to create a joyful home that reflects you, sourcing with integrity, supporting makers and tapping into the beauty of your heritage.

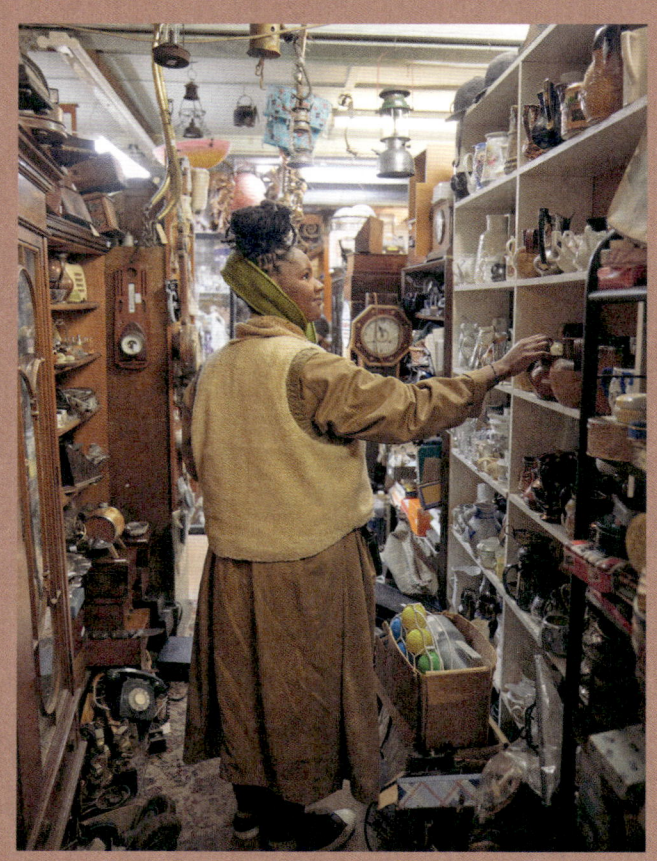

CHAPTER 8

PROCESS AND PROVENANCE

Many of us are coming round to the idea that we need to source items with a more considered approach, whether that's the food we buy (or even grow), the clothes we wear or anything else that we bring into our home. Over the years, I have deliberately moved towards being much more mindful of the provenance of my purchases as well as the process by which I shop. This allows me to make considered acquisitions, keeping sustainability and accountability at the forefront of my mind, without ever becoming too overwhelmed with guilt about my individual impact on the makers and the climate.

The non-negotiable need for inclusivity is also central to my buying practices now, particularly for the (increasingly infrequent) times that I buy something brand new. The 'Great White Unlearning' of 2020 really saw brands being held accountable for their lack of inclusivity. It became increasingly easy to spot 'token' archetypes and even easier to call out problematic tropes, and PR companies had to dig deep to right that wrong. What followed was a complete U-turn in terms of advertising strategy for many notable brands. Several years on, you'd be hard pushed to find a brand that doesn't have a diversity marketing strategy. While this is certainly a step in the right direction, it is important for consumers to still scratch beneath the surface, to see if a brand follows through in ensuring equality and support for its all of its staff.

For some of us, a sustainable method of sourcing will be a new way of approaching consumerism and it will be a considerable learning curve until it is an integrated part of who you are and how you buy for your home. I hope this chapter gives both the new and the initiated some guidance on how we can source in a way that supports creators and supply chains. The issues raised here aren't always comfortable ones, and, while I don't pretend to have all the answers (I'm on this journey too), what I am sure of is a need to identify problematic practices and call them out, while continuing to ask questions.

You'll discover an added bonus when you shop with your values at the forefront of your decision making – you'll be creating a home that's more representative of you, with pieces that are meaningful and moving, and which last longer because they are better made.

Authenticity

If it's new and seems super cheap, there's usually a reason why. Someone, somewhere is paying the price for your bargain purchase. It's that simple. There is a trickle-down effect, from the products of haute couture and bespoke interiors to fast fashion and fast furniture. The modern retail system is all about the bottom line, and increasingly, brands are skipping as many steps of the traditional creative process as possible with little care for the authenticity and quality of the end result, or the lives that they impact.

Take, for example, the popularity of rattan, used to make all sorts, from seating and lamps to smaller pieces like trays and baskets. Some brands have invested in going back to where the raw materials and highly skilled workforces originate. With an understanding that sustainability is an intricate balance between environmental, social and economic needs, good retailers are constantly looking for ways to achieve a balance between all three. This comes at a cost – a higher price to the consumer and likely a lower retailer profit – but this approach keeps communities working and artisanal skills alive. Other brands at the faster end of retail may choose to use the same materials, but not compensate the workforce fairly, and as their business model is trend-led, they won't be offering these communities any promise of longevity in production or job security. Another more common sight is retailers simply mimicking natural fibres like rattan in their construction, such as moulded plastic baskets with realistic indentations to look like the natural fibre. Examples of this are seen across the board in home fittings and furnishings, as well as fashion. With the rise of online shopping, it can often be hard to tell the difference on a highly edited website thumbnail.

The higher price need not be a barrier to purchasing what you love and need. Sourcing second-hand, which we'll explore in more detail later, may take more time but often results in finding a unique piece with its own interesting history.

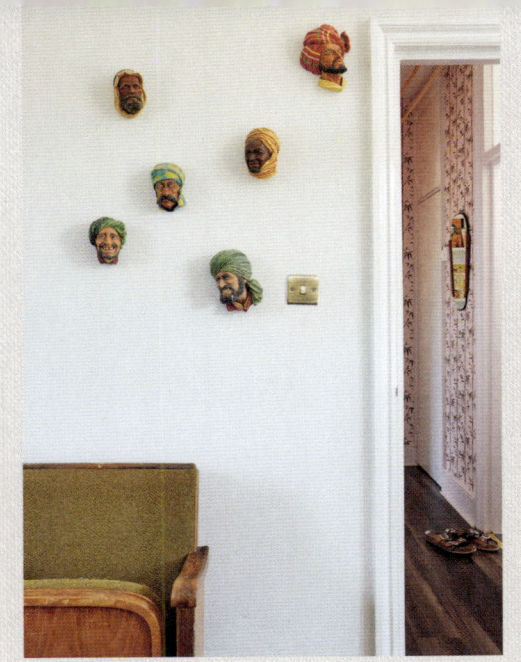
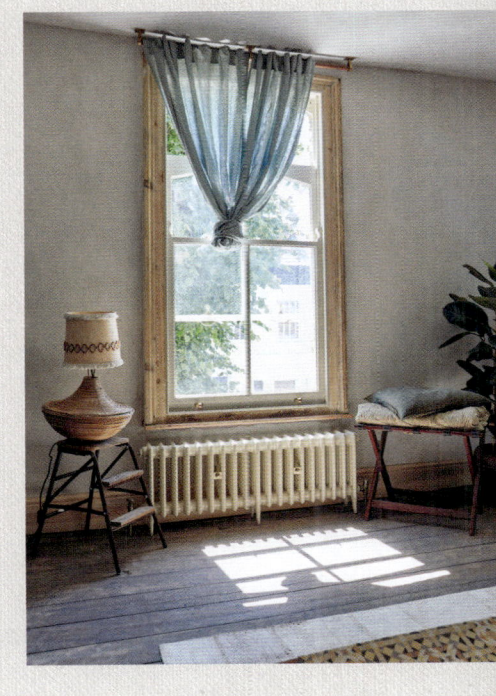
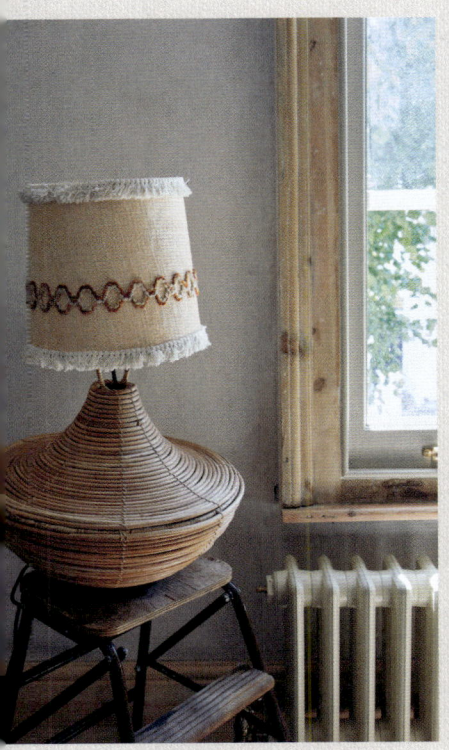
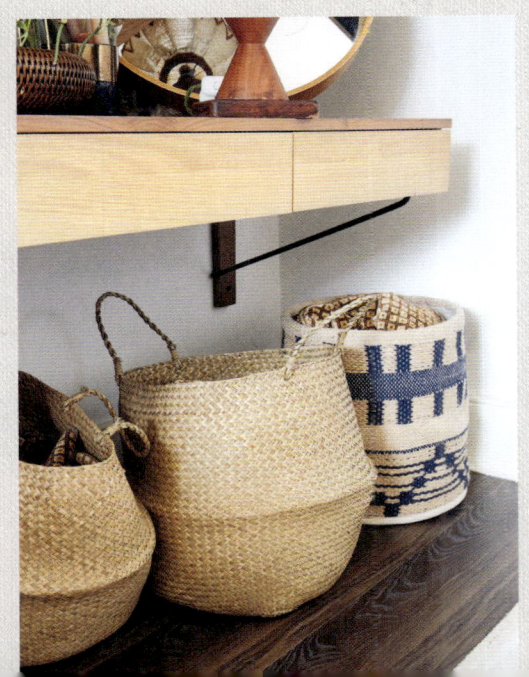

Ethical sourcing

I was raised to see the value in quality craftsmanship but haven't always had the funds to invest in such beautifully crafted wares. Because of this, the skill of sourcing vintage items at the right price has always been invaluable to me. If buying new, I prefer to hold off and save for a beautifully made, durable piece rather than buy a cheaper knock-off.

You have power as a consumer, and you can exert your agency by choosing to shop with brands whose values align with your own. Something that it took me far too long to learn: that your values don't have to align with mine, but we should both have values. For me, this might mean choosing brands whose policies support the kind of Earth I want to live on, who are not complicit in propping up inequality and underrepresentation and who do not exploit their workforce or have a cavalier attitude to the environment.

Also, I often like to look at a brand's leadership teams – simply google their executive team and ask yourself, is this a business that is inclusive, or heterogenous and exclusionary? Does the CEO actively encourage an inclusivity at every level, or is there a concerning pattern of ethnic minorities making up a large part of the lower-paid end of the workforce? Where are their wares produced and are the pay and working conditions fair? Have they actively chosen a location that treats workers with dignity, or do they select territories in order to exploit their lack of safety regulations, human rights or minimal wages?

Keeping these considerations at the front of my mind makes it difficult for me to switch off and enjoy items in my home that have been made by people in exploitative conditions. We can't go back and un-buy the items we bought before we began to shop with awareness and integrity. But when you know better, you do better. Keeping that in mind helps me source with my values at the forefront.

Being accountable

I've found that approaching purchases with a few questions in mind helps guide my decision-making by sparking deep thought around the subject.

- What am I OK with in terms of manufacturing? E.g., manufacturing outside of Europe isn't a no-go for me if the staff's wellbeing is prioritised and salaries are comparatively fair.
- What am I definitely not on board with? E.g., using animal products in production.
- Why might certain things not bother me? E.g., does a confirmed child labour workforce leave me unphased because I can pretend it doesn't exist? Is it easier for me to turn a blind eye if the children don't look like me?

The questions I ask myself aren't always comfortable and I have really had to confront some choices I've made that were totally unacceptable in retrospect. Dissecting these things over the years has allowed me to home in on a framework of rules before I make a purchase. The result is buying less, feeling proud of what I own and having a naturally more cohesive style.

Understanding provenance and the ethical origins of artefacts is an integral part of cultural appreciation. Before bringing an item into our homes, we should inquire about its journey and ensure it has been obtained through ethical means. This practice not only respects the culture it comes from but also supports fair trade practices and encourages responsible consumer behaviour.

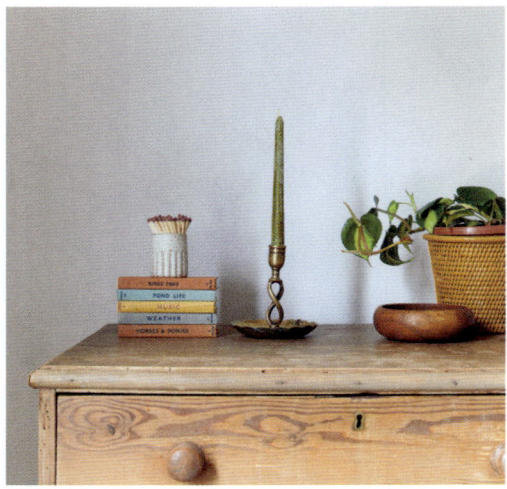

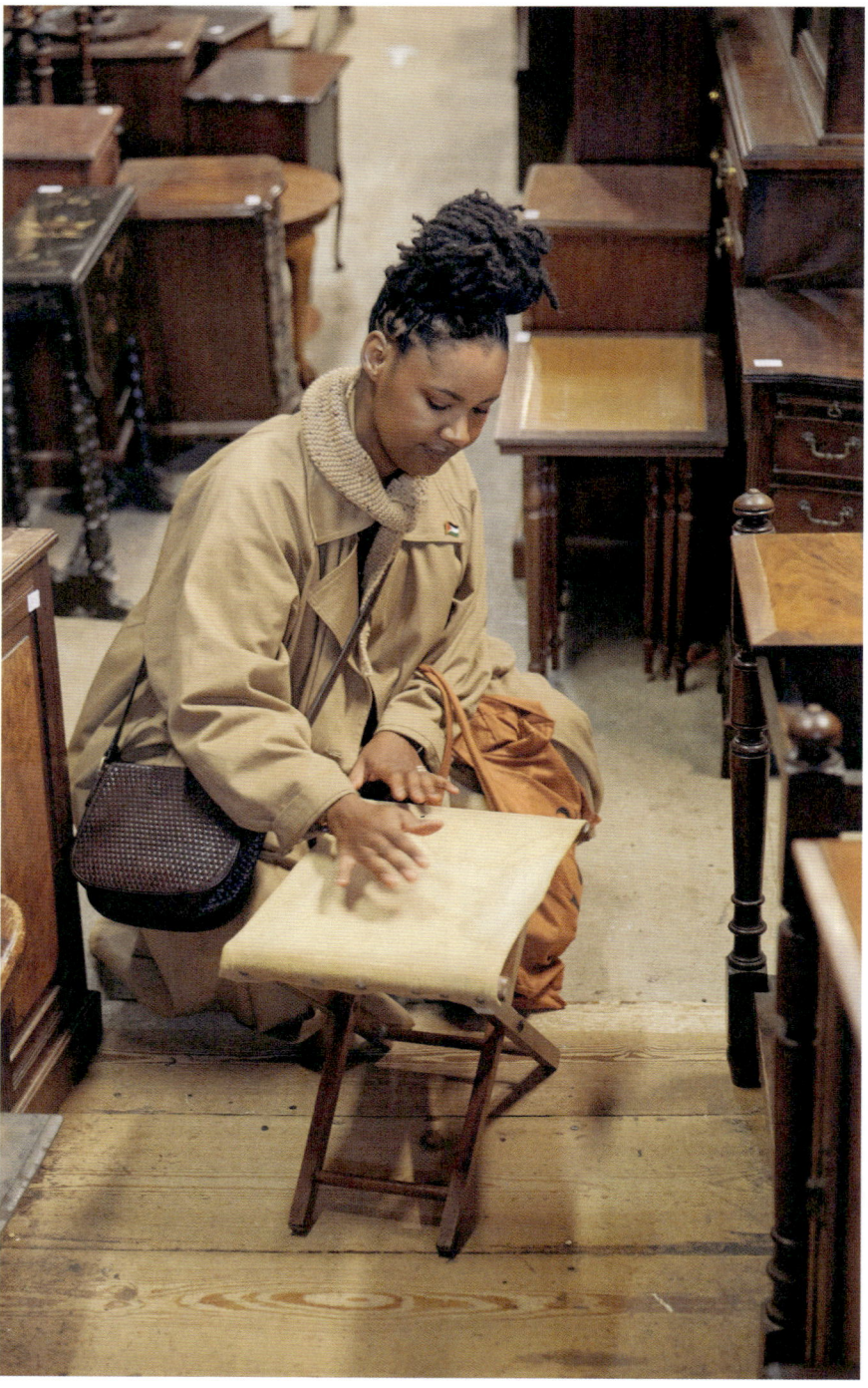

Appropriation versus appreciation

Cultural appropriation is a thorny issue. It arises when elements of one culture are 'borrowed' by another without proper contextualisation or recognition. Instead of treating cultural items as trendy décor, we should strive to learn about their origins, traditions and significance before taking them into our homes. This education can lead to a richer appreciation of the world's diverse cultures and histories.

At this point, it is crucial to differentiate between appropriation and appreciation.

Cultural appropriation refers to the act of taking elements from a culture, usually a marginalised or historically oppressed one, without proper understanding, respect or acknowledgement. It involves taking elements purely for aesthetic purposes, separating them from their original cultural context (and, in the case of certain hairstyles for instance, often without experiencing any of the stigmatisation that a more marginalised person would experience doing the same). This can lead to the commodification of cultural symbols, the reinforcement of stereotypes and the perpetuation of cultural insensitivity. In the context of fashion and interiors, examples of cultural appropriation might include using sacred symbols or traditional clothing as mere objects of décor, without considering their significance or meaning. This can be offensive and harmful, as it reduces someone's heritage to a superficial trend.

Cultural appreciation, on the other hand, involves genuinely recognising, respecting and learning from different cultures. It entails seeking to understand the history, traditions, and significance behind artefacts and themes before integrating them into our own style. In fashion and interior design, it can mean drawing inspiration from diverse cultures with a deep understanding of their history, customs and perspective, and crucially, giving credit to them. This might involve incorporating traditional patterns, colours or motifs in a respectful and fully cognisant manner. By acknowledging the origins and meaning of these elements, cultural appreciation fosters cross-cultural understanding and celebrates the richness of global heritage.

By appreciating, we can embrace the diversity of cultures in an informed and sensitive way. Designers, retailers and consumers can draw inspiration from different cultures while giving credit and acknowledging their origins. This can lead to creative and unique designs that honour and celebrate the beauty of cultural diversity. In essence, the key difference lies in the depth of understanding and respect. While appropriation can lead to harm and perpetuate inequalities, appreciation promotes cultural exchange, mutual respect and a celebration of our global human tapestry. It's essential to approach interior trends with a conscious awareness of the significance behind the elements we choose to incorporate, ensuring that our choices come from a place of genuine appreciation and respect.

Here are some starter questions to determine where we might have unwittingly disrespected someone's cultural heritage in our homes:

- Does an item in your home hold religious significance for someone else but no specific value to you?
- Does using said item in your home bring any disrespect to a culture or religion?
- Is this item mass-produced or an original? If an original, was it purchased directly from an individual/company representing that heritage?
- Is there a chance that the item was stolen or taken without consent (even if many years ago)?

One example is the display of Buddha heads (without their bodies). These serene faces, often used as decorative items, have a deeper spiritual and historical significance in Buddhism. The separation of the head from the body not only distorts the intended message of unity but also represents a dark history of pillaging. During colonial times, many artefacts were looted from Asian countries, and their detachment from their original context strips them of their cultural and religious resonance. It is crucial to consider the implications of showcasing such items as mere ornaments, as it perpetuates the idea that one can pick and choose elements of a culture without honouring the full significance (or acknowledging the shameful parts of our history).

In a similar way, the use of Native American or Indigenous-inspired motifs and homewares, such as dreamcatchers, tribal patterns and feathered decorations, are often incorporated into interior design purely for their visual appeal, overlooking the spiritual and historical meaning that these symbols hold for Native American and Indigenous cultures. Dreamcatchers, for instance, are believed to protect individuals from negative energy and bad dreams. When these symbols are used as mere decorative items without respect for their cultural context, it diminishes their importance and perpetuates a shallow understanding and fetishised approach to that culture.

Similarly, tribal patterns and motifs from various Indigenous cultures are often appropriated without consideration for their origins or meaning. These patterns may carry specific stories, traditions, and connections to the land for the communities they belong to. Appropriating these designs without proper research can lead to cultural insensitivity and misrepresentation.

If you are drawn to incorporating these motifs into your home, I suggest you take time to learn about and understand their cultural significance and origin. Engaging in fairtrade practices by sourcing items directly from Indigenous artists and communities can also help ensure that your choices support and respect the cultures you admire. Prioritise purchasing work from them over those who historically have had more exposure. Finally, if you aren't in a position to support them financially, share their content as recommendations, engage with their social platforms and amplify their work.

Rectifying wrongs

Cultural appropriation is complex, but taking steps to rectify past mistakes demonstrates our commitment to growth and cultural understanding. I shudder when I recall some of the egregious ways that I appropriated various cultures in the past, before I began to prioritise listening to communities that were marginalised by my own. As a 1990s babe, much of our home décor was appropriated from Indian culture and I carried that into my personal style by rarely being seen without a Bindi for much of the next decade. Another choice in particularly bad taste was having a Native American-inspired headdress custom-made for a 'hat' party. When I started to connect with and learn from Native American educators online just a few short years later, I was hot with embarrassment but committed to ensuring that similar blind spots didn't trip me up in the future. By making informed and respectful design decisions, we can avoid perpetuating cultural appropriation and instead contribute to a more inclusive and appreciative world (not to mention, interior design landscape).

If you're reading this with an open heart and mind, and realise that you, like me, have made mistakes along these lines in the past, rest assured that you can acknowledge and rectify cultural appropriation in your home designs. Here are some positive steps you can take towards fostering cultural sensitivity and respect.

Educate yourself

Take time to educate yourself about the cultural elements you've incorporated without understanding fully. Research the history, traditions and meaning behind these elements. Understanding the context is crucial to rectifying the situation.

Acknowledge

Recognise and admit that you've engaged in cultural appropriation. Acknowledge that your previous choices might have been insensitive and harmful (even if unintentionally). This self-awareness is the first step towards positive change.

Reflect on intent versus impact

Consider your initial intentions and how they might have clashed with the impact of your choices. Recognise that, even if your intentions were harmless, the impact on the cultures being appropriated can be negative.

Remove or repurpose problematic items

If you've incorporated items that are particularly offensive or inappropriate, consider removing them entirely from your décor. Alternatively, you could repurpose these items in a way that respects their cultural origins. For example, if you have a decorative dreamcatcher, you could research its significance and display it in a respectful context. In terms of offensive items, for example, anything depicting golliwogs, it's always important to acknowledge the power we have to end an item's lifespan rather than sell or pass it on. With that in mind, I always advise disposing of offensive items entirely.

Learn and share

Share what you've learnt with friends and family. Educate them about cultural appropriation and the importance of cultural sensitivity in design. It was a social media follower of mine who first prompted me to research the cultural significance of the Native American headdress. We had both attended a clothing fair and one stall was selling a toy that depicted a cartoon of a naked white baby proudly wearing a headdress. The toy was very much of the 'Cowboys and Indians' era. This follower petitioned me to use my voice to persuade the seller not to re-stock the toy, but, being uneducated on the subject at the time, I failed to see what was wrong with it. I then made short work of researching and am so grateful for having had that prompt. By spreading awareness, you too can contribute to a more informed and respectful community.

Support authentic creators

When adding new cultural elements to your interior, support makers from the cultures you're interested in. Purchase items from Indigenous artisans, local craftspeople or fairtrade organisations. This ensures that your choices contribute positively to the cultures you admire.

Embrace cultural exchange and appreciation

Moving forward, focus on embracing cultural exchange and appreciation. Instead of appropriating, learn about and celebrate the cultures that inspire you. This could involve integrating cultural elements in consultation with experts from those cultures or creating spaces that reflect diverse global influences.

Seek feedback

If you're uncertain about whether a design choice might be appropriate, seek feedback from individuals who belong to the culture in question. Engaging in open and respectful conversations can provide valuable insights and guidance.

Drawing from *your* identity

I like to draw on the warmest childhood memories I have and make space for them in my own home. I've mentioned how, when I bought those Le Creuset saucepans years ago, they weren't a status symbol for me, rather they represented lovely memories of summers spent at my grandma's home in West Yorkshire. This nostalgia is so easily evoked by the sight of those bright cast-iron casserole dishes. I see my grandma too in our collection of mismatched china (an abundance of generously sized bright mugs hanging on display), although none of it was actually hers. The memories and feelings evoked are just as important as the objects themselves.

For as long as I can remember, in the entrance hall of my grandma's home we have been greeted by a dozen or so decorative Bosson's chalkware heads. My grandma didn't travel until she was forty (though she has made quick work of making up for lost time in the three decades that followed) and she has a selection of busts depicting men from the various places she has either visited or still hopes to visit someday. The manufacturer itself has some less than savoury (read: racist) depictions that my grandma steered clear of, and in our last home in London, it felt right replicating that selection of Bosson's heads in a prominent spot in our home as a little nod to my grandma.

I often refer to my style of interiors as what the homes of Indigenous Caribbean people might have looked like had Christopher Columbus and his ship of plunderers sunk on their way to the West Indies. A joyous celebration of the local landscape, drawing on local materials. When I watch interiors shows and someone hints at wanting a nod to the Caribbean it always feels so stereotypical – gaudy bright colours, plastic faux plants, animals and the like. That's not the Caribbean I know, nor was it embodied in my relatives' homes in Grenada or in the homes created by my immigrant grandparents here in

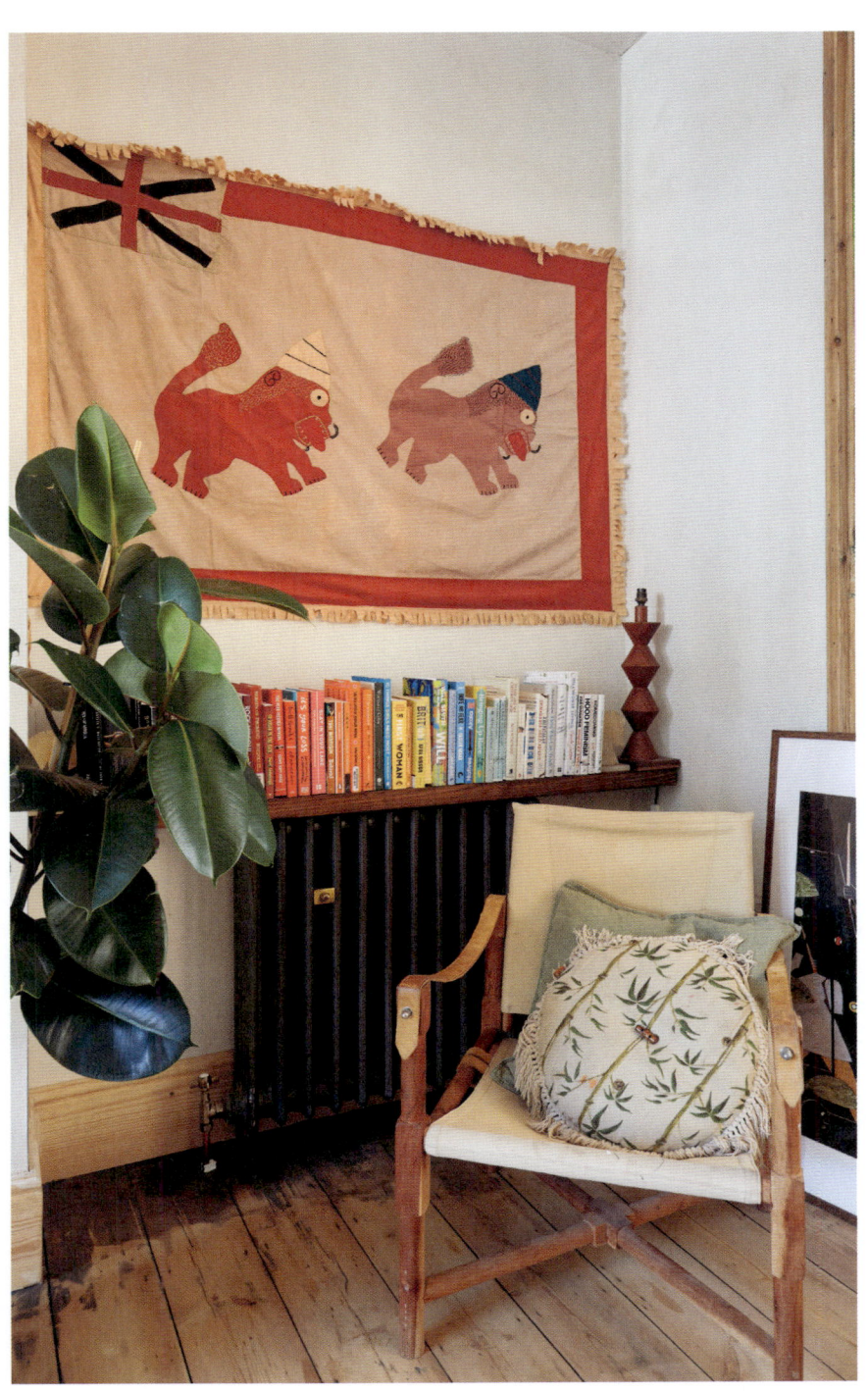

the UK. They were far more drawn to mid-century design, warm pattern clashes, busy, durable textiles and little patriotic nods to their homeland dotted throughout. As a result, these have influenced the design choices that I've brought into my homes over the years.

What parts of your identity might you want to bring into your home? Are there particular people or places that you want to invoke? What messages about your own heritage would you like your children, or other people in your home, to take from your belongings? How comfortable do you feel with sharing your heritage at home? If you have some reservations, then the next section may be for you.

Embracing your heritage

We are living in a time when more of us than ever before identify as being mixed heritage. How beautiful. It can sometimes be tricky to feel confident enough to have the licence or agency to represent these heritages in our homes, particularly if/when our lineage partly stems from a parent or grandparent who didn't play an active role in our lives. Many individuals proudly carry multiple heritages in addition to the one they are raised in. However, for those who haven't had the chance to explore or connect with a side of their heritage, there may be a powerful journey awaiting them – one that involves research, and embracing and incorporating that missing piece into their identity. If this is a journey you want to take, it's time to take charge of your narrative and create a home that reflects your complete heritage. Embrace your cultural multiplicity and recognise that your identity is a beautiful mosaic of different factors. By celebrating all sides, you can create a space that honours your complete self and the diverse influences that have shaped you.

The first step towards incorporating your missing heritage is embarking on a journey of discovery. Research the culture, traditions, history and values of the heritage(s) that you're less familiar with. Dive into books, documentaries and online resources, and connect with individuals who share that background. Understanding the essence of the culture is fundamental to integrating it into your life.

My maternal grandma has always known her father was from Co. Monaghan, Ireland and her mother was from Fulham, London. Less than a decade ago, my grandma discovered that her mother, my great-nana Daphne, was actually an Armenian immigrant. It explained so much, including the family's unquestioning love for all people from all backgrounds (a scarcity in 1940s West Yorkshire). It also explained the beautifully rich complexion of my grandma and a handful of her siblings. The news came as such a beautiful shock to my grandma, but we made every effort to immerse ourselves in learning about this newly discovered heritage.

Personalise your space

Your home is a canvas waiting to reflect your full identity. Incorporate elements from your heritage – it could be artwork, photography, textiles or artefacts that symbolise the culture's essence. By surrounding yourself with these reminders, you create a sense of connection even if you haven't been introduced to the culture in a traditional way.

Don't wait for an introduction

One common misconception is the need to wait for a formal introduction to said culture. While that can be a wonderful experience, it might not always happen. Don't let that hold you back. You have the power to initiate your own exploration and research.

Seek out community

Connecting with others who share your heritage can be incredibly enriching. Whether online or in person, engaging with a community that understands your experience can provide support, guidance and a sense of belonging.

Be patient with yourself

Embracing a new heritage takes time and effort. There might be moments of confusion or challenges but remember that this journey is about growth and self-discovery. Be patient with yourself as you navigate uncharted waters.

Incorporating your missing heritage into your life and home isn't just about aesthetics either – it's a profound acknowledgement of your roots and an empowering act of self-expression. By taking the initiative to research, embrace and incorporate your heritage, you're shaping a narrative that's uniquely yours. Remember, your heritage is a gift, and your home can be the stage where the beautiful tapestry of your identity unfolds.

Practical steps to adjust our sourcing habits

Earlier, we looked at how we can manifest our values in our homes through the ways in which we source homewares and furniture. In addition to educating yourself and choosing authenticity, take time to reflect on your values and the type of home environment you want to create. Research ethical brands and artisans who prioritise ethical practices, fair wages and respect for cultural heritage. Yes, this might all sound like quite a lot of work when buying an item, but when I compare it to the hours that I could spend on Pinterest trying to get inspo for a single paint colour, it's really no time at all! And what you find in your research is bound to unlock even more inspiration! Look for certifications or information on vendors' websites that demonstrate their commitment to values you admire, and keep in mind these points:

- Avoid fast fashion and fads by incorporating items with timeless appeal rather than following fleeting trends. Have a dose of healthy suspicion around any stores that appear to offer amazing value through their permanent sales or 'free' shipping; in reality, these costs are worked into the price you pay for the product.
- Research sustainable materials, support local, marginalised and Indigenous creators, and prioritise quality over quantity. Consider buying second-hand as a first option or upcycling items currently in your home.
- When travelling or exploring different cultures, opt for souvenirs and artefacts that have a meaningful connection to your experiences. Avoid mass-produced souvenirs that lack cultural authenticity. Engage in conscious design by thoughtfully and respectfully incorporating cultural elements into your home.
- Periodically reassess your home décor choices and reflect on whether they align with your values and goals. This practice helps you maintain a sustainable and culturally appropriate living environment. I like to operate using the one-in, one-out rule,

particularly in my children's spaces where it can become so easy to just . . . keep . . . buying, so I only purchase an item after I've sold or donated an item.
- And finally, remember that change takes time, and it's OK to make gradual adjustments to your habits. Incorporating these steps into your lifestyle allows you to take on a more respectful and environmentally conscious approach to creating a home that reflects both your identity and your commitment to positive change.

The upcoming two chapters offer practical advice for sourcing and finding new second-hand pieces you'll love.

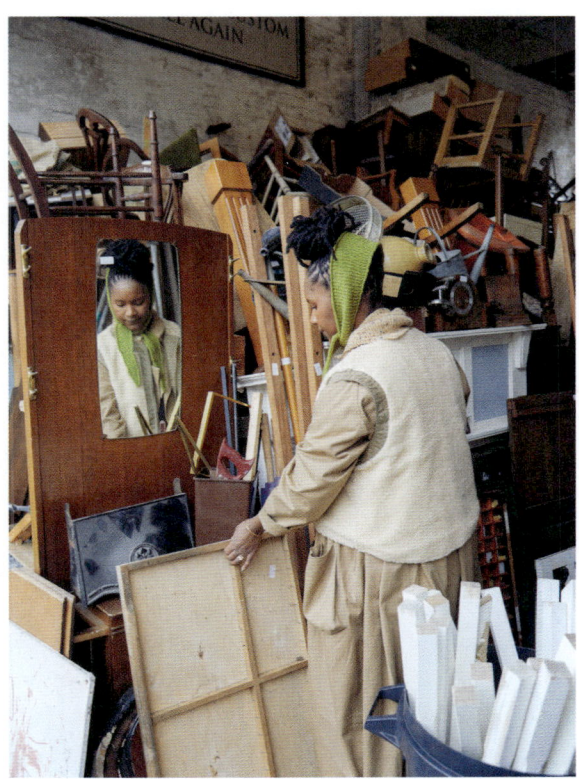

CHAPTER 9

SOURCING MATERIALS

Later, I'll give you my advice on sourcing furniture and other second-hand items, but this chapter gives a closer look at how to consider and source specific materials and fixtures for your home improvements. I have focused on the things I get asked about most often, which are options for kitchen and bathroom updates, as well as flooring and tiles. You'll find that the broader sourcing principles can be applied to any other material you need for your home, so take inspiration and begin to look outside the box. I hope this chapter gives you confidence to look past the supposed convenience of the giant superstores and embrace items that bring history and personality to your living space.

I've mentioned (oh, just once or twice!) that I love sourcing older pieces for my home, as they tend to make for a more relaxed, lived-in feeling, and because the patina of wear and tear often makes for a much more beautiful finish. This is an approach I'm increasingly taking towards the fixtures, fittings and furnishings of my home, becoming more mindful of choosing sustainable options where I can. I would rather spend on a good-quality second-hand bathroom suite, robust kitchen unit or reclaimed hardwood floorboards than buy new, less durable equivalents, even if they cost me the same or a bit more. Fixtures that have already lasted a generation or more, are made from solid materials and are still in good condition indicate that they have plenty of life left in them. Sadly, you just don't get those assurances anymore when you buy new, as so much is designed to last only for the short term.

There's an approach I've often observed, particularly among landlords, of prioritising quick fixes over longevity. I certainly found this when renting from various housing associations in London. This tendency might look like buying the cheapest fixtures, usually in the knowledge that they won't withstand daily use and will need to be replaced in a few years. It leaves tenants living in homes with subpar fixtures that often break, while landlords have to go through the disposal and sourcing of materials on a regular cycle. I believe we need a change in our culture to ensure that using and re-using quality materials becomes our first port of call when it comes to fixtures (and everything else, to be honest). Best for our homes, better for the planet.

Kitchens and Bathrooms

You'd be forgiven for thinking that a new kitchen needs to come from one of those sleek showrooms that invests heavily in marketing campaigns featuring beaming families beside large bowls full of lemons. In reality, shop-bought fitted kitchens are a relatively new invention that have only come to the fore in the past couple of generations. Before built-in kitchens were the norm, it was common to have a kitchen where a table and some free-standing cupboards were used for decades – and if one of them needed replacing, there was no need to replace the entire kitchen.

The even more recent phenomenon of replacing kitchens every ten years or so – either because the materials have not lasted well or due to the residents' desire for change – is a big contributor to environmental waste, and also a sign that decisions were not made with longevity in mind. In all of this, there has been a move away from more hardy materials like solid wood towards cheaper alternatives like MDF, which can be damaged more easily and can be trickier to repair, shortening the overall longevity of the kitchen.

There is a huge range of kitchen suppliers out there, from well-known high-street names to the deluxe aspirational kind. There are, of course, benefits to going down the one-stop-shop route: in the short term, you may find it quicker and simpler to buy from such suppliers, as they can deliver all aspects of a kitchen, from units and worktops to hobs and fridges. Depending on the quality, though, you may consider it a worse investment in the long term.

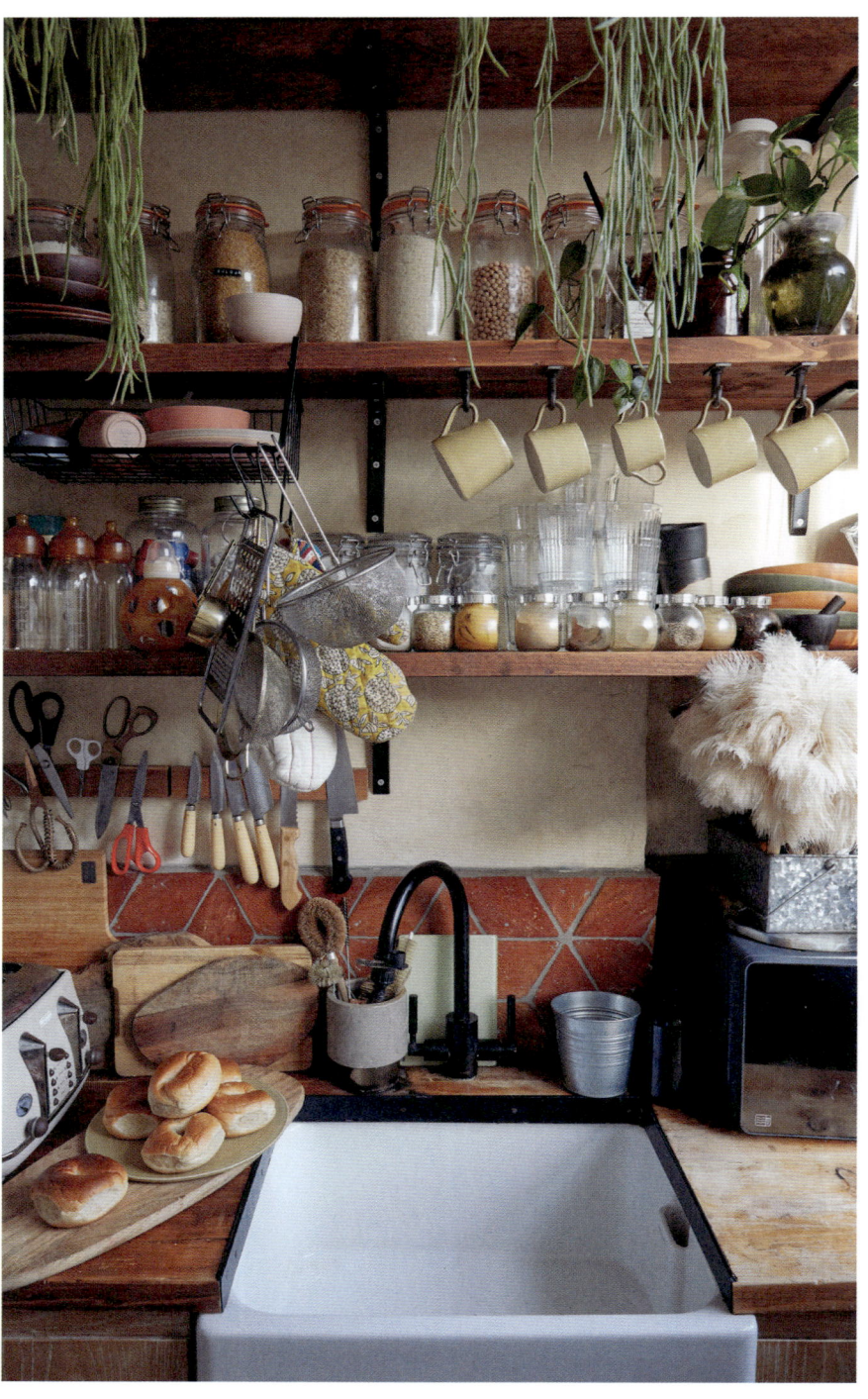

Kitchens

Reusing

If a fitted kitchen is of decent quality to begin with and has plenty of wear left in it, there's no reason it can't be carefully removed and re-used, donated or sold on. This can be hit and miss with cheaper kitchens, which aren't usually designed with movement in mind, and there might be a certain amount of risk about whether it will survive being dismantled (its age may impact this too). You might find local tradespeople who are skilled in removing kitchens and preserving them in the process. These tradespeople are an excellent resource for kitchens that have the potential for a new lease of life. Depending on the material of the re-used kitchen, you may be able to paint or stain the doors, or even replace them with cheaper curtains in your favourite fabric.

Free-standing

I love a free-standing kitchen because they often have so much soul, especially if the elements aren't all matchy-matchy. Free-standing kitchens can come together over time as you buy different elements, and are often a bit of a labour of love because you may have to wait until you find all the pieces to suit your space and budget. Since free-standing kitchens tend not to be as fixed in place as fitted kitchens, they offer more flexibility over time. You can swap things in and out as you wish, for example, a little old prep table might tide you over until you see the vintage butcher's block that you have your heart set on. If you are sourcing well-made solid pieces, like a Welsh dresser, you're unlikely to have any trouble reselling them later should you need to. There are many lovely examples online of people breathing new life into older pieces, whether a school lab table becomes a breakfast bar or a haberdasher's cabinet houses pots and pans. The bonus is they can come with you if you move.

Bespoke joinery

Having a carpenter make something unique to your space, whether a kitchen or bathroom, is a great luxury. The idea of getting to choose the material and having something fitted to maximise my unique space, following my exact specification, brings me huge contentment. You might assume that anything bespoke would be way beyond your budget, but I have often been surprised at how reasonably priced bespoke joinery can be compared to buying off the rack at kitchen showrooms, where the quality is likely nowhere near as long-lasting. If you are tackling a kitchen project, I'd encourage you to speak to some joiners and get a ball-park figure to see if it might be an option.

In addition, bespoke joinery offers you the ability to create space for the pieces you already own, rather than having to make your belongings fit into standard fixtures. This allows you to have a home for everything, even the awkward objects, and it helps keep your home feel calm and clutter-free.

It doesn't have to be all or nothing when it comes to having fixtures made for you. Many people successfully mix off-the-shelf units with individual parts made by a carpenter, creating doors for shop-bought carcasses, for instance, or open shelving, or solutions for tricky areas (perhaps too small or awkwardly shaped for a shop-bought option but potentially really useful for a bit of extra storage or even seating). Joiners are also adept at coming up with ideas for saving costs, such as using types of wood you may not have considered.

Remember that the small details go a long way. As mentioned in the Embrace section, let lighting, switches and door handles be the icing on the cake of any room – these can easily be sourced second-hand and if using materials such as wood or brass, they will continue to build an attractive weathered patina over use. And you'd be surprised at the difference this can make. Even the most basic kitchen can be refreshed with some thoughtful touches that make a space feel like yours, instead of a look that has been simply bought off the shelf.

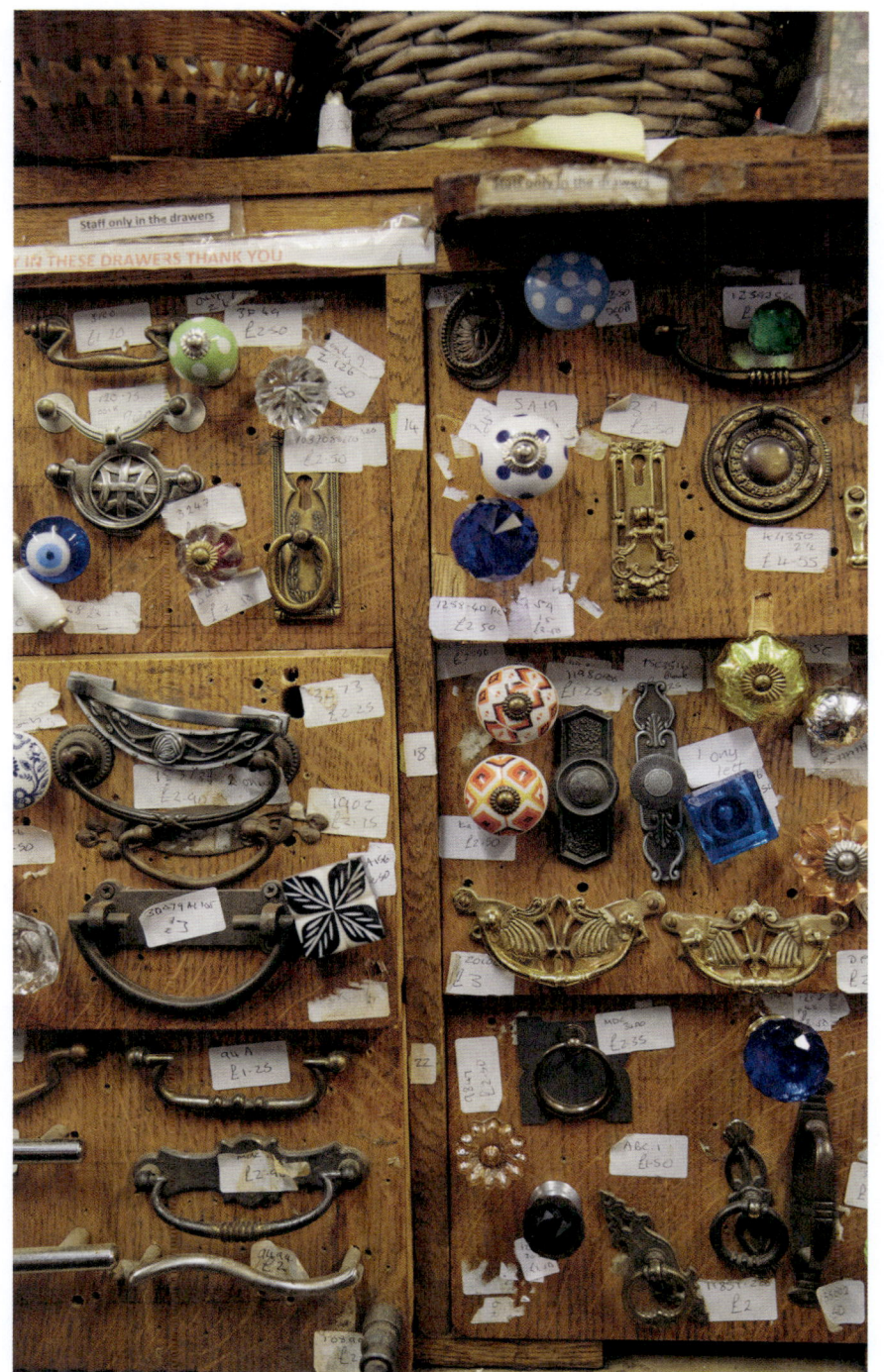

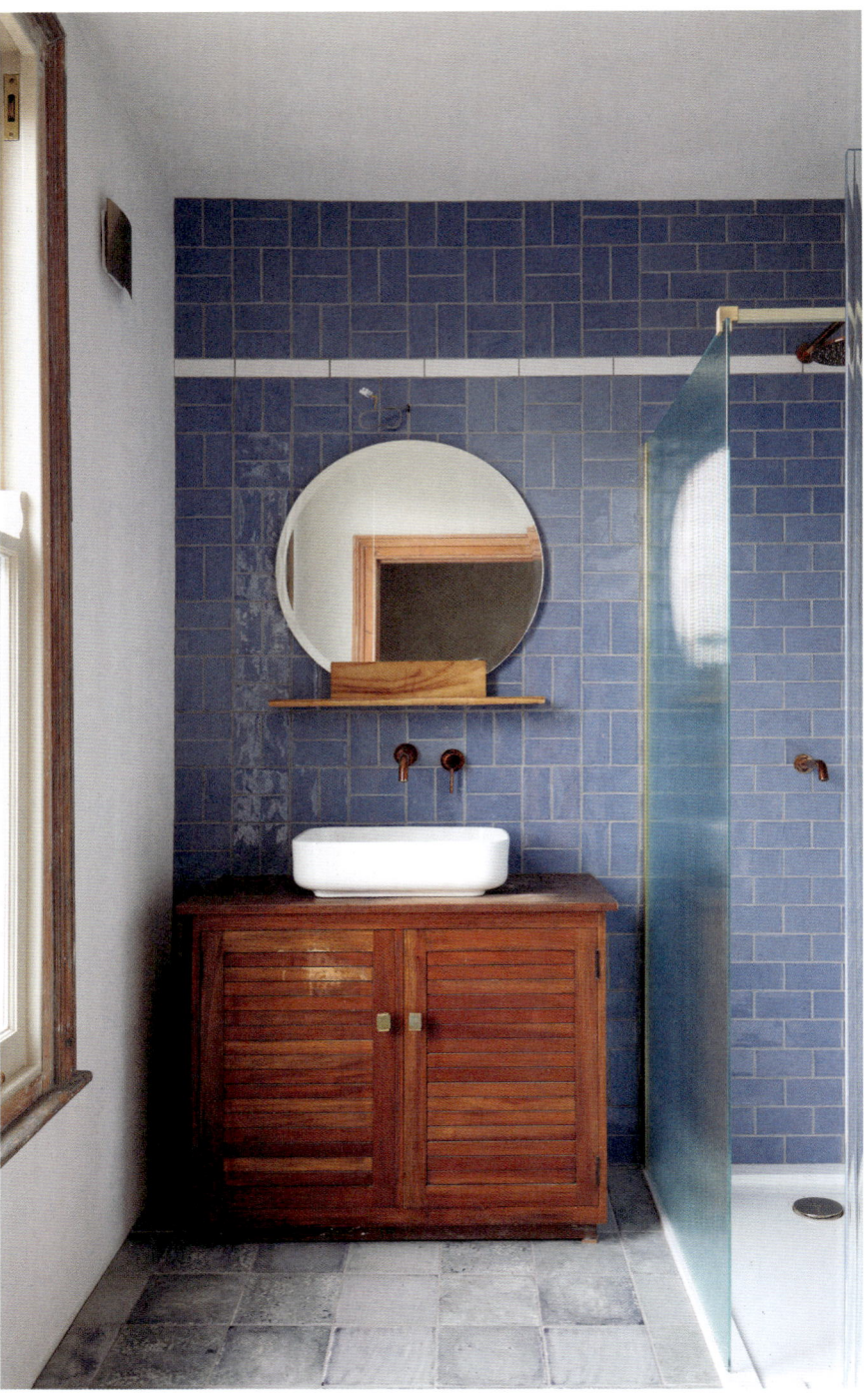

Bathrooms

In the past, bathrooms were often given less attention than other rooms in home renovations. They were dreary spaces, forgotten about or left to the end of a project when the budget had run out. Recently, there has been renewed investment in these spaces, which I'm thrilled to see.

As with kitchen fittings, bathroom fittings like toilets, basins, baths and tap hardware can absolutely be reused, and, if made from robust materials like ceramic or cast iron, with a bit of care can last generations. You will find plenty of second-hand options for bathroom fittings online or at reclamation yards, house clearances or even in skips! Some people don't like the thought of using someone else's old bathroom suite, but I am very much not of this mindset, and would always favour an older piece that will offer longevity over a new, low-quality alternative. If you are creating a bathroom from scratch with a retro feel (I love an avocado basin), you'll likely find even better value when you source a three-piece bathroom suite over individual fixtures.

If you are in any doubt about the value of second-hand bathroom fixtures, try leaving an old cast-iron bath outside your home in any urban area. I can promise you it will be taken within hours, if not by your neighbours, by builders and scrap metal merchants.

Kitchen and bathroom fixtures

I've put the sourcing tips for kitchen and bathroom fixtures together as there are so many similarities between them. Although you're free to get as creative as you like in your home, I've found that in a small space such as a flat where the kitchen and bathroom may be very close to each other, using similar fixtures in both can create continuity in the space as a whole.

Hardware

Taps can be a real focal point in a kitchen or bathroom, and when I have designed rooms that include them, they've always been one of the main priorities for me. Wall-, deck- or even floor-mounted, I'm always drawn to older taps, which tell of a life given over to the selfless service of washing!

Be mindful that older taps were sometimes manufactured to different environmental standards than they are today, so ensure you buy them from someone who is experienced at refurbishing them (asking about the refurbishment may help to identify a pro from a novice).

Questions to ask include:

- What are these made from?
- Will the finish stand the test of time?
- Does it require maintenance to keep its appearance, and can I commit to that?
- Do I have existing holes in my sink that will work with this fixture?

Ideally, any taps you source will be fitted with an aerator or flow restrictor, which slows the flow of water as it emerges from the tap, reducing water wastage. Make sure the inlets are compatible with modern plumbing standards.

Sinks and basins

Vintage sinks are so characterful and often have beautiful detailing like bullnose edges or built-in backsplashes that you frequently see replicated in new models (usually to a lesser effect!). Salvage yards and online sites tend to have a steady supply of reclaimed sinks and you can search either by using brand names you admire (for example, I search for Lefroy Brooks or Catchpole and Rye), or by other attributes such as the type (e.g. a Belfast sink) or location. If made from materials such as ceramic, cast iron, enamel or natural stone, cosmetic damage such as scuffs and scratches can often be repaired (whether you take the time to do it yourself or find a specialist). There are many clever ways to work an older sink into your space, such as setting one into a repurposed free-standing dressing table or placing one atop an old chest of drawers (complete with handy built-in storage ready to go). My advice is to go local when salvaging sinks and basins, due to the potential transport limitations because of weight.

When searching for a sink, check its pipe diameters are compatible with your drainage pipes, and if using heavier materials like cast iron, ensure that the surface it will be placed on can withstand its weight. If you find yourself with an old sink that you can't reuse in the home for whatever reason, I've found they can make lovely garden planters – just keep the plug open and set the sink's bottom corners on top of bricks or stones to allow for drainage.

I've seen some antique sinks and baths even placed on footpaths and used as beautiful guerrilla gardens in public spaces.

Work the floor

In my opinion, flooring is the aspect of a home that can make the biggest immediate impact (for better or worse). Just like how mowing the grass in a scruffy garden can have a transformative effect (although perhaps this isn't the best analogy as we are avid no-mowers!), a pleasing floor can help appease the shortcomings of a room. Flooring is also one of the areas in my homes, past and present, that has elicited the most queries – both curiosity from those who want to try something similar and shock from others at the effort we've put into flooring in our rental homes!

We were lucky enough to have the original Victorian floorboards lurking underneath the carpets in our current home – a real find as we'd only ever been able to use cheap laminate in our rentals.

Coming up are some options for sourcing flooring, as well as points you may wish to consider. They are by no means exhaustive because of course there are far too many options to list here, so I am homing in on the material and sourcing options I am asked about most often.

Wood

A wood floor, in my humble opinion, is something to get excited about. Wide-plank, skinny European-style, parquet – every type is wonderful in its own unique way. As well as looking characterful with an ever-changing patina that reflects the movement and energy in your home, I find wood practical too – warm underfoot and easy to clean. Pine, oak, ash, Douglas fir, walnut, cherry, the list goes on and your choice will come down to your preference and budget. Remember that wood needs to acclimatise to its environment before being laid, to avoid it warping or splitting, so speak to your supplier about this well in advance. This can mean you have to leave the floorboards in that space for up to a week, so ensure you've factored that into your schedule.

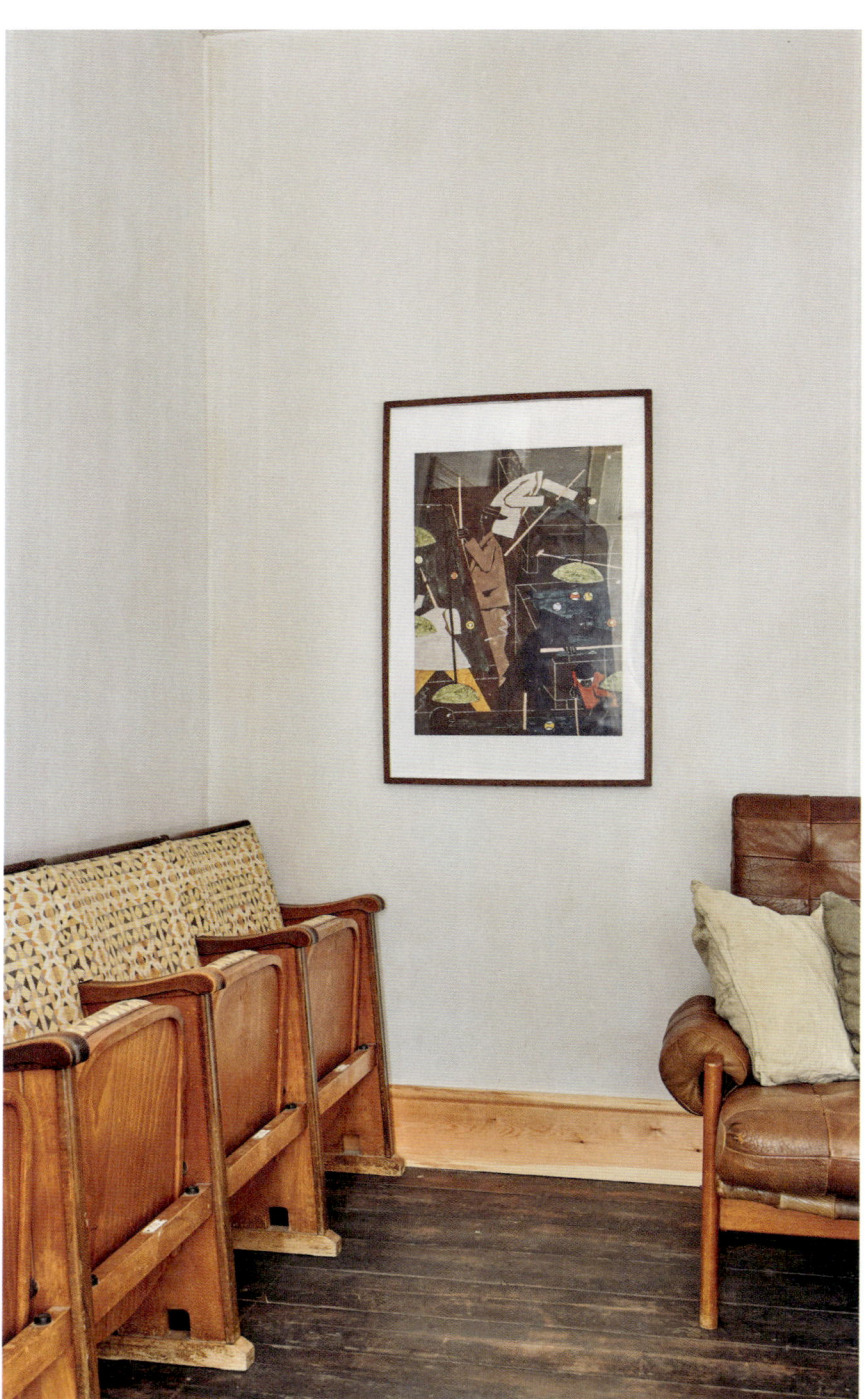

If you are living in an upstairs flat, always check any potential restrictions about using bare wood, because it can make it much nosier for anyone living below you (so much so that some leases forbid it, even if you own the property). Adding underlay beneath the floorboards will help with sound-proofing but it still may not be as effective as any carpet you've pulled up.

Reclaimed wood

There's something very special about a reclaimed wood floor, it tends to steal the show in a room. Old boards often come from large buildings such as schools, libraries or hospitals and it can feel very special to bring a piece of another building's history into your home. More's the better if they originated near you and don't have to travel far. Some people feel strongly about only bringing materials into their home that match the era in which their home was built, and so having, for instance, Victorian boards in a modern flat would be a faux pas for them. I personally like an eclectic approach to fixtures and fittings so that doesn't personally concern me. Reclamation yards, or sites like eBay or Gumtree, always have options for reclaimed flooring – when sourcing them, take into account that they might need to be treated once laid (sanded, treated for woodworm and then stained), so be sure to enquire about this before purchasing.

Engineered wood

These boards tend to be made of composite woods bound together under a top sheet of hard wood, giving the illusion of a solid wood floor. They often come as tongue and groove, making them straightforward to lay, so you may not even need a tradesperson to fit them for you. There are many variations in material, finish, quality and price with some options on the scale looking incredibly realistic. Ultimately though, engineered boards are unlikely to last as long as hard wood boards because there are limits to how much they can be re-sanded.

Laying new boards

Going direct to a timber merchant for untreated boards can be quite a cost-effective approach to new flooring. Depending on the merchant, they're likely to stock different options for hard and soft wood, and they can cut them to size as per your dimensions. If you're a confident DIYer then have a go at laying the boards yourself, but an expert flooring professional could also be hired if the budget allows.

Sanding

I'd always recommend working with what you've already got, if possible, particularly if you're in an older home which still has its original floorboards. That might mean finding floors which are structurally sound but need a bit of cosmetic treatment. Sanding floors can be such an impactful way to breathe new life into a floor that has perhaps been covered with carpet for many years or has been uncovered but is a bit worse for wear. You can hire a sanding machine and tackle this yourself or book a professional.

In our own home, my mum, in an attempt to help us out, hired a heavy-duty sander, and to my horror it removed all the patina from the floorboards in the living room. So, for the other rooms I just did a light sanding by hand, followed by applying a light coat of oil. It really depends on what you're looking for – if it's a uniform look then a heavy-duty sander is effective, if you want to maintain some of the natural patina of the wood, I think that can only be achieved by doing it by hand, whether that is done by you or a professional.

Remember, boards will need to be treated after they're sanded to protect them, usually using oil, stain or wax, depending on the finish you're after.

Painting

Painting over old floorboards, using specialist wood primer followed by floor paint, can hide a multitude of imperfections. Painting tends to be quicker and cheaper than sanding (hiring a sander can be expensive), not to mention less dusty! However, in high-traffic areas, painted floorboards will likely need repainting and touching up from time to time, unless you don't mind scuffs. I love seeing people get creative with floor painting, such as creating a diamond or chequerboard pattern, a bit like a tiled floor.

Vinyl and laminate

There are so many options for vinyl and laminate flooring with a huge range in type and price. If you're living in a rental, you may well already have a vinyl or laminate floor. They are prevalent materials as they tend to be cheaper to buy and lay compared with other options such as wood or linoleum (a natural, more hardwearing material that was more common before cheaper alternatives were invented). You often see vinyl or laminate used in a faux wood style or in jaunty patterns. I can see why many people use them – laid well, they can look quite smart and are easy to clean. Laid inexpertly however, and depending on their quality, they can soon look scruffy and shiny, often warping and sporting some weird-looking bubbles underfoot. I find they are a great quick fix, but they tend not to be a long-term solution for flooring as they can tear and come away from the skirtings. Be mindful too that noxious adhesives which give off a harmful gas are usually used to stick this kind of flooring down, meaning it wouldn't be the most eco-friendly choice. So, vinyl is not a material I'd necessarily recommend you use, however, if it's what you've got and you're not about to tear it up, don't fight it – consider rugs to be your greatest ally.

Carpet

Fashions in flooring preferences have changed a lot over the years – where wall-to-wall carpets were once a mainstay throughout homes (including often in bathrooms!), there has been a move towards embracing flooring that is cooler underfoot, lower-maintenance and easier to clean. My grandparents' generation tended to favour a cosy fitted carpet, often lifting it up and taking it with them if they moved house, particularly if it was made from a good-quality material such as wool (a high-quality wool carpet can last decades). Apart from in our play room, we don't have plans for any carpets in our current home, but I do think they can be lovely additions. Like other soft furnishings, they help absorb sound, which is why carpet or carpet runners are often used on stairs. Carpet doesn't just have to mean wool or artificial materials. Natural fibres like jute, seagrass or sisal offer a beautiful, earthy look and look great layered with rugs. Be warned though that these natural fibres can stain very easily, tend not to be water-repellent, and aren't always suitable for homes with pets (sharp claws not working harmoniously with the fibres!).

    There is a huge range in the carpets on offer and prices vary massively according to the material(s) the carpet is made from. Although we've gone for wooden floors and vintage rugs in our home, I love the idea of eco carpets, like the ones made from recycled plastic or even food waste. Remember also to consider the cost of underlay and professional fitting when it comes to carpeting your home. Carpet-fitting takes skill but of course, many committed DIYers have a go themselves. If you're considering this, remember that some carpets, particularly those with natural fibres, have a tendency to shrink away from the walls and so need to be placed in situ for up to a fortnight to acclimatise before being laid.

If you are planning on installing carpet anywhere in your home, be sure to get a sample of the fabric to add to your mood board – colours and textures can vary so much from product to product.

If you have moved into a home with carpets that are not to your taste, but you aren't able to remove them for whatever reason, I would recommend cleaning them or having them professionally cleaned (if possible) using environmentally friendly products. When moving into our current home, we did the maths and it worked out cheaper to purchase a top-rated carpet-cleaning vacuum ourselves than to outsource the job as a one-off. Now, we have the ability to regularly clean our carpets! Cleaning can make a big difference to not just lingering marks but smell too, as carpets really hold on to odours, such as smoke or pet smells. If, even after a good clean, you're still not a fan of the carpet, layering some rugs should help.

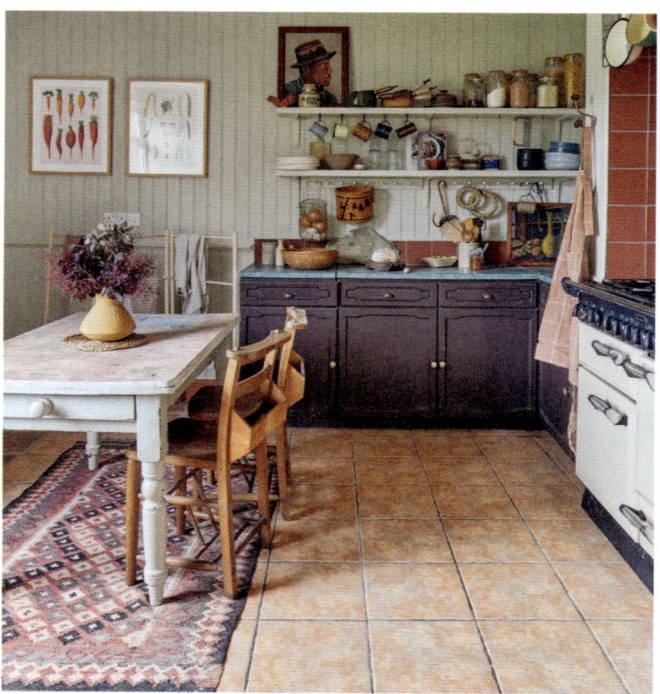

Tiling

I couldn't write a book without giving some attention to tiles. Oh, the hours (days? Years?) I have spent searching for the perfect tiles for our current and previous hallways and bathrooms. Suffice to say I am a tile obsessive, and I think that a lot of my online community are too, judging from the comments I get.

I just love the grandeur and texture that tiles bring to a room. There's something about them that feels luxurious to me, but I find them practical too – easy to clean and hard-wearing. Luxury and practicality are a killer combination. A tiled floor is a great way to introduce pattern and colour which you can continue up the walls, or pair with a more restrained look. Large quantities of tiles can be pricey to buy and lay, but you can also achieve a striking effect using tiles in a small area, such as a used or disused fireplace or a recess by your front door, or you could even have a few loose tiles propped up on a shelf or used as coasters or pot stands.

Sourcing tiles

When sourcing tiles in the past, I have tended to veer away from the usual big-brand suspects, not because I don't rate the quality (many high-street stores do stock good-quality tiles; many sadly don't, despite their high price points), but because I have never quite found what I've been looking for. This has meant a lot of time asking around or digging online, staring into my phone for solutions to my tile search woes. The dreamy terracotta tiles I finally found for the bathroom in our former maisonette had a lead time of four months (much to our tiler's horror), which is why planning as far in advance as possible is always helpful. Some things are worth the wait. With many beautiful tiles being manufactured outside of the UK – in Spain, Portugal, Turkey and Greece to name a few countries – I have noticed that typical lead times have become longer in recent years, so do plan accordingly if you're working to a tight schedule.

Something to be mindful of is that many high-street stores actually sell the same tiles, sourced from the same tile-makers, but market them under different names and for different prices, so be sure to look around for the best offers.

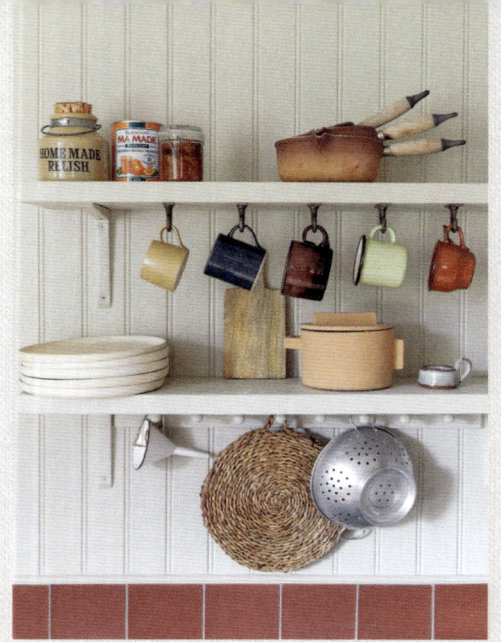
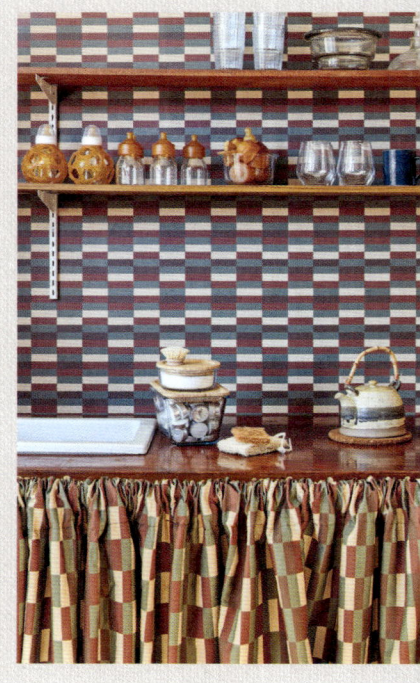
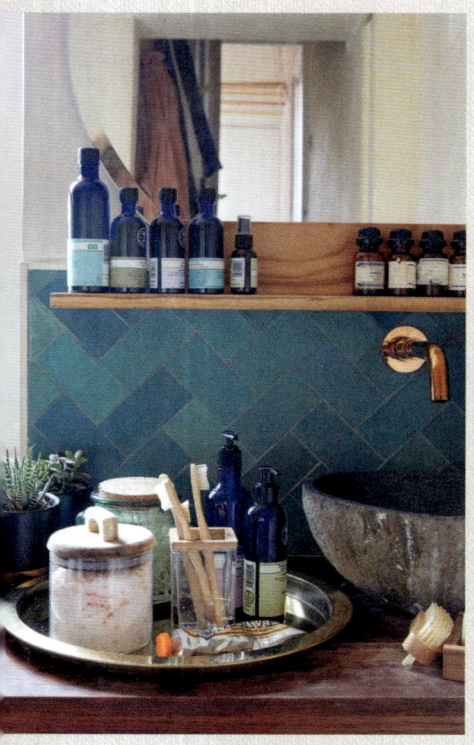
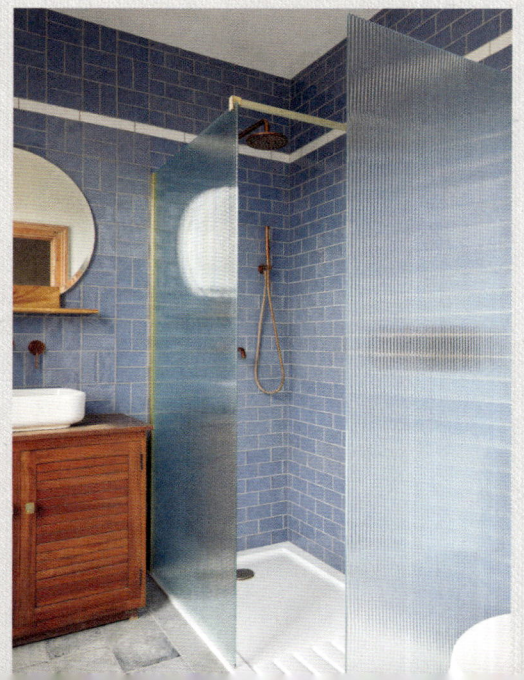

I recently noticed a very hip, aspirational tile brand with a sleek website selling the exact same tiles as another lesser-known online store, for much more money.

You can find beautiful vintage tiles in a stunning array of colours and patterns, and often for a song on eBay or other second-hand sites. I always check these second-hand sites before sourcing directly from a traditional seller just in case it's my lucky day. It's quite likely you'll find some nice options for smaller tiling projects where fewer tiles are required, if you are willing to be flexible. Be mindful though that reclaimed tiles often come with old adhesive on the reverse that will require careful and painstaking removal if you're hoping for a smooth installation.

Porcelain

Porcelain tiles tend to be a more wallet-friendly choice compared with other tiles, and the array is endless. They are usually suitable for walls and floors, come in all shapes and sizes and are generally straightforward to install (at least more so than the other options in this list). 'Straightforward' often equates to cheaper too, since if you are hiring a tiler it will take them less time. Square and rectangular tiles tend to be quicker to lay than hexagonal ones, for instance, and produce less waste, so both factors will affect your budget.

Terracotta

You'll be bringing a warm Mediterranean feel into your home with terracotta's rich orange-red tones. Reclaimed terracotta is lovely too, quite reasonably priced and often used in a previous life as roof tiles.

Encaustic

I love the chalky finish of encaustic tiles – cheaper versions often have a pattern or colour printed onto the top of the tiles, which can fade, unlike more expensive ones where the colour is set in. Even though encaustic tiles need sealing, they are often relatively porous afterwards and so are prone to marking a little, particularly the lighter shades. An environmental impact to consider is that they are very thick and heavy, so transporting them will require more packaging and boxes, more space on a van or truck and therefore more fuel. As with everything, buying locally if you can will help to offset this.

Zellige and bejmat

True zellige tiles hail from Morocco where they are handcrafted so each tile is unique, with tonal and textural variations. They're my favourite of all tiles. The aim for the tiler is to ensure that the grout lines between tiles are as thin as possible so they look like they're almost overlapping. Beware of some high street brands selling factory-made 'zellige' or 'zellige-style' tiles, sometimes with a lack of transparency which may make you think you're buying genuine zellige. You'll likely spot something is amiss as they tend to be much cheaper than the real deal.

Terrazzo

Look down in a train station or museum and the chances are you are walking over a form of terrazzo flooring. Made from natural stone chippings set in concrete or resin, terrazzo can be a durable and cheering option found in many colourways.

Natural stone

Beautiful stones like marble, granite, slate and limestone have something of a timeless feel, perhaps because they're often found in grand old buildings. They are more expensive than other options but will last a lifetime if you don't mind some visible cosmetic damage in higher-traffic areas (I personally love the lived-in look). So, think about sealants carefully and be sure to choose appropriate cleaning products once they've been laid.

Mosaic

These come in an array of colours and shapes, and I enjoy their swimming pool vibes. If you source these by the sheet, they will be simpler to lay.

More sustainable tiling options

Nowadays, more tile companies are working with interesting methods to recycle old materials – often waste headed for landfill – transforming them into amazing tiles. Terrazzo is a great example of this kind of tiling, using marble scraps and recycled glass, so if you're keen to find sustainable tiles start by searching for these.

Instead of or in addition to tiling, experiment with other finishes. You might have noticed the rise in popularity of an aged plaster effect that is often achieved with a lime wash paint such as Bauwerk. We used this a lot throughout our Islington home to add texture to the walls.

Continuous covering finishes such as microcement and tadelakt are becoming increasingly popular (I say 'increasingly' but actually in some parts of the world they have been around for thousands of years). Rather than separate tiles, they offer a smooth finish to a wall or floor. These are skilled techniques that to my mind look beautiful, understated and luxuriously spa-like. It can actually be more cost-effective to have microcement or tadelakt rather than expensive tiles (some laypeople even go on courses to learn the skill, and then save by doing it themselves). The added benefit of these materials is that there is no grouting to maintain, and it can be warmer underfoot (unless you have the luxury of underfloor heating beneath your tiles).

Installation

I hold my hands up that I have never attempted tiling myself (I know my skills and their limits!), but plenty of dedicated DIYers are successful in doing so. Keep in mind that tiling is a skilled job and there can be a lot of preparation and specialist kit required, such as a tile cutter, and space to cut them in (ideally outdoors, if possible, as it produces a lot of dust).

Remember

- Order enough tiles for cutting excess – the percentage you will need to over-order will depend on the shape of your tiles and whether they are patterned or not.
- Factor in costs for adhesive, grouting and sealant.
- Grouting colour is important so check this carefully against the tiles you're using. Tile stores often recommend complementary shades, but you can go rogue if you prefer another.
- I'm stating the obvious here but be sure to check that your tiles are suitable for where you're laying them (some tiles are suitable for both floors and walls, but not all, and you need heat-resistant tiles if using them near an in-use fireplace).

- If using on the floor, check the slip rating (some floor tiles are not suitable for the bathroom, where they can be hazardous when wet).
- If you're laying over an underfloor heating system, check that the tiles are suitable.
- Take into account how the depth of your tiles might impact the thresholds in any connecting rooms. For example, encaustic tiles are very thick, so this may result in there being a slight step down onto the adjoining floor, rather than it being flush. The discrepancy can be softened with a threshold strip, which can be ordered in a variety of materials like metal or wood, and can come cut to size. Full disclosure, we forgot to do this, and so the tiles in our ensuite bathroom remain unlaid until we can come to terms with removing the underfloor heating we have already installed.
- Little finishing details such as 'pencils' (thin pencil-shaped tiles to fill in edges), border trims or skirtings can add lovely next-level finishes (though they can be pricey!).

I'd recommend keeping a few tiles if you have any leftover, in the unlucky event of any later damage. Leftover tiles can sometimes also be cut and used as skirting, which can work well in bathrooms.

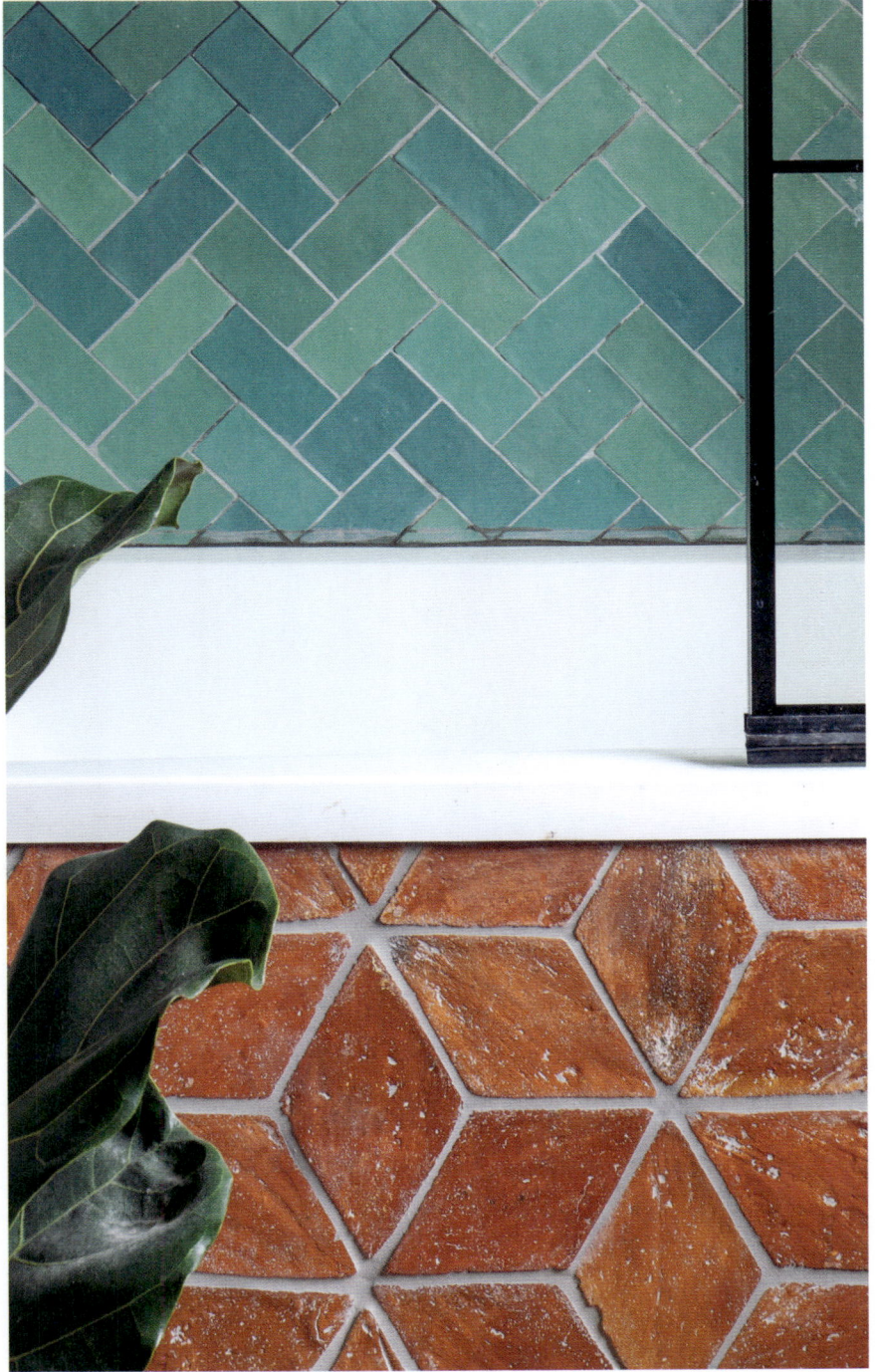

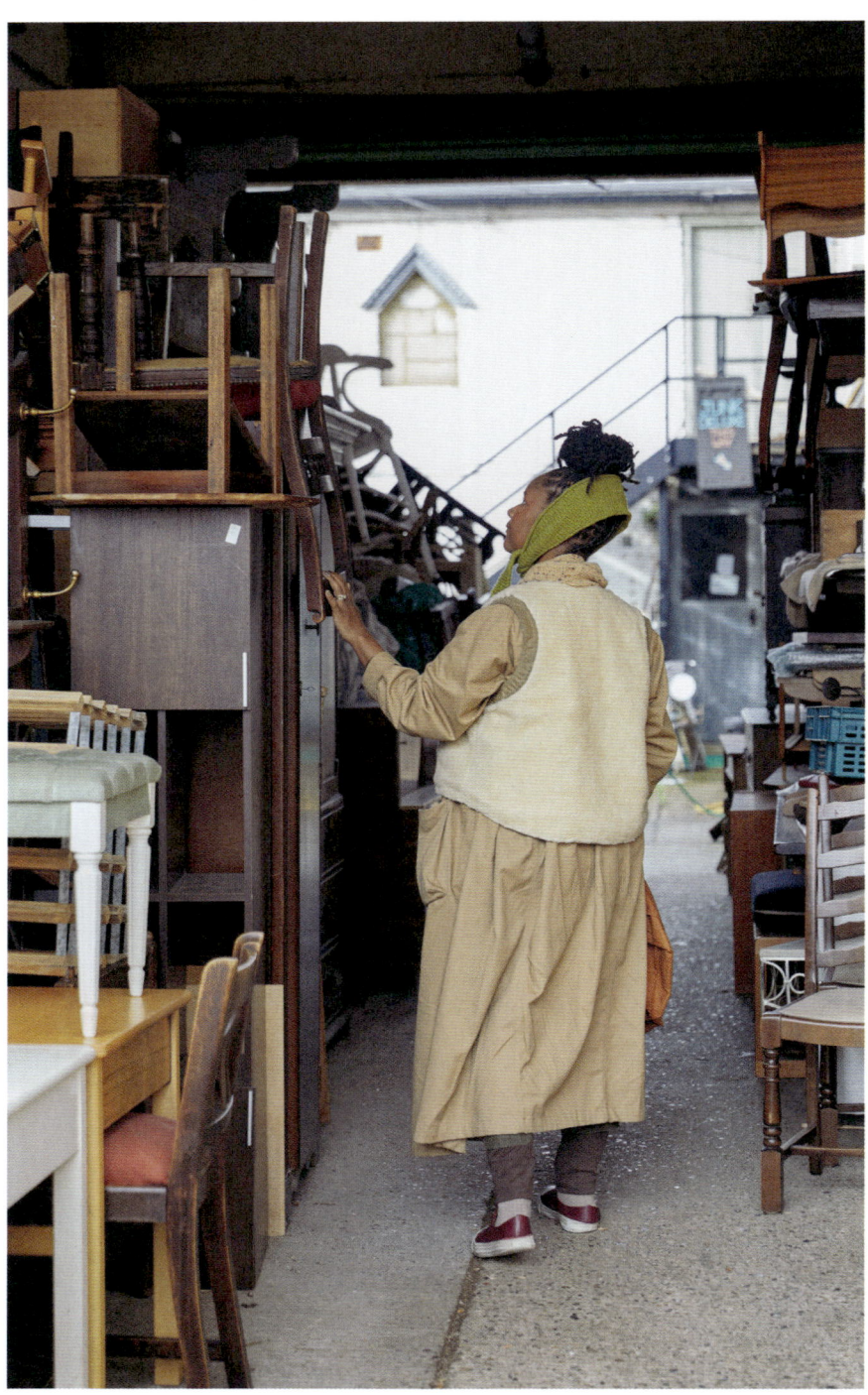

CHAPTER 10

PRE-LOVED: SOURCING (AND SELLING) SECOND-HAND

Thrifting, antiquing, scouring neighbourhood sale sites and even skip-diving: this chapter looks at some of my favourite ways to source second-hand. Here I put into practice some of the theory mentioned earlier, as I apply broadly the same principles to whatever I'm sourcing, whether furnishings or clothing. Not everything I buy is pre-owned, but it is almost always my first port of call and to my mind second-hand is the backbone of a relaxed, lived-in look. Not only are such elements more sustainable to re-use, but good-quality older pieces are often better made and longer-lasting than many newer equivalents.

I learnt from the best how to find treasure – my mum is a magpie and as a young kid, I used to accompany her to her market stall on Portobello Road. I get a real kick from offering new life to a piece and I like thinking of its history, imagining where it has lived before or who has worn it – thinking of its previous lives and owners, and knowing I'm just part of the journey, a custodian. Maybe it's because I'm an old soul that I am drawn to things that have had a bit of a life already by the time they reach me.

Sourcing second-hand isn't always the easiest choice and often it takes longer than buying brand-new. I believe the process of furnishing a home shouldn't be about box-ticking, quickly buying anything suitable just to get it done. Sourcing items you love may take years and, like my childhood homes, there may be a revolving door of pieces coming in and going out again as life evolves. Let's take our time, slow down and be considered in our purchases, both in terms of getting only what we need and also respecting provenance. Being more deliberate in our sourcing decisions can lead us to making better choices.

Many of us are coming round to the need to shop with integrity and consider the impact of supply chains. Being more intentional about how we fill our domestic spaces grants us agency and ensures that we're not becoming victims of rampant consumerism. Just being aware of how high-street brands manipulate us with their offers, sales and 'free' shipping (spoiler: it's built into the price!) is a step in the right direction, and the more I keep this in mind, the more resilient I find I am to being swayed into generic purchases that certainly don't fill me with joy.

I hope this chapter convinces you of the merits of buying pre-owned (and re-selling in future if you so wish) and offers you lots of practical tips to do so. Go forth and source!

Consider your mindset around cost

For some people, there can be a mental block around buying something that has belonged to someone else, perhaps because they hold a perception that second-hand means lower-quality. This might be for a variety of reasons, but one common rationale is that for some, second-hand was a necessity growing up rather than a choice, and there may be some lingering, unresolved shame associated with that. Many working-class adults are trying to process the remnants of feelings of going without in their youth, and now providing their own safety nets in the form of secure homes that no longer lack material possessions. Additionally, buying new can feel liberating to those who grew up in homes that faced financial unpredictability. In either case, buying second-hand can feel like a step back, since it is no longer a necessity.

A scarcity mindset can occur for a whole host of reasons, not all financial, and you needn't necessarily have grown up poor to have experienced it. A lack of quality time with caregivers, unmet needs or living in transient circumstances can sometimes lay foundations for this. So, it'd be flippant for me to say 'forget any taboos around buying pre-loved and just go for it' if you hold deep-seated feelings, conscious or unconscious, that may be holding you back from taking this approach. Try to reframe your thoughts, focusing on second-hand being the more sustainable route, more beneficial to the planet than buying new. Speaking to like-minded people in your community can also be a good way to share your experiences. Start out by gently easing yourself into the second-hand marketplace – second-hand books for example can be a good gateway. Go from there and at your own pace.

Many of us were raised to be very adept at seeking out the furniture or clothing we love at a fraction of the price, because it's all we knew. This feels so second-nature to me that even if I won the lottery tomorrow, I still wouldn't change these buying habits. I will always favour good-quality second-hand over a lesser-quality brand-new item, whether I'm buying a dining table or school uniform. But even for seasoned thrifters, there can be a bit of a psychological barrier to spending the same amount or more on a used item as you would on something brand-new. I want to challenge that, if only because longevity will be the true marker of value. A second-hand solid oak wardrobe in good condition should cost more than a brand-new chipboard equivalent: it will last longer, it will retain its value and it will likely outlive us. Once we can get our heads round that, we'll increasingly come round to second-hand shopping.

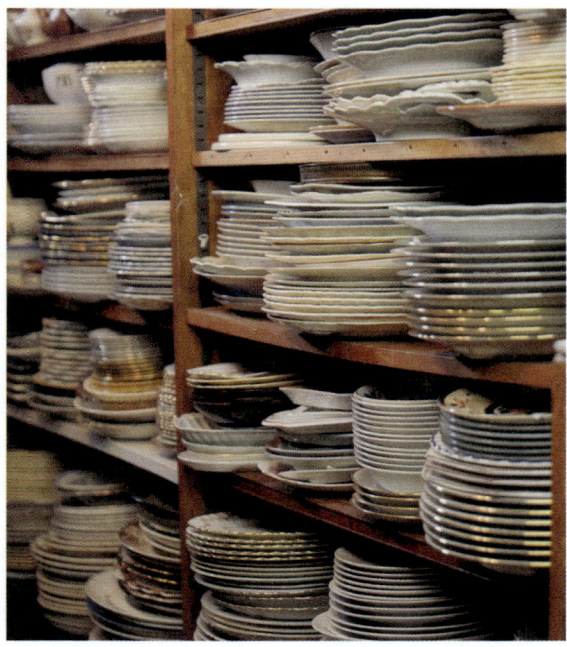

Shopping with purpose

Of course, just because we're buying second-hand it doesn't prevent us from falling down the consumer rabbit hole of mindlessly shopping, wasting energy and cash buying random things we don't need. We can just as easily use second-hand shopping the same way we do buying new – to fill a void or to counterbalance a lack of emotional safety. Buying for the sake of it could be a symptom of hoarding, so before you acquire something, ask yourself if you love it, if it will be useful, if it fulfils all your criteria – or whether will you still be on the lookout for a better item and whether it will still be useable several years from now (either by you or someone else). If not, walk away.

Getting something new (albeit second-hand, so new to me) can provide a quick thrill and a bit of a distraction from daily life and its issues, especially if I get the dopamine hit of scoring a great bargain. It's so easy to spend a few pounds here and a couple there, justifying each expense as being so small it doesn't really matter. But it all adds up, both in terms of the expense and the accumulation of stuff. I am really trying to get better at resisting these unnecessary purchases because I know that before long each one will be yet another object in my home to clean, tidy away and eventually to drop off to a charity shop. Knowing when to pass up stuff is a skill in itself.

Process and provenance when sourcing second-hand

In Chapter 8, we looked at the importance of the origin of what we buy, but what about those times when the precise provenance is unknown (often the case with second-hand sourcing) or where a maker may have been from a marginalised community?

Purchasing items for our homes from marginalised communities is no bad thing. The systemic exploitation of those communities for profit on a mass scale is. For me, unless a second-hand item is clearly problematic, for example it's offensive or it has religious ties that I don't feel I can honour, I am more relaxed knowing I may not get to the bottom of its provenance.

There's still an element of responsible shopping needed, though. For example, recently my mum sent me a photo of a gorgeous piece of art she had found in a charity shop. It was two women under a giant plantain tree. 'Do you want it?' she asked. 'Only £14.99!' I asked her to zoom into the picture so I could inspect what clothing the women were wearing and then again to zoom into any text on the print – my concern was whether this was a plantation scene or simply two women basking under a plantain tree. She sent me the photo and within a few minutes, Google had pulled up all I needed to know about the print and the artist. It's now got pride of place in our living room.

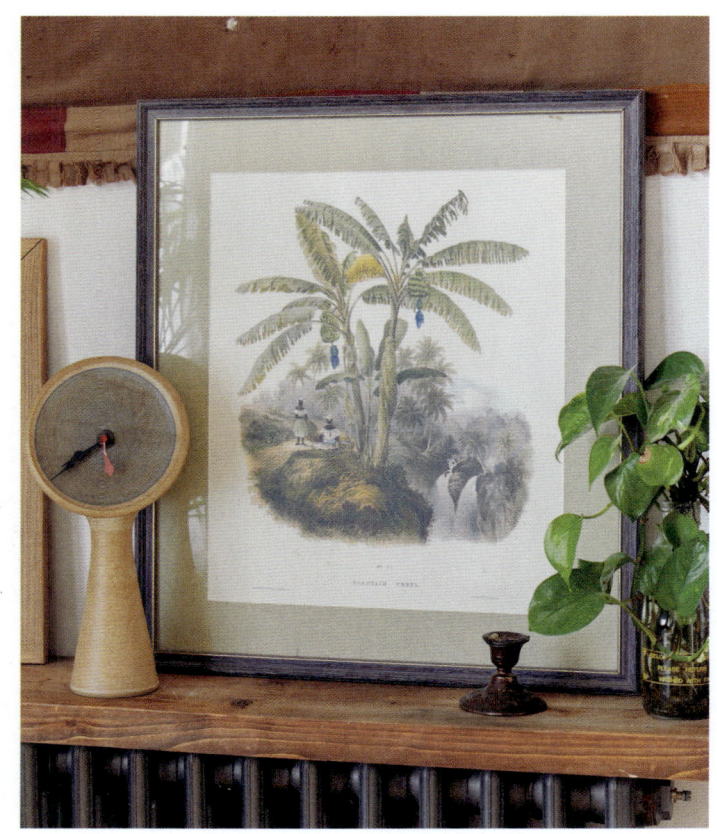

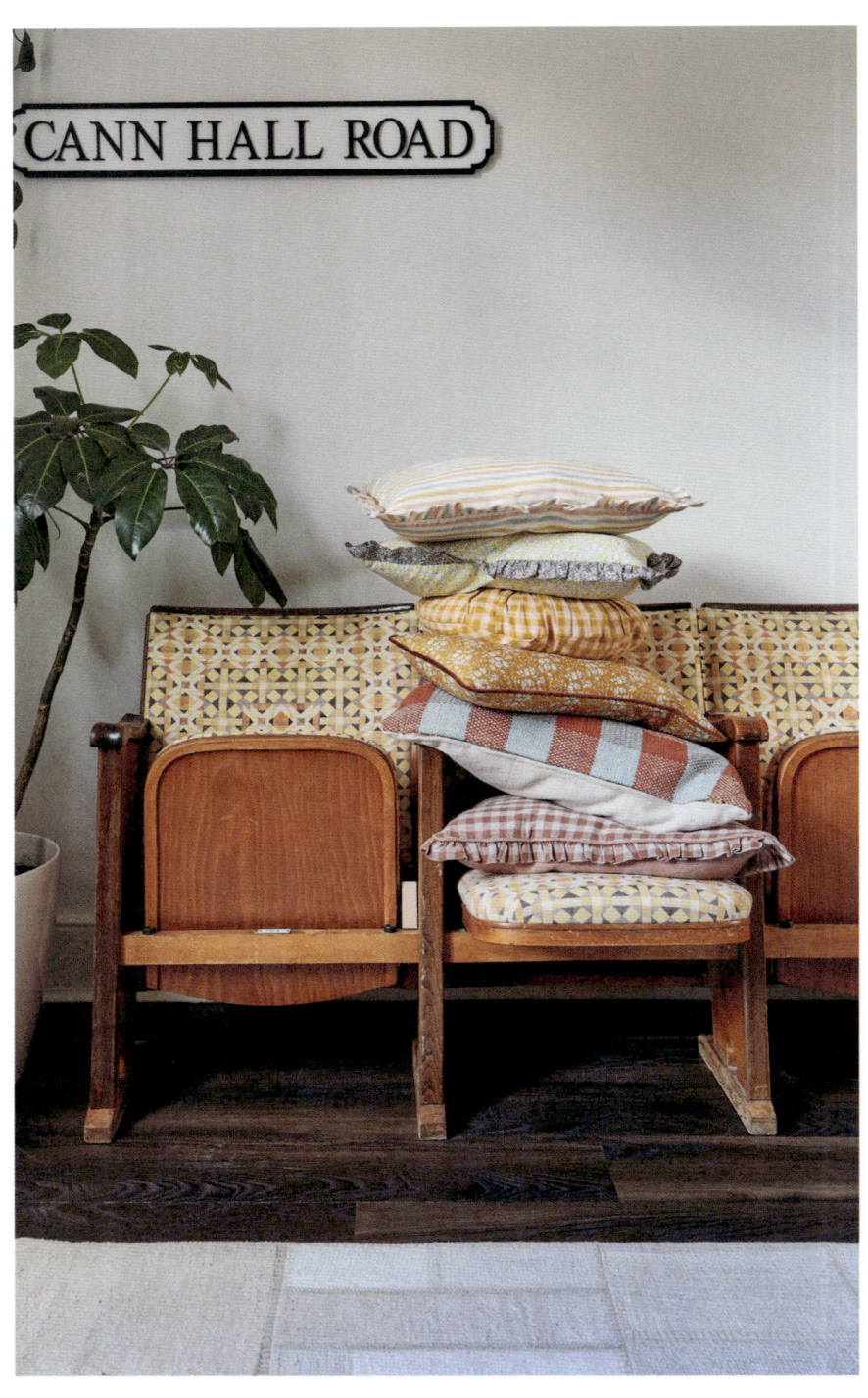

SOURCE

Repurposing

As I've said, my mum has an incredible knack for vintage sourcing and repurposing these discoveries. I marvel at how she finds one-off treasures to fit a brief and she always keeps an eye out for the things that she knows I'm looking for. Some years ago, I tasked her with finding a moquette fabric for me and she came through in spades. Moquette is a woollen fabric that is often found on public transport seating such as train or tube seats. I initially thought it could work to re-cover our second-hand theatre chairs, but when my reupholsterer saw the fabric, she said that it didn't have quite enough 'give'. Instead, we repurposed the material as the backing for our handmade banner that reads, 'We are our ancestors wildest dreams', which was also my grandfather's epitaph. The moquette fabric reminds us of his working life as a bus driver, so this tribute to him hanging in our home feels incredibly fitting – another connection to our past that also utilises a repurposed item.

Think creatively about what you might already have in your home that can be repurposed into a more practical application and loved a little more. Keep an open mind too when you are sourcing pieces for your home, as what you purchase may be perfect for a very different use. When our green vintage theatre chairs clashed with our second-hand green leather sofa, we took them to be reupholstered in a busy yellow Liberty of London fabric that picked up on the tones of the display books in the shelving opposite. It's striking, unique and the pattern has done a great job of hiding inevitable stains over the years. I love that nothing else quite like it exists.

If you're willing to make repairs, either yourself or by outsourcing to a specialist, you will often find pieces at amazing prices. You are unlikely to find an antique in pristine condition – it doesn't quite work that way – but common defects like ring marks, scratches and scuffs on wood, tarnishing on metal or tears in fabric can usually be repaired without too much faff. Reupholstery and repairs to leather, wicker or other natural materials like rattan or cane do tend to be time-consuming and therefore costs can mount, but if you have found a piece you love, it may well be worth the effort. When compared with new high-street equivalents, you may be pleased to discover that your one-off piece, made good as new, may still come in significantly cheaper. If you can, contact two or three contractors to get quotes (most should be able to offer you a ballpark figure based on photographs, dimensions and a description of what you want). Remember to allow for material costs (such as fabric, lining, webbing or similar) and courier fees if needed – always a stinger!

When repurposing, look beyond the description, for example, a small chest of drawers could double as a bedside table where space is at a premium, vintage Tupperware could be the perfect storing for small toys, a cutlery divider could work for stationery. Further to this, you might think about any pieces you have that could be upcycled to suit your needs, like placing side tables or wooden storage boxes on castors or reusing any textiles or soft furnishings for a children's play space. The possibilities are almost endless.

Hello, goodbye

If you see something you truly love, I think there usually is a way to find a spot for it in your space (even if that means calling on the one-in, one-out rule). My home, much like my childhood one, is a space in constant evolution as we say farewell to some pieces and embrace new ones. Nothing in your home has to be forever. While I am committed to longevity for the sake of an item's quality, I am all for pieces coming in and out of our home to suit our changing needs and selling on when necessary. I view my investment in pieces almost like a rental charge, which is usually minimal, as the vintage items I've owned tend to sell on for around what I bought them for (unless they've been damaged), or even more in cases where I know more about the item than the original seller. This is in stark contrast to a new piece, which devalues greatly the moment you take the packaging off. This approach to the objects in your home also allows you to take a chance and even make mistakes, because you can always resell with the peace of mind that your investment shouldn't have decreased too much. I get such pleasure from wearing something well-crafted or using an item that is many years old yet works as well as the day it was made. True craftsmanship is something to celebrate.

If you do need to source pieces for your home that you already know will be short-term solutions, such as packing boxes and clothes rails (handy for moving), or toys and baby equipment (barring car seats and cot mattresses, which are not recommended to use second-hand), be sure to check local selling groups, where items like these are perennially available as families outgrow them. If you are fortunate enough to get any bits for free, consider giving them away too when the time comes, rather than selling on.

Tips for selling on

Sell in season

For homewares, things like wool blankets or slow cookers will have more appeal to buyers in cooler months, and few people are looking for garden furniture in mid-December, so apply this logic to your selling window.

Quicker online selling

If you don't like the hassle of selling, consider grouping items together in bundles or job lots which will cut down on your dispatch admin. You may not fetch as high a price, but you are likely to save time and energy. If you find re-sale sites fiddly, try setting up a re-sale Instagram account, with basic information on each piece.

Yard sales

If you aren't a fan of selling online, an old-school yard sale can be a simple way to have a clear-out. These work best if you have some private space outside your home, like a front garden, and I'd recommend you price your items attractively to catch the eye of punters! Some neighbourhoods organise an annual jumble trail or similar sales, with lots of people selling disused items.

Car boot sales

My husband and I live for a car boot sale. They can be great fun to do (unlike eBay it's a good day out), and they're a way to get rid of a lot of big objects in one go. Be flexible and prepared to haggle!

Charity shops

If you haven't had luck selling and/or you want to donate instead, some charity stores offer collection, especially for larger pieces, if you don't have the means to drop them off yourself.

Your sourcebook

When you are sourcing homewares or clothing in a more conscious way, the approach is a little different than clicking the 'add to basket' button – it can take longer and I can't pretend I don't always find the wait frustrating. When I consider the alternative though, I know that holding out for a pre-loved gem will always be more fulfilling. I have a rolling wish list of pieces I want and hunting them down is part of the fun. I literally cannot walk past a charity shop, second-hand store, car boot sale or similar, without having a little browse. Coming up are some other second-hand sourcing options to keep in mind.

Auction houses

Auction houses can be a brilliant way to find a variety of vintage pieces, from affordable art to furniture, musical instruments, textiles, ceramics, you name it. We haven't always had a car and so often, this option felt inaccessible to me as we had no way of getting bigger pieces home. Now, however, many auction houses can be accessed remotely, giving you much broader access to auction houses here and abroad (many will organise international shipping). If you can though, physically visiting one can be really inspiring, with many having much more treasures to discover in situ than what's advertised in their online catalogue. There is usually so much on offer at an auction house – large spaces filled with mountains of historical objects and curiosities – it can help to stay focused on any specific pieces you're looking for. As in any auction situation, decide on your top limit in advance and don't be tempted to exceed it in the heat of a bidding war. Bear in mind that interior designers and other tastemakers often rely on auction houses for their finds, so you may face fierce competition from some of the professionals. Seeing what sells and for how much is always useful for gauging trends in the making.

SOURCE

Salvage/reclamation yards

If you are looking for fittings or materials for your home or garden, salvage yards can offer an array of weird and wonderful reclaimed options, often at great prices. From materials such as timber, bricks and stone, to kitchen and bathroom fittings, fireplaces, radiators and outdoor bits and pieces, such as gates and guttering, salvage yards are treasure troves to be explored. Like auction houses, nothing beats a wander round in person if you can, seeing materials in the flesh, feeling their texture and patina, and assessing whether they'll work in your home. There tends to be quite a high turnover of stock at these yards, and I've found that stock online runs out quickly, so visit in person if you can (many are only open by appointment, so call ahead). If you are searching for something specific, go armed with the precise dimensions of your space (along with photos on your phone for good measure) and bring a measuring tape. Remember, if you are looking for a piece of furniture to fit a particular space in your home, such as an alcove, measure from skirting to skirting, rather than higher up from wall to wall.

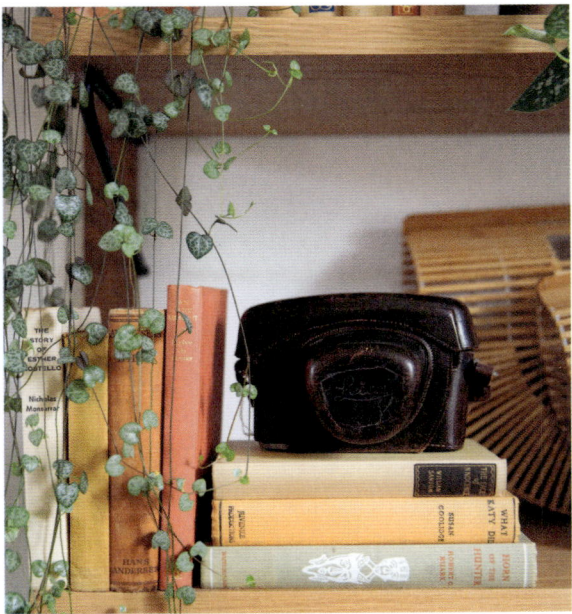

Sourcing online

I am the first to admit that I love trawling through my phone once the kids are in bed to hunt for vintage gems. Some of my favourite places to search are online: English Salvage, Etsy, eBay, Gumtree, Retrouvius and Vinterior.

I always try to get as much information about a piece's history before purchasing – online sellers specialising in specific vintage homewares tend to be fountains of knowledge on their subjects.

Here are a few things to keep in mind

- Set search alerts for your favourite styles (rather than brands, which often ends in a dramatic bidding war) or anything you're looking for. For example, my most frequent search is 'leather mid-century Danish sofa'! Be creative in your terminology (remember, one person's 'cupboard' is another's 'cabinet'), set different alerts and use a variety of phrases so as not to miss out. It's often worth trying out typos and alternative spellings too – sometimes an object you're seeking is hiding under a slightly different name, so search for 'mid-century' as well as 'midcentury' and 'mid century'.

- Modern designers often base their designs on vintage creations, so if you fall in love with an item on a contemporary website, the product name (or the description) may reveal a little more about the original design that it's based on. Use that to your advantage by going straight to the source, where a vintage item may well be better value than any current It-brands.

- Get specific with your searches using filters (most online sites have them) as this will make it easier to stay focused and avoid scrolling through hundreds of mismatches. Depending on what I'm searching for (usually homewares, toys or clothing for myself or the children), I filter by size, colour and material, and then I organise the results by price. Most of the sites I use allow me to save these searches, keeping things more manageable than if I were just scrolling aimlessly. Searching in this way will save you time (and from being overwhelmed).

- Think multi-purpose – a coffee table might work brilliantly as a children's desk, a lovely old wooden ladder might offer ideal towel storage in your bathroom, a pretty desk caddy might be a wonderful home for your make-up. Don't limit your searches by being too literal in what you're looking for.

- On many sites, you can filter by location (as well as the price and date added). Depending on what you're looking for, postage can sometimes be pricier than the actual item, and in those instances it might be cheaper to collect it yourself, if you have the means, or to organise your own courier. If booking your own delivery, some couriers – such as AnyVan or Shiply – combine pick-ups and deliveries to other customers and tend to be cheaper and are often more environmentally friendly. They occasionally take a bit longer but if you're not in a rush they're a good option.
- If you see something you like, always look at an online seller's other items for sale as you might spot something else you fancy, and they may well be open to offering a discount or consolidating postage.
- If they're nearby, see if you can view an item in person before purchasing.
- Don't be afraid to make a fair offer, or better yet, ask them first if they'd be open to an offer but don't suggest a number just yet: leave it up to them to kick-start your negotiation. This can be especially handy if you can see that the item was listed a while back. The seller can always say no!
- If sourcing items from abroad, remember to factor in potential duties, as well as shipping.

You will have seen throughout this chapter that I advocate for a shift towards investing in quality second-hand items, fostering a sustainable and lived-in aesthetic. There is, however, a fine line between collecting and hoarding, and even when sourcing second-hand it's worth considering each purchase carefully and with consideration. Don't let enthusiasm for thrifting, or the lure of a bargain, mean you abandon your purpose-driven and values-inspired goals for your home.

    I hope this section will have left you convinced of the merits of buying second-hand, even for spaces such as your bathroom where we often feel like new is the only option. Let go of the old stigma linked to pre-owned items and embrace heritage and provenance alongside purpose, and create a home that feels fully reflective of you. Thoughtful sourcing means a thoughtful home.

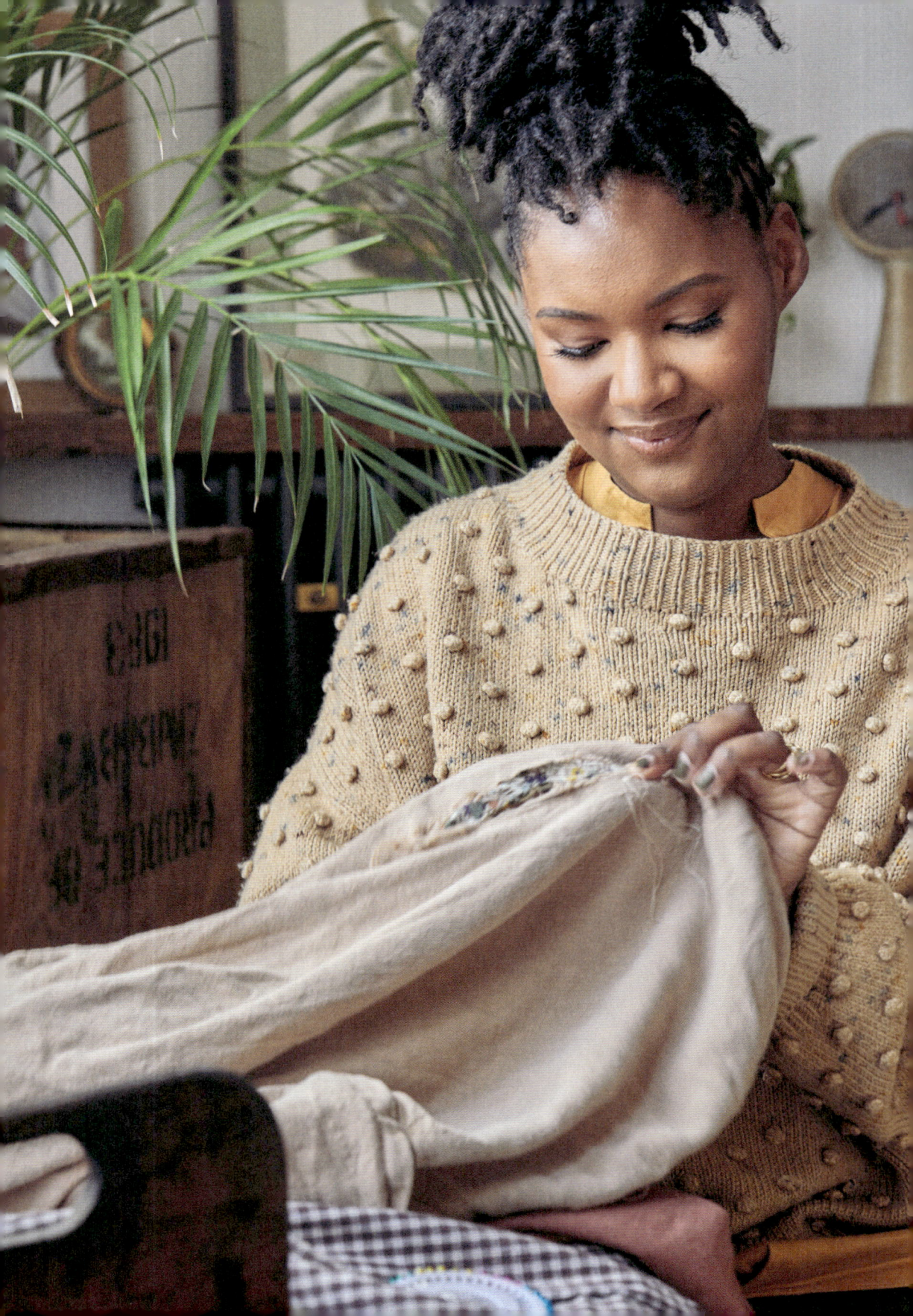

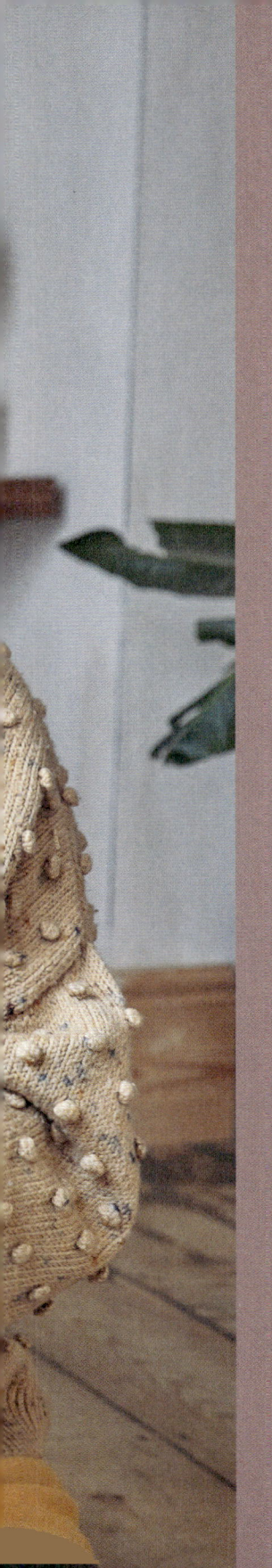

CREATE

I believe a home should nourish our creativity. It should be a safe place where our imaginations can flourish and passions can be ignited. In a world that isn't always easy to navigate, where the reality of adulting and its many demands can somehow be both over- and underwhelming, where we're more likely to scroll on our phones than to read a novel or doodle on some paper, giving our creativity space to be expressed allows us to forge our own little worlds.

It stands to reason that there is a direct link between our homes and our mental health. When we feel on top of things and have arranged our space in a way that flows with our life, we feel more inspired, at peace and creative. Juxtapose that with how our homes may look when our mental health is low. In my case, that's likely to be mountains of laundry, a neglected fridge, piles of unopened mail and soft furnishings that have all just kind of migrated to a sad pile in a corner of the room. Try as I might to be creative during those times, it's just not possible, such is the mirror effect between my mood and my surroundings.

So, this section of the book looks at ways in which our creativity at home can support our wellbeing, while remaining within the bounds of realistic planning and budgeting. How we prioritise our investment of time and money in our homes isn't always obvious, and I have certainly not always got this right. We'll be looking at how to approach jobs with a longevity mindset, by not scrimping on the important things, but doing them once and doing them well. If you are undertaking any renovation work or DIY, try not to let the process become a chore: celebrate every tiny bit of progress because it'll help spur you on.

When you have worked hard to create a home filled with meaningfully selected pieces that hold purpose or sentimental value for you, you'll want to take care of them. This doesn't mean being fastidiously tidy and keeping everything just so, but rather showing our homes lots of behind-the-scenes attention, ensuring that it's a pleasant and functional place to spend time. I include simple tasks for weekly and monthly maintenance that help bring order to my space.

To me, building a home also means finding ways to create communities that we are proud to live in. Serving our communities as best we can and rallying around local initiatives will make a huge difference to the place we call home, both in terms of bringing practical improvements to a neighbourhood, and also encouraging bonds with those around us. Progress starts with us and with normalising a generosity of spirit, kindness and the importance of connection so that it becomes ingrained in the next generation. It is the gift that keeps on giving. As with all aspects of life, you get back what you put in: love your home, love your community and they will love you back.

CHAPTER 11

CREATIVITY IN YOUR HOME

At their best, our homes shape us, fill us with inspiration, nurture our relationships and help bring our ambitions to life. On the flip side, when they're not supporting us as they might, our wellbeing and creativity can be hugely strained, leading to a sense of life being put on hold. When I've lived in homes like that, I felt as if my lungs didn't ever allow me to take a full breath. Can you relate? A poor home environment really takes its toll.

This chapter looks at two aspects of home that have probably had the biggest impact on not just my creativity, but my overall wellbeing. The first is light. The reality for many of us is that we live in spaces with compromised light, but I promise that you can transform even the gloomiest of rooms into cosy, fully functioning living spaces if you work with what you have. Dark doesn't have to mean dreary.

The second element that we have found fundamental for our family has been carving out a play space for our children where their creativity can run wild. The way in which a space is set up can have a huge impact on how children use it, depending on their age and stage. I am a big believer in adults cultivating their creative sides by incorporating play (and silliness) into their lives too, so I hope that even if you don't have children, you'll find some of the advice here useful. I've really loved creating child-led spaces wherever we've lived so our kids can really let loose – this chapter includes simple steps to set up a space that encourages creativity and unstructured play.

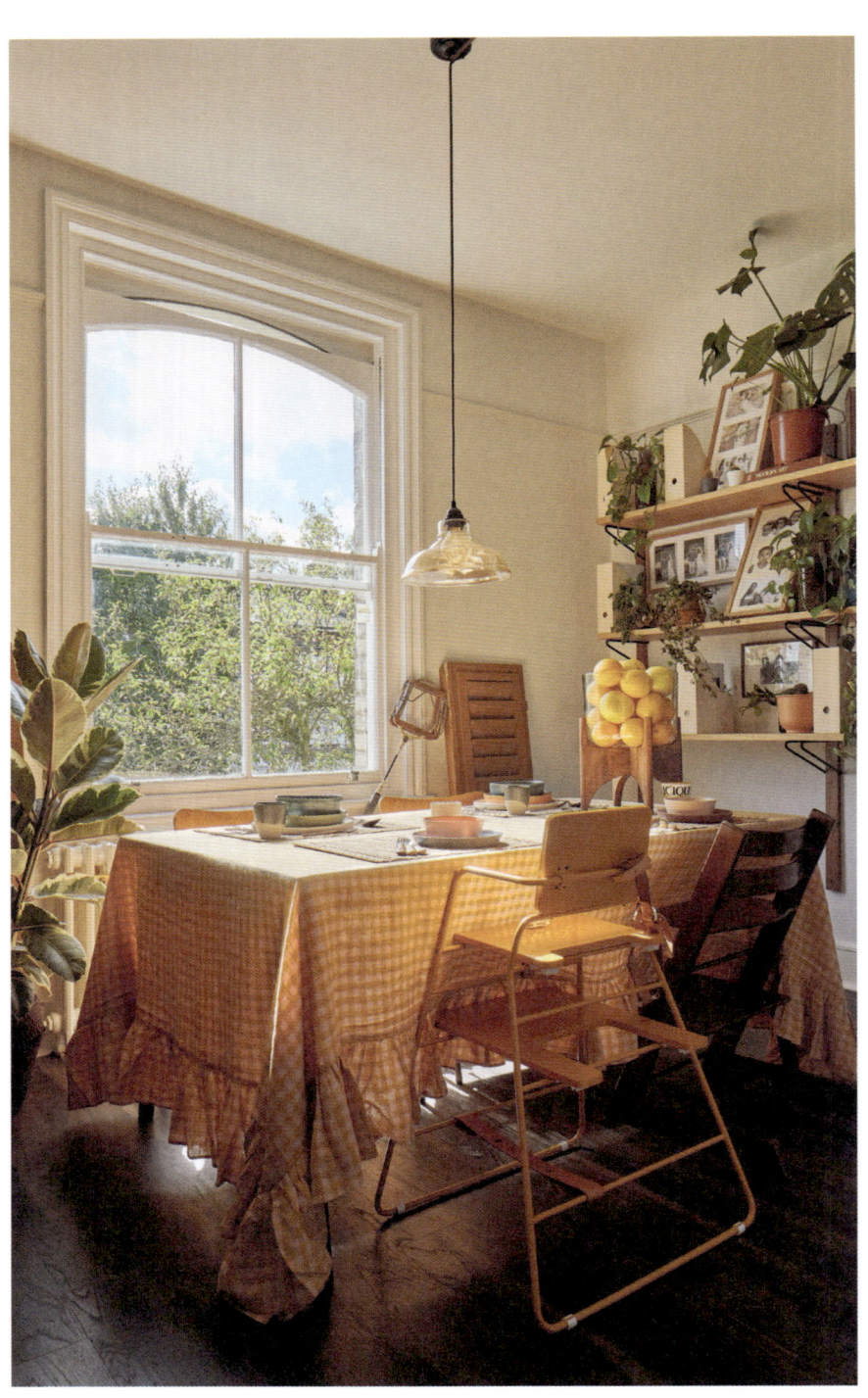

Let there be light

For decades, researchers have investigated the ways in which we are affected by light, often with a focus around the link between light and mood. Getting enough daylight has been linked to higher productivity at work, better sleep quality and a boost in overall wellbeing, which are not always easy to experience, particularly in the winter months of the northern hemisphere. Years ago, our one-bedroom flat in King's Cross was so starved of light that I truly believe it contributed to my depression as a first-time mum at the time. I wish I had known then that I could have implemented some simple changes to create a feeling of more light, as perhaps it could have helped. When we came to view the home we live in now, the fact that the living room was dual aspect with glazed doors leading into the playroom was such a selling point in our eyes. The light this created felt worth the other compromises that came with the house.

I am hugely influenced by light in my home and often find that I chase it throughout the day, moving about to try to work within its rays. In the darker months, I am meticulous about incorporating multiple artificial light options, always selecting warm bulbs and lamps of different heights (retractable wall lights can work well, particularly in smaller rooms). There's no doubt that light has a transformative effect on a room and therefore our moods, which in turn can absolutely affect our creativity and productivity to boot. In order to support our wellbeing then, we need to maximise our exposure to natural light where we can, but when that's limited (due to the season or our home's layout), we need to try to bring it into our homes another way.

In an ideal world, we'd all be living somewhere with high ceilings and large windows to let in vast amounts of light (preferably all day long!) but the reality is that we need to work with what we've got – basements, tiny windows, north-facing rooms. Rest assured there's plenty we can do to maximise light even if our living space is naturally dim. Here are some ideas:

Consider your set-up

Try to set your home up in a way that maximises any natural light available. For example, I've often seen living rooms where the TV is positioned in the sunniest part or the dining table in the gloomiest bit, which feels to me like a waste. Take note of the light in your rooms at different times of day and consider moving your furniture to ensure you make the most of it. For instance, placing a table beside a window can really help you to follow the light throughout the day if you decide to eat there, work from home or carry out other tasks. If your floorplan facilitates it, consider using the darkest rooms for bedrooms and the brightest for living space (this is why upside-down houses, with the living space on the upper floors, often work so well).

Clean

Cleaning your windows, inside and out, can make a dramatic difference to the feeling of a room, as well as light-flow. This is particularly true if you live in an urban area where traffic pollution can contribute to a murky build-up.

Reflect

Mirrors maximise light, bouncing it around rooms. In darker spaces, consider hanging mirrors beside and/or directly opposite a window.

Go green

Bring the illusion of the outside world inside by adding plants such as ferns, which naturally grow from the forest floor and so do well in dimmer spaces. Ferns like to be watered from the roots and kept moist, and also misted every few days, otherwise they have a tendency to go brown and crispy (if this happens, just cut away the affected leaves from the roots and move to a shadier spot, such as on a shelf away from direct sunlight).

And of course, going back to the previous advice on paint colours can also help a room feel lighter.

Practical lighting tips

Overhead lighting

If you ask me, there should be a law against having a naked bulb hanging from the ceiling, and yet, as I look up to my own living room pendant light, I'm indeed greeted by a naked bulb! For me, an overhead light is really harsh and contributes to a clinical or sterile feeling in a room, even if the light itself is warm. Fortunately, this is easily remedied. You can either go the whole hog and replace the light fitting (I'd recommend using an electrician for this, and if renting, you'll need the landlord's approval first), or use a clip-on shade. One easy-to-fit option is a paper shade; these are often very reasonably priced (and can often be found second-hand) and I love the origami feel they bring to a room. They can also usually be folded down concertina-style once removed from the ceiling, meaning you can easily take them with you if you move later on.

Battery-powered

In dark spaces, it can be hard to see inside a cupboard. Adding sensor lights to cupboards that switch on when you open the door have given me a (rather sad?) great amount of joy. Place them anywhere and everywhere, to illuminate linen cabinets, loft spaces or dark kitchen cupboards. You can also get magnetic ones or teeny ones that you can affix to door hinges. And of course, you can take them with you if you move.

Lamps

In Denmark, where there is very little sunlight over winter, homes embrace what author Meik Wiking calls 'pockets of light', using low lamps with warm bulbs in all corners of the rooms, which you can select depending on which 'zone' you're in (reading, working, watching TV, etc.), or enjoy them all on for a warm radiance. There's a simple pleasure to switching on three or four lamps in a room instead of the main overhead light. Lamplight offers a softer glow, creating a cosy atmosphere. Further to this, there is a biological upside to using lamps in the evening, as a darker space can help signal to our brains that bedtime is on the horizon, helping the sleep hormone melatonin to kick in. Many people deliberately keep all lighting to a minimum a couple of hours before bed (some eschew lamps altogether in favour of candles) to help ensure a good night's sleep.

Switch clever

Use an inexpensive smart plug to control all the lamps in a room from a single switch, meaning you don't have to turn on each one individually.

If you are doing major work in your home such as wiring, have overhead lights placed on a dimmer switch so you can control the levels of brightness, reducing it as evening turns to night.

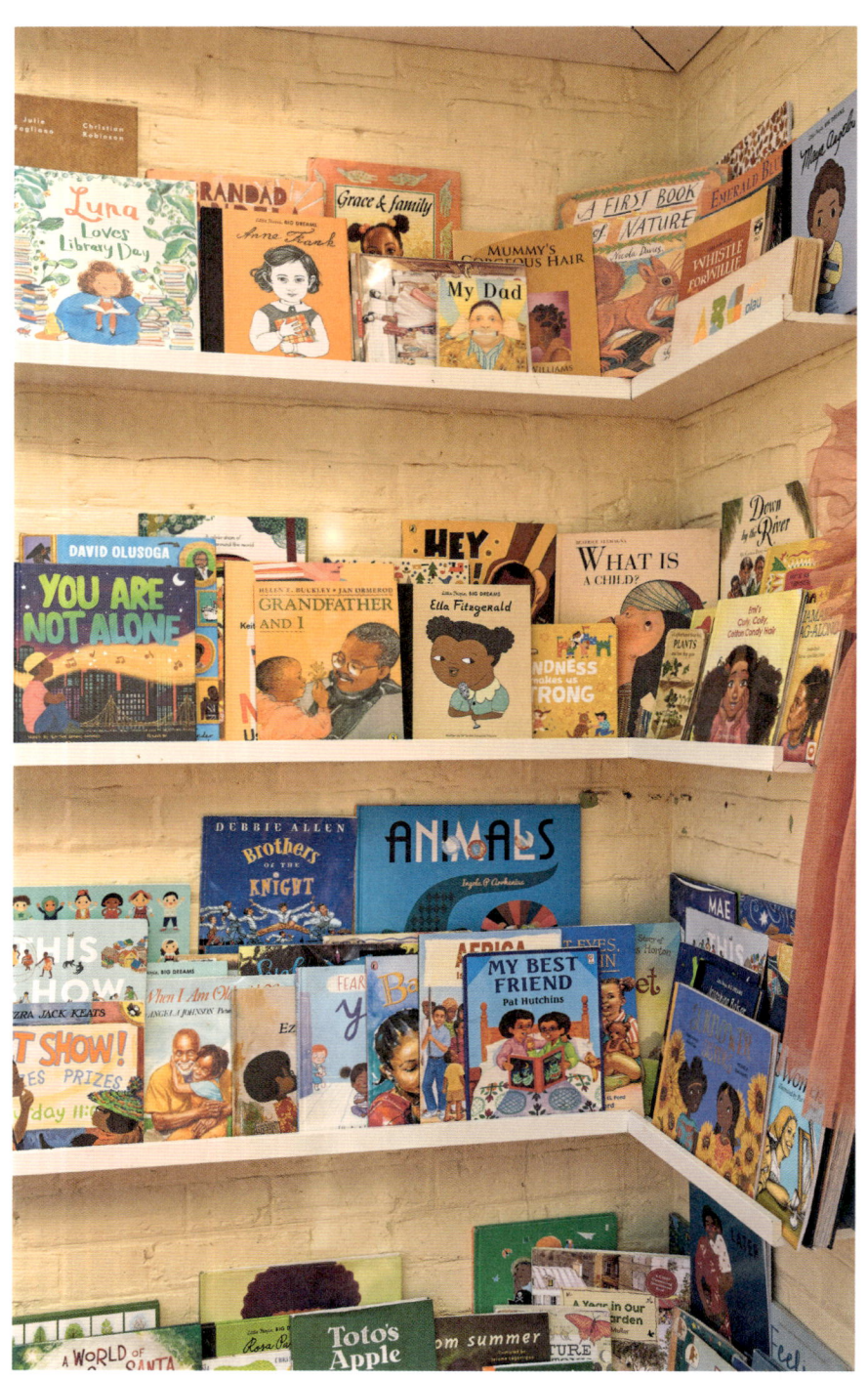

CREATE

Creating space for children

Putting together inspiring spaces for my children to unleash their imaginations has brought me so much joy. The first home we shared as a family of four was a one-bedroom flat; it was a challenge carving out sufficient space for an energetic toddler along with a baby, whose play needs were rather different. Even in the smallest of spaces though, whether that's in a bedroom or a sliver of a living space, you can create an area of wonder for children to explore.

Making your values count

After the birth of my oldest child, I remember looking for inspiration for how to organise our space at home to nurture learning through play. I was keen to invest in brands of toys that were ethically made, and crafted in a way that I knew would stand the test of time for any siblings down the line. The same brands I was drawn to though were often the ones that felt exclusionary to me as a Black mother, because of their total lack of representation of families that looked like ours. I used my small online presence to challenge that, adding photographs of our play space to communicate the reality of Black family life that is so often overlooked or misconstrued.

Starting out

A lot of parents can feel extra pressure to make a space 'perfect' for children, especially the first baby. Brands are well aware of how easy it is to play on this, targeting and guilt-tripping susceptible new parents into buying a whole load of stuff they don't actually need, much of it not even recommended by paediatric health professionals. The reality is that babies aren't fussed about the perfect shade you paint their walls or the perfect nursery wares on their shelves – really they just want to get on with the important business of being babies (i.e. stealing your sleep and growing at the rate of knots). When making spaces for our children I've found it helpful to keep in mind:

Cohesion

Think about your baby or child's space as being an extension of the rest of your home, rather than a separate entity. Cutesy nurseries in traditional pastel shades with white flatpack furniture do look very sweet but you don't have to go down that route if you don't want to. When setting up a space for our youngest, we ended up combining bold colours and rich textures with moody aged woods. It certainly doesn't scream nursery but to us it feels just right and meant that the items of furniture could be easily swapped out and used around our home.

Long-term

As ever, approach your children's space, whether that's a corner of your kitchen, a cupboard under the stairs or a little patch of garden, with longevity in mind. Where possible, I have tended to avoid sourcing items that I know will only be used for a short amount of time. For example, rather than a changing table, could a chest of drawers with a changing mat on top work? You may find you have lots of smaller bits in your home that can be repurposed as baby apparatus (for example, cotton tote bags are handy for storing nappies, wipes and cream, baskets can house bibs and muslins).

Viewing from a child's height

So often we place wall prints or shelves at adult height, meaning kids don't really see what's on display. Consider hanging bookshelves, picture ledges or corkboards low down, or even use some string tied up like a washing line so that children can proudly display their works of art and 'redecorate' whenever they like.

Let them join you in creating their space

I'm not a fan of eradicating signs of my children's existence in our home and there's evidence of them in every room, not just the playroom and their bedrooms. As they get older, I feel it's important to let them join in on how they

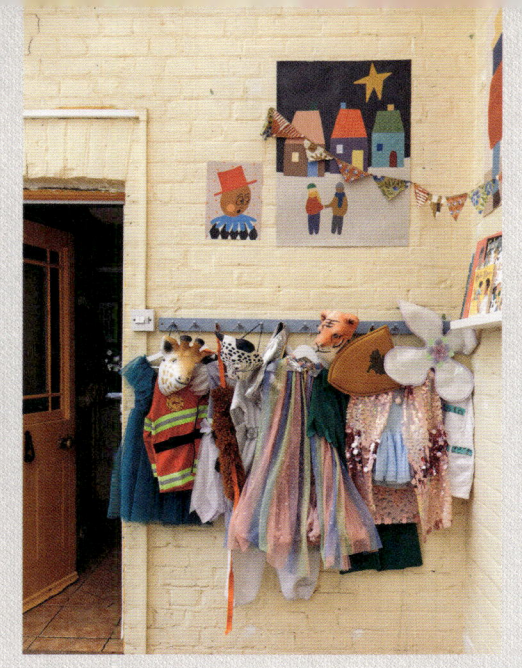
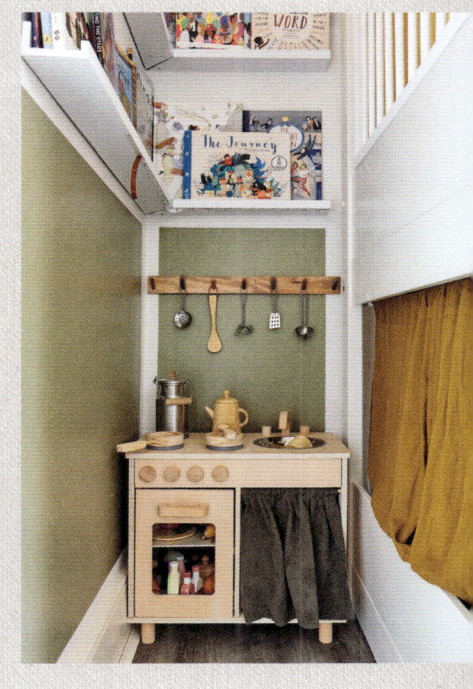
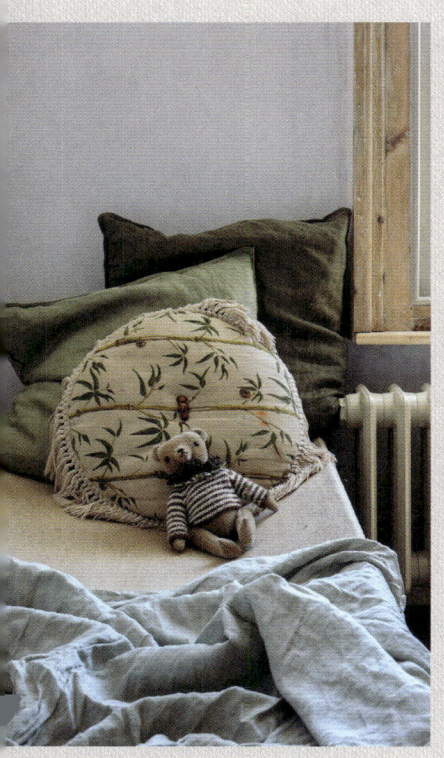
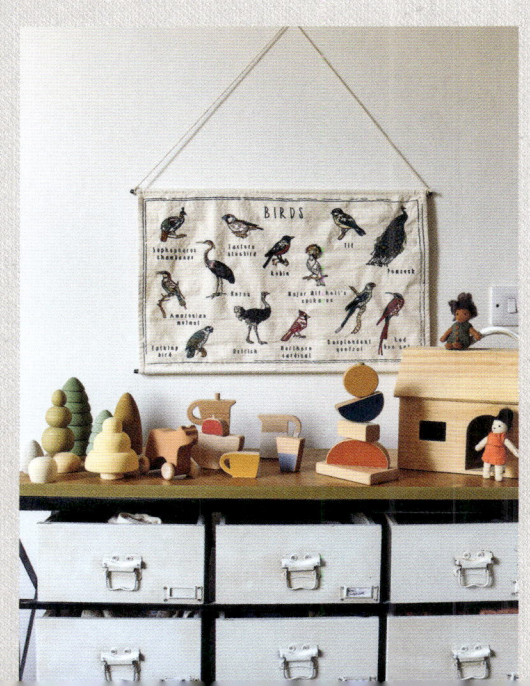

decorate their spaces, giving them a sense of ownership and the feeling that our home represents each member of our family. Just like our work in the garden, planting fruit and veg and play areas for them, we want to build their skills and confidence by getting them stuck into the process of creating spaces, not just the 'ta-da' moment of the end result.

Facilitating play

My two older children attended a Montessori nursery and when I first saw their set-up, I recognised that I had instinctively been trying to arrange our space at home in a similar way, without necessarily realising it was a thing. There was a lot about the Montessori approach that appealed to me – the soothing neutral shades of the spaces, and often the toys too, the open storage ideas with the focus of everything having a place – perhaps my neurodiverse mind found it calming too.

The way we set up play spaces for children will not only benefit them, but as they grow older their setting will encourage more independent play (often an age-related milestone), helping them become engrossed while giving caregivers a bit of a reprieve in the process (amen to that). Playing independently can be such a gift as it encourages creativity in a child and it's why I have no problem hearing my children complain, 'I'm bored!'. Great, I think, boredom is an opportunity for creativity! There's something beautiful about observing children in their flow state – that level of focus when they are totally absorbed in play, oblivious to the outside world – something for adults to aspire to!

Flow

I steer clear of fixed furniture in the children's spaces and encourage them to move things about to suit their play needs on any particular day or hour. Rainy days often see us pushing all our furniture against the walls and setting up little play stations in our living room.

Surface

Ensure there's a surface they can use for play, at a height that works for them, either standing and/or sitting on the floor. This can be multi-purpose – an area for building with blocks or flicking through books, a prop during imaginative play or a surface for arts and crafts (just slip some old newspaper underneath). The storage we use in our home for toys also doubles as a table for play.

Accessibility

Make sure children can access plenty of toys themselves: this will make everyone's life easier as they can choose what they play with and then put it away once they're finished. This won't always be possible in smaller spaces where you're relying on storage higher up, so toy rotation (see below) can help with that. Some families keep individual activities on trays for kids to help themselves to, but my storage (and organisational!) capacity has not managed this yet.

A place for everything

As I've mentioned before, having a place for everything is helpful for children and for you. Maybe that's a box for building blocks, another for doll's house pieces, yet another for stuffed animals. There can be a lot of anxiety for children when they're told to be 'tidy' or not make a mess, but there isn't actually a place for them to put their things. It can help to create a calmer home environment by being clear with everyone about what goes where.

Toy and book rotation

If you can, divide toys up and swap them out at a pace of your preference (every few weeks works well for a lot of families). This prevents kids from becoming overwhelmed by choice and allows them to concentrate on fewer toys in a more focused way. When you make the swap, they also feel excited to see toys, books and games that they haven't played with for a while rotated back in. Plus, I find it helps me make informed choices for my one-in, one-out rule as we are only letting go of things that are less loved.

Let them make a mess

Provided my children are safe and respectful of the space so that nothing will get irreversibly damaged, all bets are off when it comes to play in our home. I want my kids to enjoy becoming immersed in play without their dad and I nitpicking about toys being out of place. As long as they help tidy up at the end of the day, all's well in my book.

Get organised, stay organised

Of course, the trend for micro-organising has extended to children's spaces and though I don't want to over-manage my kids or obsess over tidiness, I am glad of the practical tips I've picked up from these organising pros.

The way that we've always organised our kids' spaces is to have the majority of pieces stored on display or in handy transparent drawers grouped by type (we use IKEA Trofast drawers, which I've often seen being passed on in neighbourhood resale groups). We like the kids to enjoy a sense of pride in their home so they are very much in control of tidying their personal spaces (with the exception of adult jobs like vacuum cleaning, mopping and changing the bedsheets).

Wall storage

As ever, walls are your friends for storage. Wall-mounted baskets can be brilliant for smaller toys like dolls, stuffed animals or play kitchen sets. Outlines can be a simple reminder for where something goes, like a toy buggy. Wall-mounted rails or hooks are great for fancy dress outfits, and as mentioned, we love a front-facing library using picture ledges.

Group toys together

Store like with like, and for pre-literate children, label your storage receptacles with an illustration or photo of what should be inside. Failing this, clear or translucent storage is great.

Slim bookshelves

When space is tight, these can make use of dead space such as behind a door. In fact, we removed the door to our girls' room in our previous home to make better use of the wall behind it.

Make it fun

You might find that sticking on a tidy-up song helps foster a bit of energy for what is, let's face it, not a very exciting proposition to a child. Similarly, I have found words of encouragement like, 'Wow, look how many dolls you've thrown into the crate already!' much more incentivising than, 'It still looks like a bomb has gone off!'

Managing children's toys

With four children, I have had to become quite strict in trying to curb the flow of toys into our home, simply because having too many can prove more overwhelming than they are inspiring for kids. I've become more discerning over the years too and found that open-ended toys (i.e. toys that can be used in a variety of ways to support creative play) are the ones my kids use most often. If you have children, you're likely to already have many that fall under the term, such as LEGO, building blocks, play kitchen sets, magnetic tiles, teddies, the list goes on. Local charity shops and online sites are an absolute treasure trove for second-hand kids' items; I always look at pre-owned options first for toys, books, puzzles and games.

Gifting

Children can accumulate A LOT of stuff, and this can be wonderful but overwhelming too, both for us and for our homes, particularly if we don't have ample storage. I'm often asked how I deal with gifting, commonly by parents who don't want to seem ungrateful offend a well-meaning friend or relative. The things our children are gifted may not always be something we'd choose ourselves and said items may not always align with the values of your home.

I believe we have a right to establish boundaries around gifting and we need not feel guilty about having respectful conversations with loved ones, preferably early on in our child's life (though it's never too late!). These conversations don't have to be awkward or recriminatory and the recipient may even feel glad to have been given ideas for future gifting. Generally, we only ever ask for books to keep the price point accessible for all.

If I am choosing a gift for someone else's child, I will often check in with the parents first to see if they have any suggestions, otherwise I have found that the ideas below tend to go down well. I make an effort to source the best single item I can for the amount I'm spending, so if I have £10 to spend, I will buy one great item, such as a book, rather than several lesser-quality ones.

Toy sets

These can work so well as gifting opportunities, where items can be added to for birthdays or other celebrations. I find that sets like play kitchen equipment or good-quality animals such as those made by Schleich (which, in our home, seem to defy age boundaries as my children have played with them as babies, toddlers, pre-schoolers and upwards) are always well used.

A book

Or a book voucher so they can choose their own from a local store.

An experience

A special one-on-one trip to a café for a hot chocolate can make a child feel really special.

While I love birthdays and celebrations, I believe we should take the pressure off gifting, both as the giver and the receiver (or parent of the receiver).

> **Many parents choose to set further boundaries around gifting such as:**
>
> - Having gift-free parties (discuss this with your child in advance so there are no surprises on the big day). This can be made easier if there is consensus, for example, if your child's class at school all opt into this policy so that no one feels left out.
> - Offering a charitable donation should they wish to.
> - Asking that any gifts are second-hand or come from a charity shop. For my three-year-old's party we mainly had older kids attend and requested they all bring a book that they had now outgrown.
> - Asking if guests would like to contribute a small amount of money towards one larger gift, which the child can choose. We only tend to do this with immediate family and godparents. In some communities, the default is £5 placed inside a birthday card – job done.

Ultimately, I think we would all do well to embrace the notion that the joy of celebrations need not be overshadowed by the complexities of gifting. By fostering open conversations and setting thoughtful boundaries, we can make these occasions meaningful and memorable for all involved.

CREATE

It's easy to feel like creativity is something that is reserved for artists or other creators, rather than for everyone. We're encouraged by big brands to believe that we have to buy creativity from professionals in the form of art or décor for our homes. But creativity belongs to each of us, and it's my hope that this section of the book will give you confidence to tap into what creativity, and a creative home, look like for you.

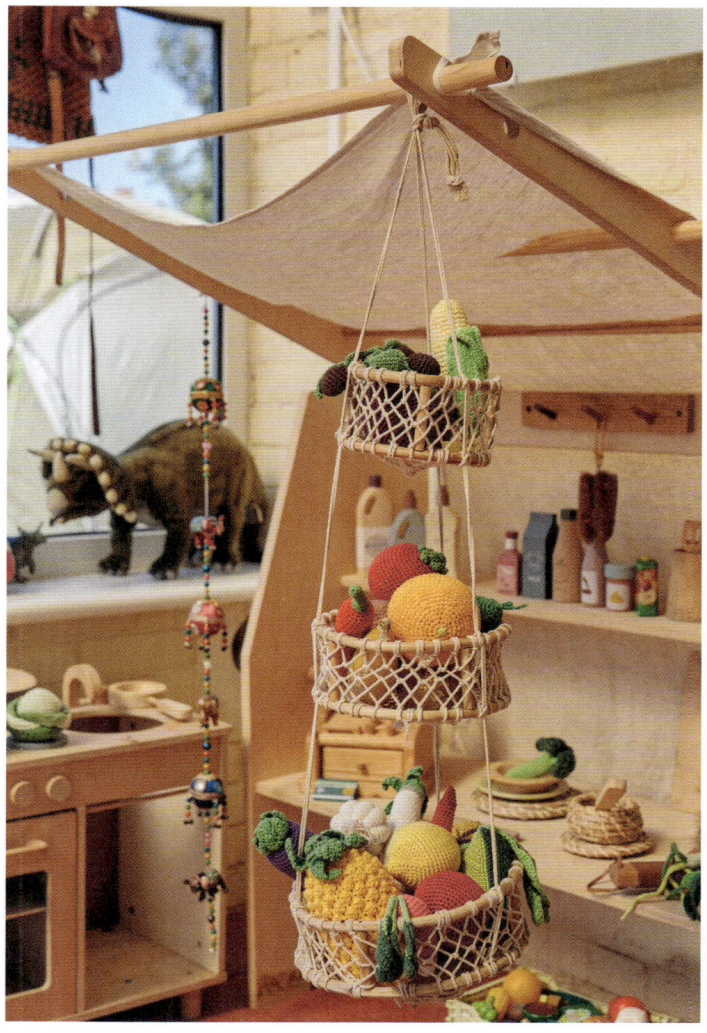

CHAPTER 12

WHERE TO START, WHERE TO SPEND

Working out how to spend your time and hard-earned pennies on your home can be a minefield, especially as there's so much conflicting information out there about what and where to invest and where to make savings. Only you can discern your priorities, determining what you can live with and what you can't live without.

I once heard a budgeting expert say that the secret to a good budget is to spend lavishly on your priorities while being ruthlessly cheap with the things that don't matter to you. So, for instance, I really care about finishes such as light switches and I'm happy to spend on those, but I personally don't think you always need to buy expensive paints so I colour-match when budgets are tight. I'm not going to tell you exactly how to part with your cash, but instead I'll give you a whistle-stop lowdown on how I have approached projects and allotted budgets in our homes. You won't necessarily agree with all these decisions and that's OK!

In our London maisonette, we tackled rooms in a mixture of ways. Our living room and two bedrooms were totally transformed with a lick of paint, cosy rugs and a change of wardrobe handles – these low-cost upgrades went such a long way to making the flat feel like it was ours. On the other hand, our kitchen and bathroom required a complete overhaul, so we prioritised our budget there. I've mentioned previously that investing in doing up a rental property can divide opinion – I still stand by our efforts (!) but I fully appreciate that it's not a road everyone will want to take. You'll know from reading the Embrace section that there's plenty you can do to improve your home without knocking walls down.

CREATE

Being intentional in your planning and décor allows you to focus on your actual needs rather than on what the trendsetters are doing or the magazines are showing. To my mind there isn't a single trend deserving of being followed over our family's actual requirements of a space.

I give a special shoutout to the entryway in this chapter, a space I feel is often undervalued and overlooked, yet it sets the tone for your entire home. The suggestions I cover aren't exhaustive but hopefully they will offer up a bit of inspiration, and also show some surprisingly cheaper options that still provide great benefits.

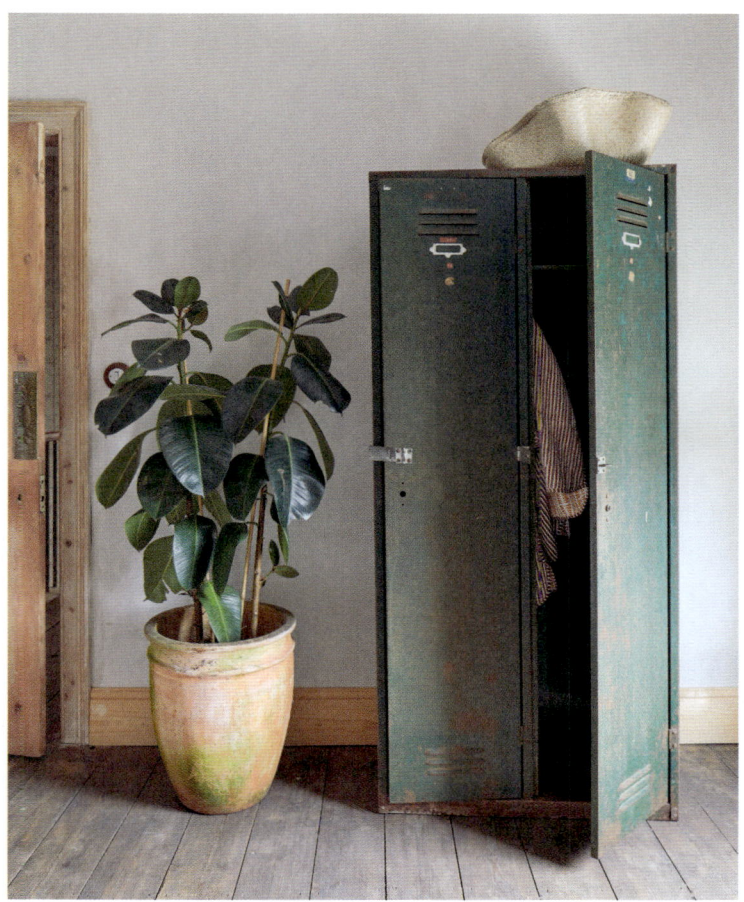

Budgeting

You're unlikely to see many pictures on Pinterest or Instagram of people popping champagne while filling in a costing spreadsheet, but anyone who's ever done up the space they live in will know you need one. A spreadsheet is not aspirational, but it is essential to work out what you have to spend – whether £20 or £200,000. Be honest with yourself and don't factor in funds that haven't yet been secured. Your budget needs to be more than a back-of-the-envelope guesswork affair, but rather itemised in detail, and, if you are outsourcing labour and buying materials, bear in mind that costs will fluctuate, so it is essential to build in a contingency of 15–20%. Brexit, the Covid pandemic and various global affairs have all had an impact on costs in recent years, with prices rising particularly for materials like timber and steel. If you ask me, this is all the more reason to try to repurpose or find second-hand where you can. This book focuses mainly on cosmetic improvements we can make to our spaces but of course there are some revamps which require much more involved work. Tasks like demolition, wiring/rewiring or plumbing are major and it's essential to get these right, so always assign funds in your budget for expert tradespeople. Invest in getting the basics in place, then let the fun begin later with the more decorative elements. For bigger jobs such as replacing windows, adding insulation or installing solar panels, check to see if your local council offers any grants or bursaries for making your home greener.

In Chapter 6, I gave some advice for how to stay focused on our needs (ahead of our wants), which is essential for adhering to a budget. But really, the most ethical thing that I can do when designing a room, and later a whole home, is to be clear on what I want and need from the space before I get started. Ensuring that I don't veer too far away from our priorities and needs is really useful for not getting sucked into fads and trends, which is the easiest way to overspend. Here it helps to go back to your list of overall priorities for your home, as well as considering individual priorities for each space.

We are constantly being sold to, often without realising it, so unless you have a limitless budget, making a plan, determining your planned expenditure and not getting distracted by shiny new things is key. Keep in mind anything you might consider giving up, to enable you to dedicate funds to your renovation. For example, you might be happy to forgo holidays for a while in favour of saving the money for your project and this might be well worth the sacrifice. Or ordering takeaways might be something you feel you could live without for a while (although they may be your best friend during a kitchen renovation). On the other hand, consider the qualitative cost of more substantial sacrifices, such as taking on extra work just so you can have a bigger or fancier home, at the expense of time spent with family and friends. There's a tipping point for effort versus loss, and this is something I've often had to remind myself when my dreams temporarily blinded me to my genuine priorities.

Here's a sample budget tracker that I've used for projects in our home, although it's easy enough to customise your own in Excel (which can add up all the numbers for you).

Renovation Tracker

Total Budget	
Actual Costs	
Remaining	

Budget vs. Actual Spend	Budget	Quote 1	Quote 2	Quote 3	Actual Spend
Wallpaper corridor					
Sand all floors					
Replace Windows					

The joy of planning

I love the planning stage of any project – so many ideas loosely or fully formed, dreaming big. Before starting any project, and particularly if you are making a significant change to your home, I suggest you make a list of what you will gain from this change and anything you might lose. For example, when J wanted to expand his vegetable growing space in our garden, we knew we'd have to lose a bit of our lawn and some of the children's play space, but we managed to make it work.

Consider which jobs, if any, you'll outsource and those you might tackle yourself. In our home, J and I have both hired professionals and got stuck in ourselves at times, learning on the job. Do your research and then just give it a go. I have found it hugely empowering watching DIY-savvy women online and it's made me more confident about approaching small-scale jobs that I would have previously set aside for my husband. We need to recognise that all the media we've consumed in the last few decades has propped up harmful gender stereotypes about who does what, and doing up your home is a great way to begin unpicking and unlearning some of those assumptions.

Have I always nailed the planning stage? Absolutely not. When we moved into our current home the plan was to focus on the bedrooms and living areas first before tackling the bathrooms and kitchen. However, two days before Christmas, we deviated from the plan. The kitchen only had a microwave and we decided to have our free-standing range installed so we could cook Christmas dinner. It felt like it wouldn't be a proper family Christmas if we weren't able to cook, and that clouded my judgement. In a rush, we paid over £1,000 for some builders to rip out existing fitted cabinets in the kitchen and hack away at the brick fireplace behind it, in order to fit the stove in on a tight deadline. What we were left with was a badly damaged exposed brick wall that then needed rebuilding entirely. For the same price we could have created a lovely, liveable space.

With hindsight, we should have kept the oven in storage until we were ready to redesign the whole kitchen. I knew we were at least two years off that, so I regret rushing the decision instead of finding a short-term solution for Christmas. For about twelve months after, we had to be really careful every time we cooked to ensure we didn't have brick dust falling in our food – how's that for added flavour! I have admonished myself a lot over this decision because I pushed for it to happen despite it going against what I knew deep down was the right course of action. We tried to turn this decision into a lesson, but it still didn't feel good until we managed to rectify it.

Phased work

If you are tackling a project, big or small, over the course of many months or even years, you may need to approach it in phases. Phased improvements can allow you to take changes at your own pace, enabling you to save up over time and often mean you can stay in your home while you or any tradespeople are working. Phasing your work will also allow you to focus on one task or one room at a time, rather than juggling multiple spaces or reaching decision fatigue. In a smaller project, this might mean painting the walls first, followed by the woodwork later when time allows. Work at a pace that feels right for you (though be warned – I've found that smaller jobs, if left too long, tend to never get finished as momentum wanes!).

For larger home improvements, phased work may mean prioritising bigger essential jobs, such as treating damp (a very boring way to spend, but an important one), with more cosmetic work happening further down the line. It may also require grouping work of a similar nature together, which can sometimes be more economical, particularly if you are using external tradespeople such as electricians or plumbers (whose quotes may be reduced slightly if tackling one bigger job rather than coming back over time to do several smaller ones). Despite the magical before and afters you see on social media, the reality is that a lot of home improvers work in this more staggered way. It takes patience though, because this approach can mean it feels like your home is never finished – which can be tough if you're naturally impatient like me!

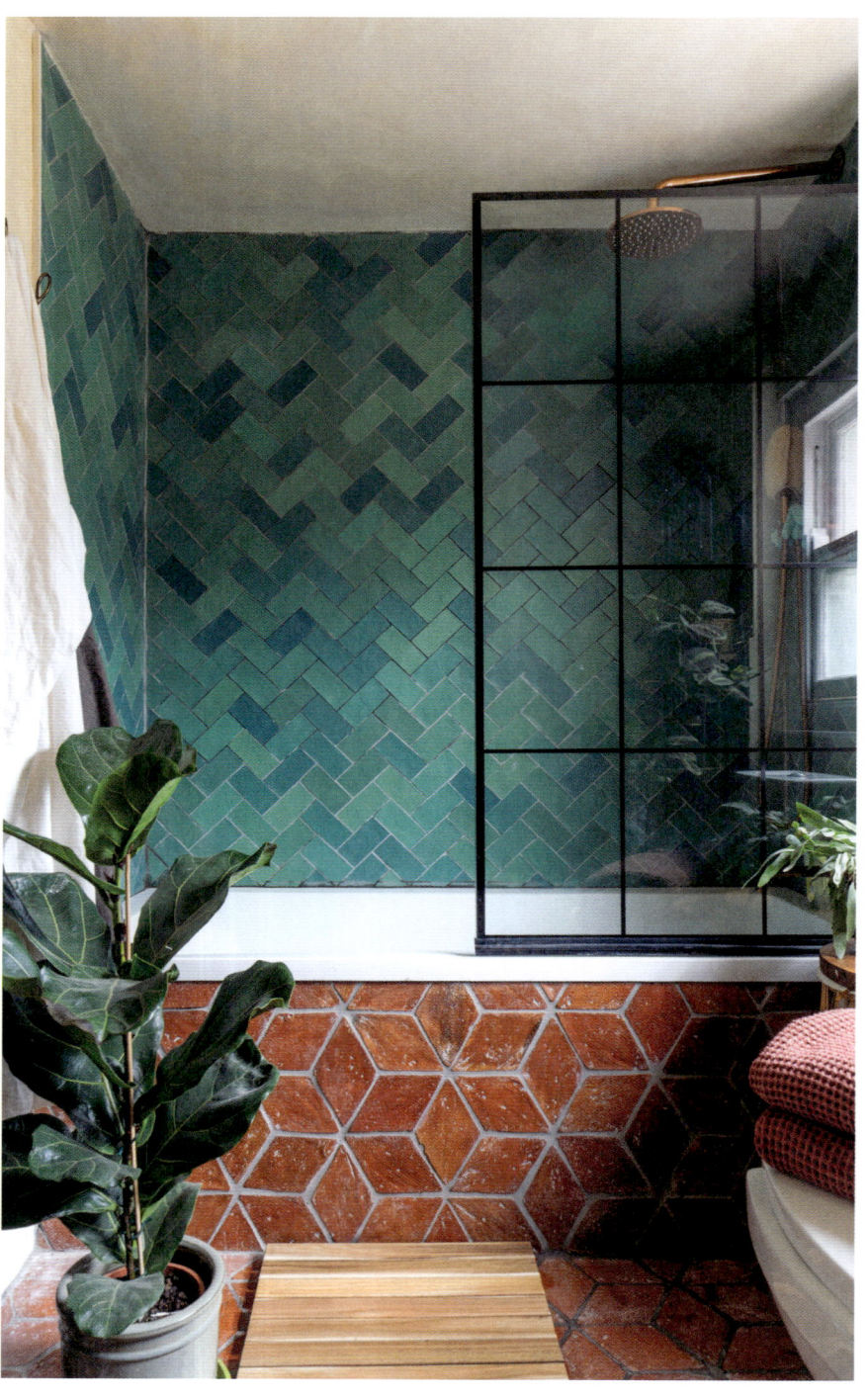

Working alongside tradespeople

If you are hiring tradespeople, a good working relationship is key. Be sure to get at least three quotes for any work you're having done, ensuring they break their costs down into minute detail, including who will be covering the cost of materials, so you can accurately compare quotes. Remember that tax usually needs to be added onto these quotes – 20% at the time of writing – so factor this into your costs. Be sure to get references from previous clients, and if you can, see if you can visit a home where the tradespeople have carried out jobs. Always draw up a contract that sets out expectations of the work agreed, the payment terms and the agreed timeline. For substantial projects, clients usually hold back 5–10% of the overall fee until several months after the work is complete, to ensure the quality is top notch, so establish this in advance.

If you are in a couple, decide between you which one person will be the point of contact between the tradespeople and yourselves, and make that clear to them too. In our home, that's me. The detail of design is a lot more important to me than my husband and so that's what works for us. Be sure to respectfully set clear boundaries with tradespeople, for example, I work from home and look after my two youngest children, meaning I can't be on call to make cups of tea throughout the day. What I can do, though, is give them a tour of the kitchen, set up a tea station and invite them to help themselves to as much tea, coffee and biscuits as they please.

I've often found that the tradespeople I've worked with are wary of new ideas, particularly when they go against the grain! Listen to their feedback but stand firm in your vision and work together on a solution. I remember when we were having our bathroom in London installed, there were lots of design concepts that made the builders anxious. One key aspect of my design was that the tiling from the floor ran up the side of the bathtub as this was my budget alternative to having the built-in stone bath of my dreams. Our installers thought it was a terrible idea! It ended up being a triumph and I've loved seeing photos of it replicated over the years since in many homes. Our tiler was also very apprehensive about the herringbone tiling placement that we'd selected for the walls. Laying tiles in a herringbone pattern requires a lot more skill than your traditional subway tiling and I recall he kept trying to encourage me to change the placement. But once it was complete he was beaming and told me it was the one job he was most proud of!

Intentional design and durability

When buying clothing, I invest the most money in items that I'll be getting the most wear out of, and it's exactly the same when it comes to objects in my home. From a shower head to a bread knife, if it's a part of my home that I interact with every day (or multiple times a day), I want it to be both highly functional and a pleasure to use. In my opinion, these everyday objects are the things to spend on. Sometimes it might cost a bit more to find a version of an item that is more ergonomic, but these little things ease niggling daily frustrations, so I think they're worth the cost.

Also remember the transitional spaces in your home, such as corridors or hallways – little overlaps that I like to think of as 'seams'. These small spaces quietly do the heavy lifting without much credit, meaning they have to be more hardwearing and functional than any other space in your home, so they deserve proper consideration. With that in mind, I see the patterned wallpaper in our hallways over the years as a real investment. Although it might feel like paint is easier to touch up, I have found a patterned wallpaper will withstand little sticky fingers, over-zealous crayoning and run-ins with a barrage of vintage furniture being scraped against it over the years.

In the Source section, we looked at seeking out pre-used fittings, fixtures and homewares. Re-using is always my first port of call but if I conclude I'm not going to be able to source an item second-hand, I start considering its shelf-life before I evaluate what I'm willing to spend. My thinking always begins with longevity. For example, if it's a large piece like a sofa I'll be aiming to get a minimum of a decade's use out of it before passing it on, so my research planning will initially revolve around one question: Does the sofa I have my eye on come from a trusted manufacturer? The following questions are asked after I've selected a supplier that I'm morally comfortable with, whittling down a potential of 500 options to maybe 10 or so.

- Is it a quality construction?
- Is it easy to care for the fibre myself or does it need specialist treatment?

- If it's a woven textile, are the covers removable and washable?
- If leather, is it a high-quality item that will only look better with age?
- Is any part of the item covered under a warranty?

I'll then move on to aesthetic questions such as, have I chosen a colourway that will work if I move the item to a different part of my home? Can it be reupholstered at a later date? You can never ask too many questions!

Thinking in detail about these points empowers us to be much more intentional in our approach and to save time and money in the long run. If a piece fulfils every criterion I have (which is rare) then it is worth the extra investment over a cheaper alternative that doesn't tick most of my boxes.

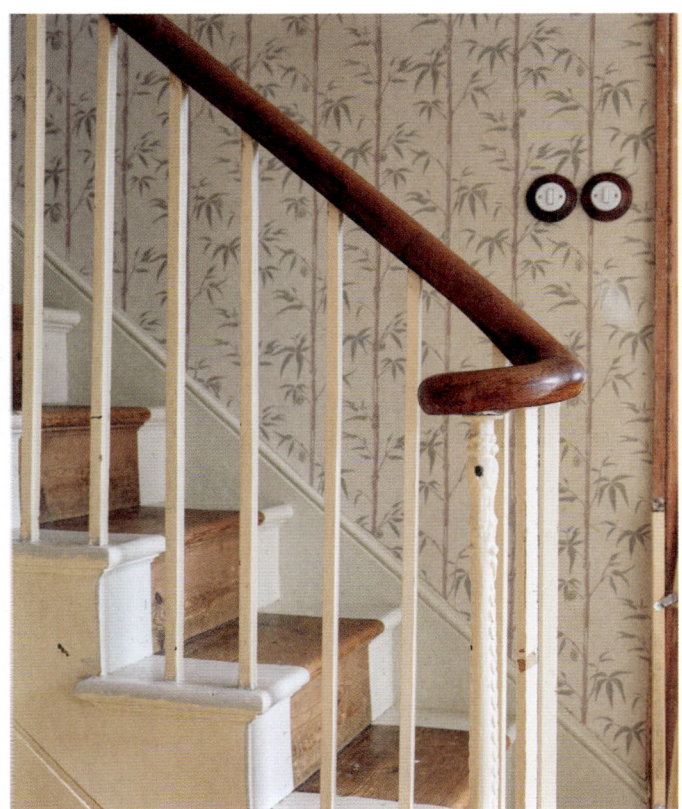

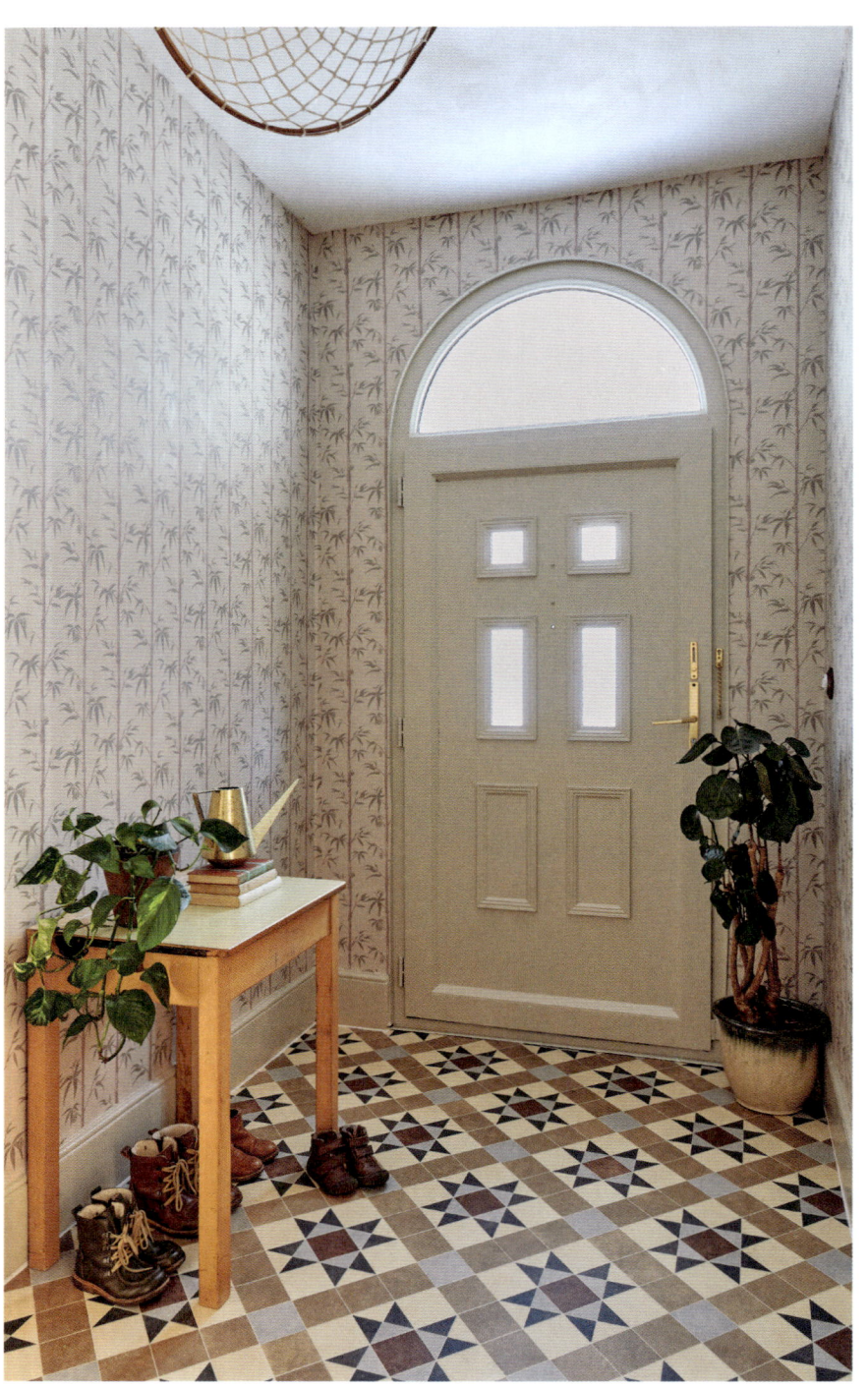

CREATE

It starts with the entryway

Thresholds are often depicted in mythology as the passage from one world to the next, sometimes with helpful or hindering deities presiding as gatekeepers. Some cultures keep shrines in the entryway and charms to bless all who step through the door (or to keep out the untrustworthy). Other faiths keep little bowls of holy water by the front door, a sprinkling to offer spiritual protection.

This section is my call to arms to show some love for our humble thresholds, the passage from outside to inside, from disarray without to sanctuary within. Whether you have a communal hallway, or your front door opens straight into your home, the instant transition from outside to inner sanctum is something to celebrate. Though you may not spend long periods of time in an entryway, you are, of course, likely to pass through it frequently, particularly if you are coming and going a lot.

When we moved to our house by the coast, absolutely everything needed doing. We had a modest pot of money set aside to tackle the first phase of the house, and we had to painstakingly work out what to prioritise and what could wait. Our wish list was long, but I was adamant about not waiting when it came to the hallway, even though it meant putting our kitchen, bathroom and bedrooms on hold. I knew I just didn't want to open my front door several times a day only to want to immediately head back outside again! If I stepped into a space multiple times a day that was enlivening and reflective of our style, I knew it would inspire us to be creative in other parts of our lives. Something had to be done. We started with wallpaper.

When we were looking to move out of London, we very nearly relocated to Scotland! I confess, in no small part because of some fabulous hallways we saw in our online viewings, the kinds with staircases and bannisters and all the fancy extras we didn't have in our flat. I fell in love with one particular hallway featuring a washed-out bamboo print wallpaper alongside a stunning grand stairwell with ornate iron balustrades. I still have the photographs on my phone, years later! That hallway of dreams led me to collaborate with iconic design duo Poodle and Blonde to create a bamboo wallpaper for our current hallway. The colourway was named 'Harvey Vale' after my maternal grandad's village in Carriacou, and I can't help but smile every time I catch a glimpse of it.

For anyone questioning my sanity around decorating our hallway before the bathroom and kitchen, you do have a point. Hallways tend to be decorated last so that building materials and furniture don't need to be lugged in and out of the house, damaging walls and floors. And our hallway very nearly was left to the end. After finishing phase one of the renovation (plumbing, wiring and re-plastering) and a fall out with the initial builders, our corridor was left in a worse state than when we had moved in. We lived with it for eight months before we could seriously feel how much the shabby hallway was detracting from the great strides we had made on the rest of our home. It was time for a quick interim fix. That meant a splash of paint on our uPVC door, wallpaper up and temporary lino down. We will certainly need to be extra careful with all our subsequent building work, taking care to put down protective floor and wall coverings. But I am so glad we made this mini investment to this space early on. I know I would have found it really demoralising to keep moving through a depressing entryway each day.

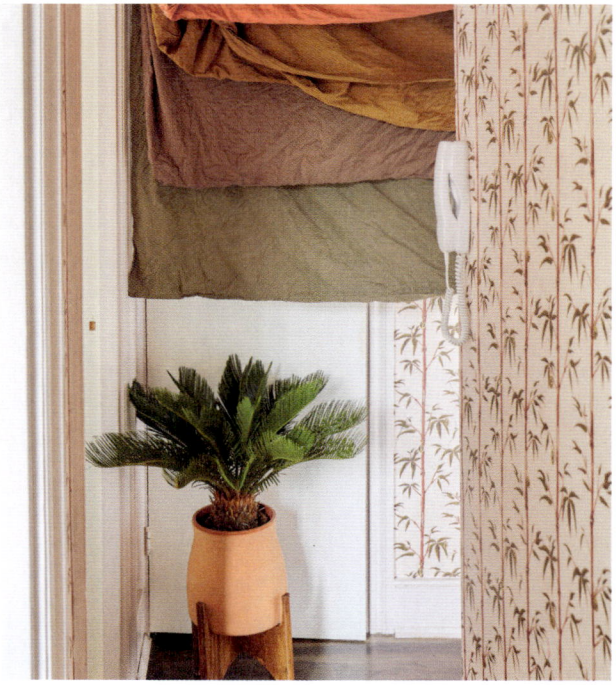

Create an entrance you'll love returning to

Think of your threshold as an energetic space, pivotal to the overall flow of your home. Treat it as importantly as any other room (if not more so). Consider its 'cost-per-use' as a factor when you're assigning the time and budget you wish to dedicate to it.

- Consider any bottlenecks and how to keep the entryway smooth and unobstructed. Have regular clear-outs to remove any out-of-season coats, shoes and the like.

- Even very narrow corridors can usually accommodate vertical storage. Shallow shoe storage (wall-mounted, built-in or free-standing), coat hooks (including low ones if children live there), a peg board that can accommodate baskets for your most reached-for items (like keys, a comb or your wallet) or trays for in- and outgoing post. A mirror is handy too.

- Panelling can work well to protect hallway walls, especially if you are bringing in anything on wheels on a daily basis or have children or pets. Typically, MDF sheets are used and can be placed horizontally or vertically, or, if you can find antique wall panelling at a price you can afford, you have struck gold.

- If your space allows, consider adding a curtain about a metre or so away from the front door. You can pull it across to hide coats and shoes from view, and in colder months it will also offer insulation from draughts.

- Think about cohesive design for any rooms leading off the hallway – consider each space as an extension of the next rather than an entirely individual space to decorate. This doesn't mean you can't go for contrasting décor, just be mindful that you will be viewing every room first from the hallway.

- Ambient lighting in the entryway is just as important as it is for other rooms. If possible, avoid overhead lighting that is too bright and opt for dimmer switches and/or lamps if you have the space (battery-powered lamps work well in places where there are no sockets).

CHAPTER 13

CARE AND MAINTENANCE

If you're like me, you'll find there's something restorative about a well-maintained home, whether that's yours or someone else's. A space that is considered and cared-for feels loved, and that seems to transfer to those within it. Looking after what you have can save money and time in the long run, and make your home a lovely place to spend time in. I like to view my home as an extension of myself, prioritising its upkeep just as I prioritise self-care.

I believe we owe it to ourselves to create spaces that are as easy as possible to live in, without making unrealistic demands of ourselves or others in the process. And sometimes the solutions to maintaining order in our homes are easier than we think. Recently, I was increasingly exasperated by my young children leaving their dirty laundry in piles on their bedroom floor each evening. It was beginning to become a point of stress for me, until I considered the impracticality of expecting them (aged 2, 4 and 6) to head downstairs, open the (usually locked) utility cupboard, battle with the hoover, mop bucket and iron and finally reach the laundry bins tucked away next to the washing machine. Simply adding a laundry bin to the bathroom next to their bedroom allowed them to have an easy, practical way to tidy up, making a world of difference to me and their dad.

This chapter looks at the small weekly and monthly maintenance gains that go a long way. I focus on clothing too (my other big love in life), showing how well-made pieces in natural fabrics can last even longer when they are properly cared for.

CREATE

Kind to your home, kind to yourself

Everyday maintenance is (or should be!) a significant behind-the-scenes aspect of the make-up and function of our homes. When making plans for any home improvements, we need to consider how changes will weather, as well as ease of maintenance. A plant placed on a high shelf may look wonderful, but if you know deep down you are never going to stand on a chair to water it, watching that plant slowly die isn't going to make you feel good. Placing a free-standing bath neatly in a recess will look incredible but have you taken time to consider how you will clean the floor beneath it, in the hard-to-reach corners? Throughout the book we have looked at the need to be intentional in our design decisions, the value of function over all else and various ways to create a nurturing environment that feels like home. But it doesn't stop there. Small-scale, frequent upkeep will facilitate the smooth running of your home, maintaining its functionality so that you can live there more easily.

Make it easy

Human behaviour researchers have shown that we're more likely to stick to habits when we make them as easy to follow as possible, a little like how when we put on our gym clothes in the morning, we're more likely to exercise that day. Don't worry, I'm not about to enforce a HIIT regime on you. It's just that I find it easier to look after our home by doing little bits every day, before the task becomes too cumbersome. I am not naturally the world's tidiest person and do have to make an effort to tame the chaos, reminding myself it's for the greater good. My husband and I try to do small bits of cleaning and tidying Monday to Friday (though in reality we're sometimes too busy, that's life), tackle DIY and gardening on Saturday and then treat ourselves to a well-deserved 'do nothing' day on a Sunday.

We all have our own thresholds for what we feel is taxing, but here are the things I find useful for making our home feel cared-for:

- Having the roles in our home clearly defined and allocated, split fairly to avoid any resentment building up. While my husband and I split most of the chores, the kids have their responsibilities too.
- A good-quality vacuum cleaner that isn't too bulky to lug about (a cordless one is the bee's knees, particularly if your home has lots of stairs).
- Keeping cleaning products accessible, such as bathroom cleaners in the bathroom (but out of reach of children), making it easy to do a quick whizz around without having to fetch a kit from somewhere else in the home.
- Having a fixed spot for tools with easy access to the ones we use for everyday jobs, such as masking tape, a screwdriver, Allen keys, measuring tape, hammer, nails and screws and a spirit level – again, all stored safely out of reach of children.
- Keeping my sewing box close by and well stocked with a variety of needles and colours of threads for quick handsewn repairs to homeware fabrics and clothes. Any buttons that fall off I collect in a jam jar for later use.

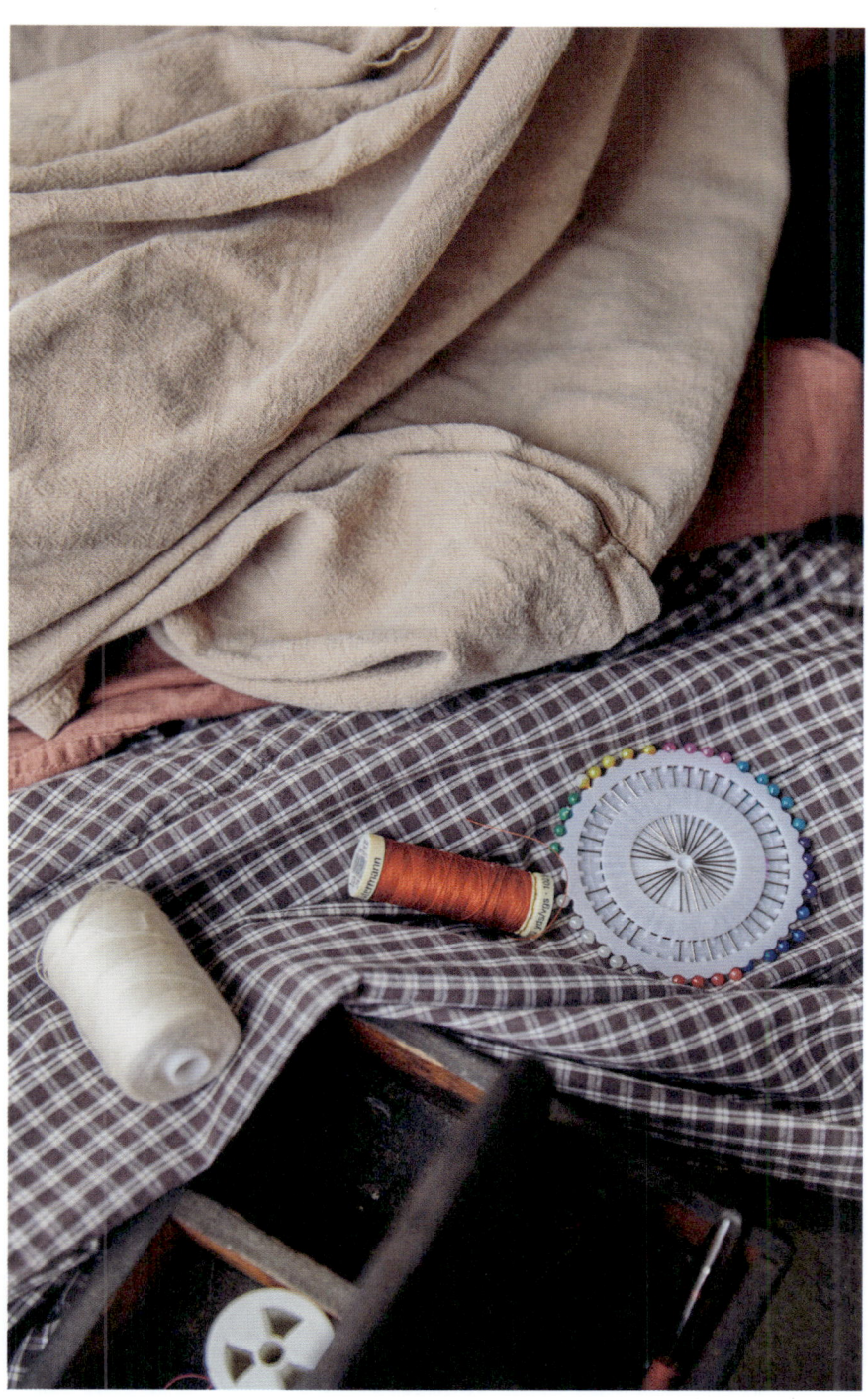

Rescue and revive

Smartening up what you already have can be a satisfying and affordable way to breathe new life into neglected areas of your home. Here are some typical parts of a home that often need a bit of attention (especially if you've just moved in), but also massively benefit from frequent minor maintenance. It's not an exhaustive list and does include more obvious tasks like regular vacuuming and mopping (which I just know you're keeping on top of!).

Kitchen and bathroom maintenance

Ovens

Use an oven mat to line the base of your oven to make cleaning up any spills and discarding crumbs easier. Oven doors can also be removed so that you can give them a good clean in the sink.

Cleaning grout

Chemical grout cleaners are effective but if you want to make a cheaper DIY version (that is also less toxic), Nancy Birtwhistle recommends making a paste of bicarbonate of soda, liquid glycerine and eco washing-up liquid. You can find full details of the recipe in her book *Clean & Green: 101 Hints and Tips for a More Eco-Friendly Home*, or on her Instagram page @nancy.birtwhistle. Apply the paste to the grout using a washing-up brush or old toothbrush, giving it a good scrub then wiping over with a damp cloth or mop.

Re-grouting

Ratty grouting can make a tiled area look far worse than it actually is. Fresh grouting is a simple makeover, and important for protecting the sealant so your tiles don't come lose. You can even choose a contrasting grout colour if you like – inexpensive plain white ceramic tiles can look really striking with colourful grout lines. Re-grouting takes a bit of time but, in my experience, you don't need to be an expert DIYer to accomplish it. There are lots of videos online showing how to tackle it.

Limescale

This is particularly problematic if you live in an area with hard water, where it often builds up around taps, among other places. Giving the affected area a good scrub with a citric acid and water mixture is a miracle worker. Shower heads, which are naturally predisposed to build-up, work well being soaked in the same solution, wrapped in a plastic sandwich bag or similar and tied with string to secure it, left for twenty minutes and then rinsed off. For limescale build-up in a loo bowl, a gentle rub with an emery board can work wonders.

Plumbing

To keep water flowing freely, carefully unscrew the U-bend under the sink (ensuring the tap isn't running!), remove any gunk (technical term) and re-screw. If your shower and/or bath drains have a tendency to clog, you can buy inexpensive unclogging tools (sometimes marketed as dredgers or much more excitingly, snake cleaners) to regularly remove hair and anything else preventing quick drainage.

Living spaces and bedrooms

Safety

Check smoke detectors and carbon monoxide alarms every month at least and keep spare batteries at home.

Mirrors

These often go forgotten but I love the difference that a sparkling clean mirror makes to a room. By 4pm, when my kids arrive back from school, they are usually streaky again!

Dust

This can affect the air quality in our homes so it's good to stay on top of it as much as possible. Always dust before vacuuming, paying attention to neglected areas where dust can gather, like shelves, curtain rails, in and around radiators, on top of wardrobes, window ledges and under the beds and sofa.

Rugs

Give these a good shake out *before* vacuuming and try adding baking soda with essential oils – satisfying!

Shutters

If you have shutters or slatted blinds, they can be real dust traps, so giving them a once-over regularly will make the job easier than leaving it to gather. You can buy specialist cleaning gadgets to go between the slats but, if you ask me, sticking a large sock over your hand works just as well.

Plants

My larger plants have a habit of getting really dusty when I forget to attend to them. Try using a banana skin (the sticky inside) to clean them and your plant will get a nutritional boost in the process (kids will enjoy helping with this chore too).

Air

If you are concerned about the air quality in your home, consider researching whether an air purifier might be worth the investment.

Love your laundry

One of the grievances I hear most often is about the dreaded laundry. As a family of six, I feel this pain. I'm convinced we don't need to wash clothes as often as we've been conditioned to believe in recent years, especially if we have desk-based jobs. So, spot-clean where you can (this will reduce your energy bill too). When using the machine, wash at low temperatures (treating any stains in advance) and with similar colours. Avoid using fabric softener as it can damage your clothes.

Drying can be a challenge, especially if you don't have any outside space for summer drying or if you don't have a dryer during colder months. Tumble dryers are expensive to run and I find my clothes look more worn after regular tumble drying, though they're certainly useful for towels and bed linen, particularly in the winter. A ceiling-mounted clothes airer can be really useful, and if you hang clothes like shirts, T-shirts or dresses from hangers you can

CREATE

usually fit more on and they'll likely dry more quickly too. Some people use a dehumidifier to help clothes dry faster and to keep damp from creeping in – they're not the cheapest to run but they're more economical than a tumble dryer.

After washing woollens, lay each item flat when drying to help preserve the shape. Use a wool comb (one of my treasured bits of kit) to treat bobbling and place cedar discs around woollens when storing (if your pieces are hung in a wardrobe you can attach the disc onto a string around the hanger).

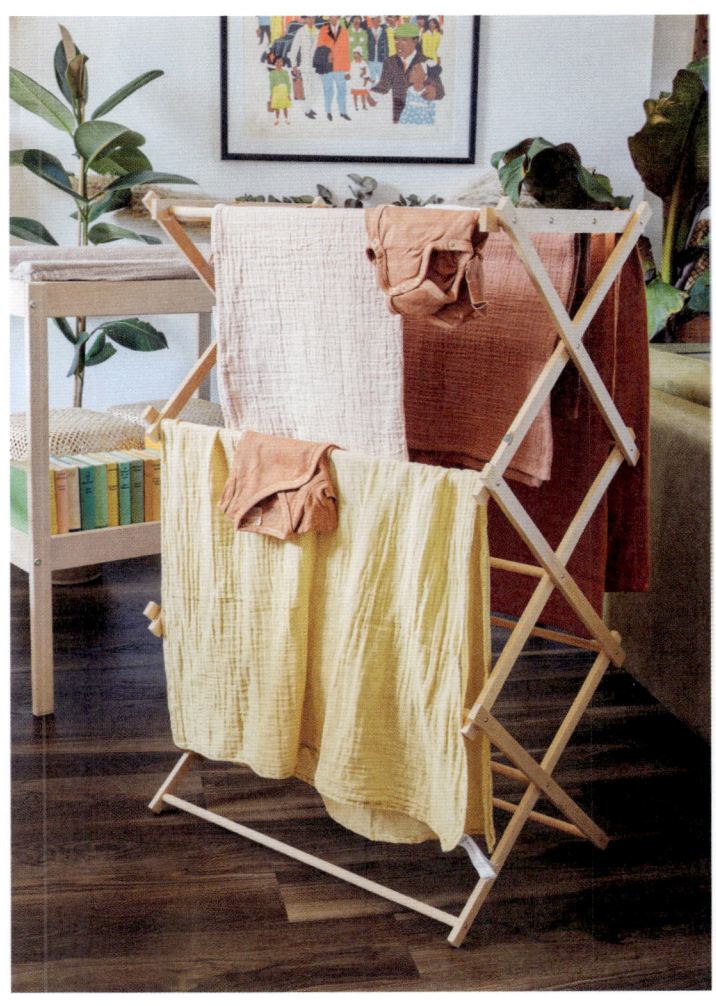

Machine care

Look after your washing machine and it will last longer (you should hope to get around a decade out of a good-quality one, longer if you're lucky).

- If you're using a highly concentrated detergent, use half the recommended dosage specified on the packaging, along with two tablespoons of white distilled vinegar in the softener section of the drawer and two tablespoons of bicarbonate of soda in the detergent part of the drawer to aid cleaning.
- Don't overload the machine. Keep the top third or so empty to allow the clothes the space to clean properly (this can help your machine last longer too). Always clip bra straps together so they don't catch on clothes in the machine, and place small items like baby socks or reusable cleansing pads in a cotton mesh bag so that they don't clog the filter and become damaged.
- Empty out the filter every month or so (usually found behind a small, concealed door in the bottom right corner – place a container or towel underneath to mop up the water and screw the cap back on tightly once finished); remove the drawer and rinse it out, and clean out any bits of detritus caught in the seal behind the door. Run an empty wash to clean the machine (some washing machines have a setting for this, otherwise use one of the longer settings, set to at least 40°C). Always leave the washing machine door ajar between washes to prevent mould building up.

While we're on the subject, let's talk about washing machine placement. Of course, you may not have choice in this matter if space, energy or permission doesn't allow much room for manoeuvre. If you do have options though, I'd encourage you to think beyond the kitchen as the best place for this essential bit of kit. On the Continent, washing machines are often found in bathrooms rather than kitchens, which many find to be a much better option (unless you have a whole separate cupboard or utility room, in which case, congratulations, you are living the dream). It needn't be a large cupboard either. In our last home, we had a plumber install our washing machine in the same cupboard as our boiler, which was the same height and width as a standard door. Washing machines can be noisy and if there are several people living in your home, it is likely to be on at least once a day, so I'd argue that adding noise and traffic to the hub of your home isn't ideal if possible.

Ultimately, caring for and maintaining your home should feel like, if not exactly a joy, at least not a huge drain on your time and resources. Again, it comes down to making your home function well for you, rather than for anyone else, and making decisions that allow you to have a home that feels welcoming and well-maintained. It's all very well being inspired by Pinterest and interiors magazines, but we also need to consider whether we want to spend every spare minute buffing those shiny metal cabinets back to a glassy sheen, or whether our own home might be better suited to a material that doesn't show sticky fingerprints. A home that allows you to relax and feel comfortable is one that isn't constantly calling for hours of your attention to look 'perfect'.

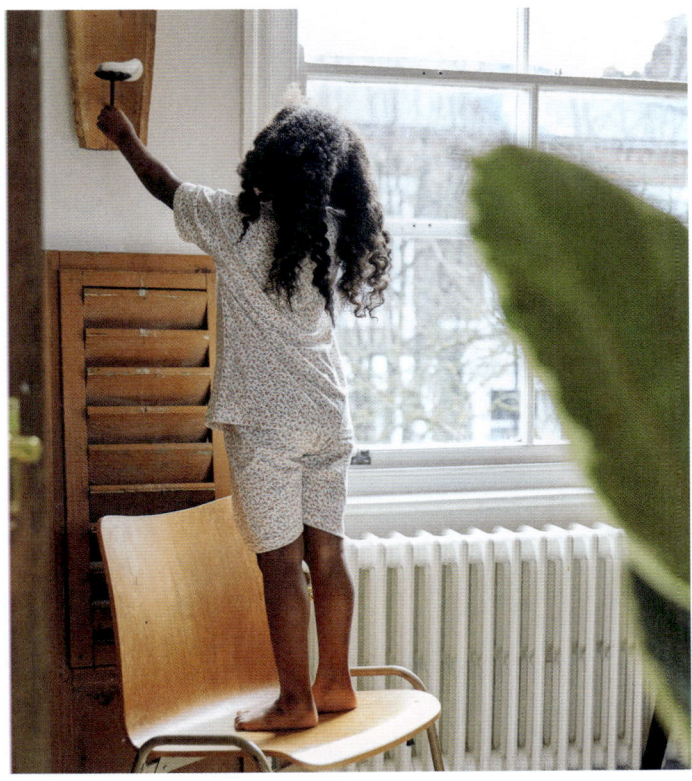

CHAPTER 14

CREATING CONNECTION

Growing up in North London in the late 1990s and early 2000s, I was exposed to a beautifully wide range of cultures, lifestyles and homes. In the bustling borough of Camden, I had friends in high rises, small estates, modest cul-de-sacs, and, at the other extreme, friends who, at the age of eleven, had their living quarters sectioned off into converted loft/basements, essentially their own mini flats! My mother spent a brief period working as a childminder as a way of juggling her own childcare needs, which meant we often visited the homes of the kids she took care of, and it was always apparent to me how wildly their experiences differed from ours. But even though we all had very different circumstances, with hindsight I was lucky to grow up being surrounded by community.

No matter how immaculate your décor or considered your purchases, I don't think it's possible to have a flourishing home without forging connections with those around us. Home extends beyond our four walls, and sometimes the more flawed our domestic environments, the more we rely on our communities for support. Increasingly, many of us are living far away from family so we need to create a community safety net, helping each other so that no one falls through the cracks. This chapter looks at our wider environs and the importance of establishing meaningful relationships with the people and organisations around us. If we want to have good neighbours, we must start by being good neighbours – let's look at how we might go about achieving this.

We are our community

I hold my hands up and admit I wasn't always a model of neighbourliness. My four years in a high-rise flatshare in my late teens made me succumb to the keep-your-head-down mentality – I barely knew who else lived in that building. Our last home in London was on an affluent street in a well-to-do neighbourhood. Our house was the only one that had been converted into social housing, and the rest – detached Victorian villas – had sold for sums unimaginable to me. That glimpse of middle-class living right on our doorstep was so far from our reality, so different to how we had grown up, despite our new home being only a few roads away from my childhood home. It was truly a place of two halves.

I moved onto that street feeling beyond lucky to have secured a home there for an affordable rent, but due to various lasting issues at play, I still brought feelings of resentment towards the seemingly 'rich' around me. I harboured assumptions about how these wealthier neighbours might perceive us and that became the catalyst for us forming a very close bond with the people that shared our building. The cast of characters was wonderful. There was the lady downstairs, just a year or so older than me – born and raised in Camden and bringing up her amazing three young children with her partner (a Rasta with a beaming smile that put anyone at ease). The elderly gentleman above us, in his late eighties, also hailed from the West Indies (as did our downstairs neighbours), and we looked out for him as if he were our own grandfather. On any given Sunday, you'd hear the dulcet tones of reggae reverberating through all three floors. Other days, we'd hear one floor play a tune and would yell out of the window for them to turn it up! It felt like a taste of communal living despite us all having our own separate flats.

I soon realised my prejudice towards our wider neighbourhood was unfounded. That chip on my shoulder quickly dissolved when we started interacting with the surrounding homeowners. There was number 13, a wonderful couple in their mid-forties; their three children went to the local schools that J and I had attended years earlier and they were emphatic about us being not just welcomed to the street, but feeling like we deserved to be there too. It was number 13 that added us to the WhatsApp group (which became

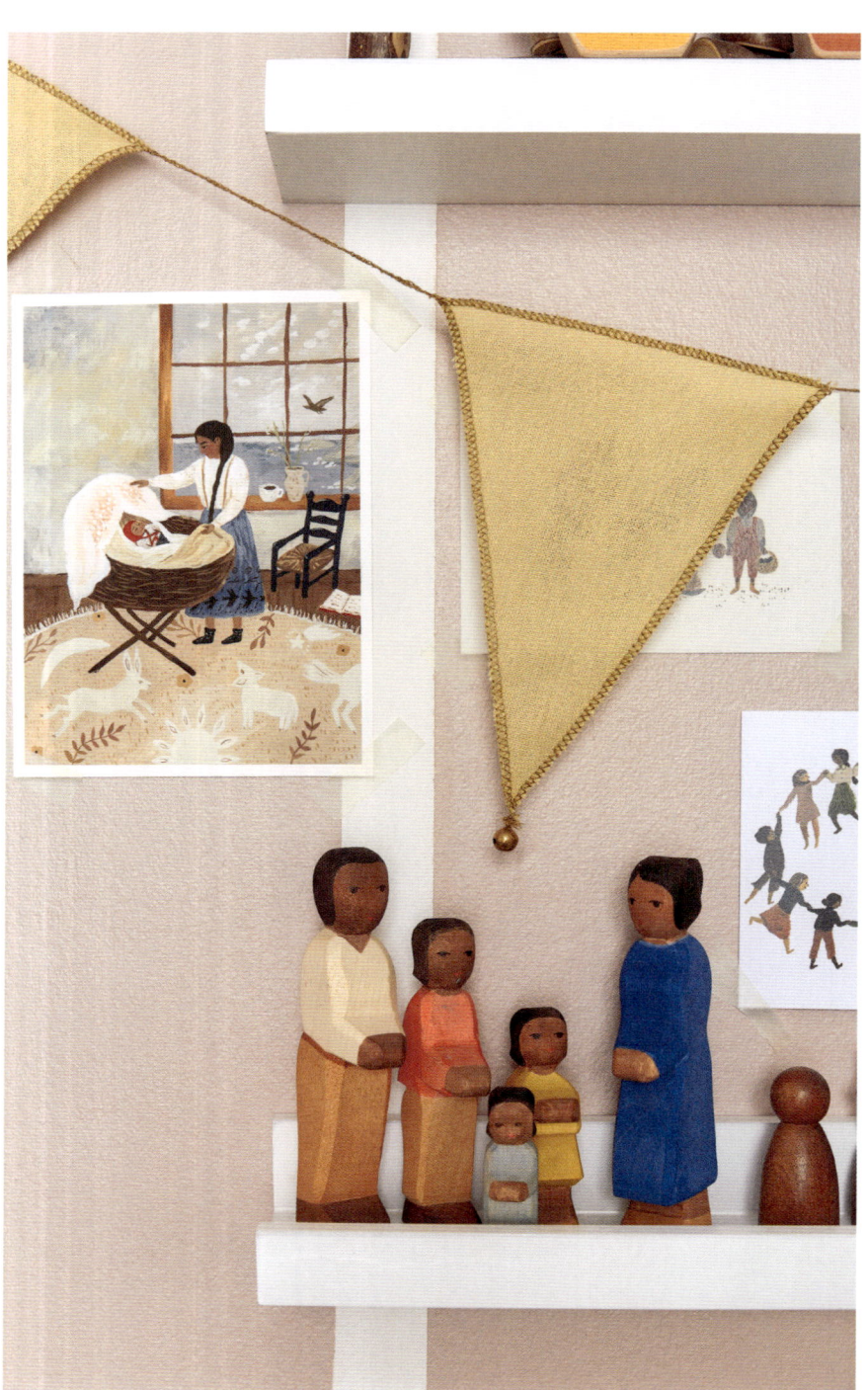

even more essential for comms throughout the pandemic). They delivered a homecooked meal after my son was born, a small act that in the throes of recovering from the birth I was so, so grateful for. They also helped to take care of our elderly neighbour, checking in on him, bringing him groceries and generally lending a hand. There was number 10, the street's answer to David Attenborough, who, on learning of my husband's redundancy during the pandemic, kept him busy by commissioning garden planters and requesting odd jobs, kindly scrunching banknotes into my husband's palm when he refused to take payment. When we started to think about leaving London in order to buy a house in a more affordable area, one of our biggest considerations was leaving behind this community and knowing how unlikely it was that we'd find anything as special elsewhere. We became adamant that seeking out community be just as important, if not more so, than finding the right house.

Community and wellbeing

Researchers across a variety of disciplines have long been fascinated by Blue Zones, those parts of the world where populations live longest and are happiest. From Okinawa, Japan, to the Italian island of Sardinia, there are many reasons attributed to populations in these places defying statistics – a healthy diet, exercise, lower levels of stress are all contributors you might expect. But there are other key factors too, including communities with a deep sense of belonging and purpose, and social circles with people who support each other. It shows that there is a correlation between community cohesion and individual welfare, meaning that the people we surround ourselves with can make a difference to how we live, how we thrive. Conversely, living in places where we feel unsettled or disconnected from our communities can have a detrimental effect on our wellbeing: a sense of unbelonging can unsurprisingly lead to or exacerbate loneliness and isolation.

In the Live section we looked at the role of emotional safety in forming the basis of a home – how feeling secure allows us to relax in a space and be ourselves. This is just as important beyond our dwellings, in the community around us, whether you live in a city, suburb or countryside. Knowing that you reside in not just a safe place, but also a place where you have someone you can turn to when the chips are down creates such a feeling of security. Our communities play a vital role in helping to prevent mental illness and also supporting recovery during times when we are not feeling our best selves.

In the Windrush era, many Black migrants initially viewed the UK as a temporary opportunity for growth and wealth and had every intention of returning to the warm, welcoming isles of the Caribbean once they had saved up enough funds. For that generation's offspring however, who had no ties to the Caribbean, knowing only this cold, inhospitable land as their home, the rise of racial tension and persecution inspired their communities to unite and resist collective oppression. Black households formed strong networks, providing unity, safety, provision and collaboration, and we see this mirrored in so many other pockets of society where migrant communities were at one point highly concentrated in certain areas and met resistance from civilians and/or state bodies.

Shortly after my youngest child was born, I was hit by a debilitating illness that went undiagnosed for quite some time. Recurrent late-night trips to A & E and compromising situations home alone with a newborn and toddler meant that it was my new neighbours I had to rely on for support. There were many times I felt so unwell that I had to literally flag someone down from my front door in desperation, and despite not knowing us well, assistance was always given. With my family no longer living close by, knowing that I could count on a handful of neighbours made a big difference to my state of mind. In turn, we made sure they knew they could count on us for anything too. It is impossible to successfully navigate life alone – let's not waste time trying to!

How to foster a sense of community

If you are in a neighbourhood that doesn't have a culture of community spirit for whatever reason, it can feel hard to make the first move. Call me optimistic but I believe most people would like to feel connected to the people around them, often we're just waiting for someone to make it happen. Maybe that could be you! Could you enquire with neighbours if they'd like to be on an email chain or WhatsApp group? You could start by slipping a note through people's doors, introducing yourself and leaving your name and number on there. From there, perhaps you could suggest a date and time for an informal first get-together, like simply congregating for a cuppa and a chat outside your homes. Start small and take it at a pace that feels relaxed. If given plenty of notice, most local councils are amenable to closing roads for neighbourhood gatherings, such as children 'playing out', tea parties (often coinciding with a national celebration or bank holiday), or sociable gatherings combined with projects like litter picking or planting window boxes. Gradually, connection will evolve beyond surface-level conversation, allowing you to forge meaningful ties with those around you.

When we moved to Kent it was the depths of winter and we had so much going on – what with our renovation, work and parenting – that it felt like we didn't properly meet the neighbours until the seasons changed. The following May I hosted a barbecue and put invitations through the door of everyone on the street, explaining that we'd love to get to know our new neighbours. I was thrilled when lots of them joined us – sometimes you have to make the first move.

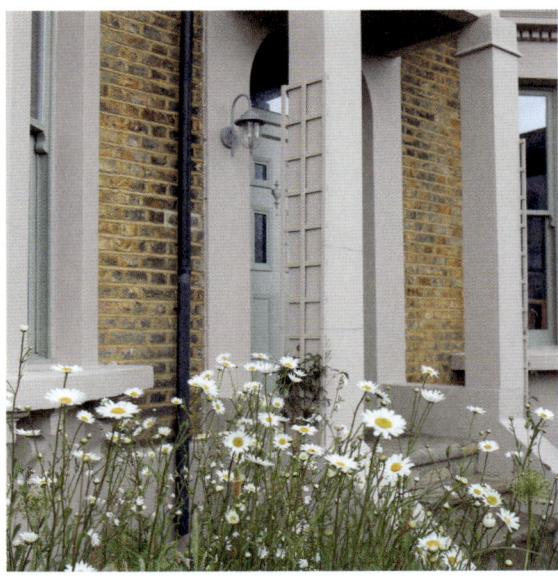

A force for good

I love hearing stories of communities doing extraordinary things, from turning defunct skips into shared swimming pools, to individuals painting tired grey buildings in rainbow technicolour to cheer up the residents. Some towns have buddy benches – public seating painted a different colour – for those wishing to engage in conversation, others have self-appointed volunteers cleaning road signs and picking up litter. What all these initiatives have in common is people taking pride in where they live and striving for purpose for the betterment of everyone.

It was our former neighbours on our street in London who first showed my husband and I what it means to be truly great neighbours. Neighbourliness isn't something that's passive, rather it requires action. We took all those tangible examples of love shown to us over that short period and extended it to our new neighbours on the Kent coast, and it really feels like we have been blessed two-fold to have landed such amazing neighbours once again.

Looking outwards

The most thriving communities tend to be the ones that support their most vulnerable members. There are official initiatives we can take on, such as joining community groups, but there are also plenty of smaller acts of kindness that can have a life-changing impact on those around us. Whether it's helping someone with mobility issues get to their appointments, supporting a neighbour who is less admin- or tech-savvy to fill in forms, or cooking a meal for someone who's unwell, these seemingly small acts go a long way to making someone feel valued. Can you think of any one-off or regular ways you can help a neighbour?

Community projects

Working together on common goals ticks so many wellbeing boxes. Not only will you be improving your neighbourhood through whatever improvements you are working towards, you'll also be interacting with neighbours to bring shared values to fruition. Think about what might benefit your area – more greenery, less traffic, a reduction in noise pollution, communal bike storage, a lending library, a monthly repair workshop (often older people have skills that have been lost in younger generations) – the opportunities are endless.

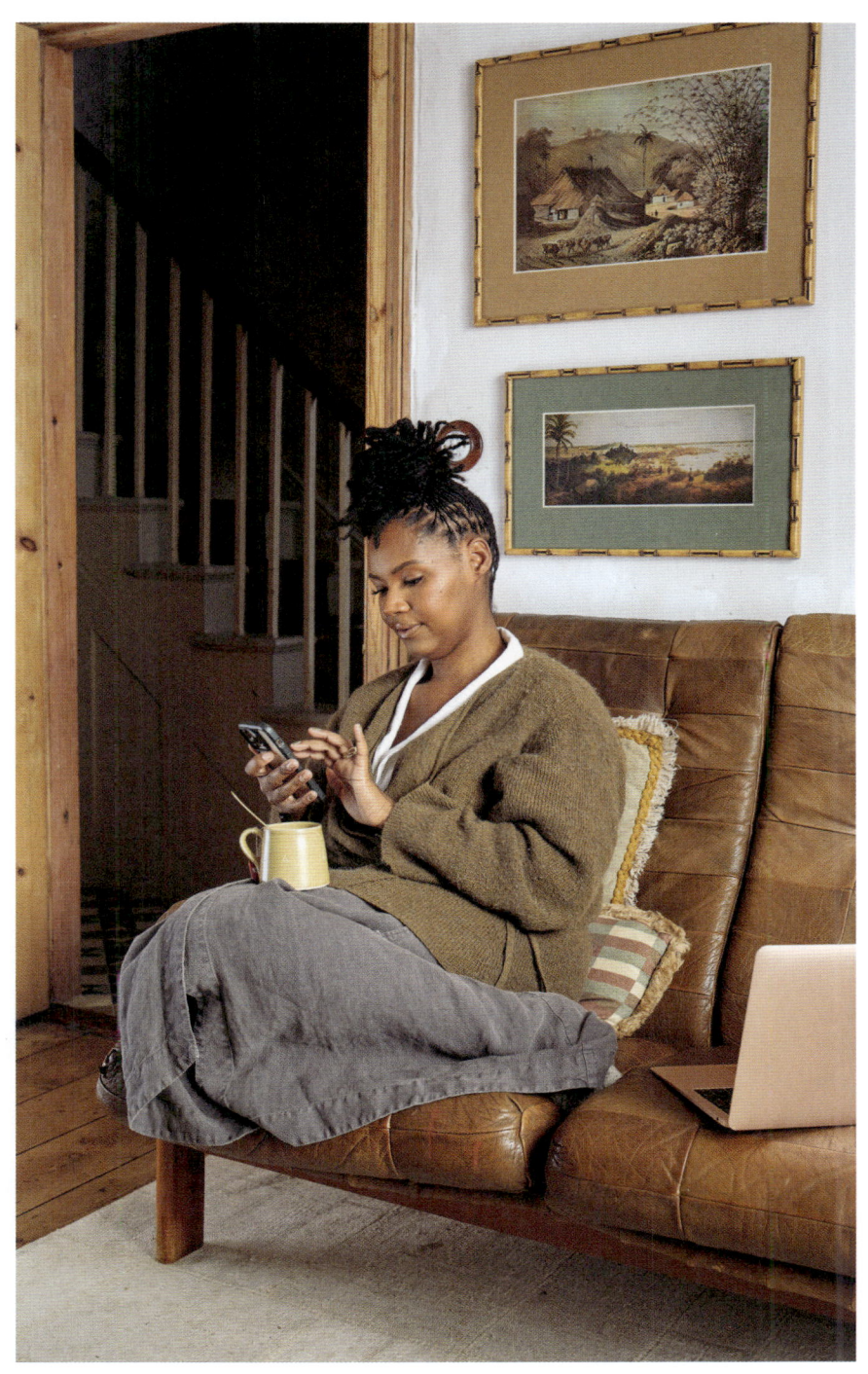

Volunteering

There are many benefits to volunteering, not just for the cause being helped but also the individual giving their time. The positive affects on self-esteem and the sense of purpose found in connecting with others pays dividends, and it's why it is often recommended by healthcare professionals as part of a wider care plan, for those looking to boost their mood. Finding a cause you feel strongly about and giving your time in service of it has been thought to give a hit of dopamine (that feel-good hormone) and reduce stress. If you are in a new area, this can be a great way of meeting new people. If you're in the UK, visit https://www.gov.uk/volunteering to see if there are any volunteering opportunities in your area.

Skill swapping

Do you have skills that could help others, such as speaking another language or being a dab hand at DIY? Consider how your talents and hobbies might be used to your community's advantage. This can be a great way to get multiple generations to collaborate. Also, lending a helping hand becomes even more rewarding when you are doing tasks you enjoy.

Pooling resources

Some neighbours share cars to keep costs more affordable and ease pressure on parking. We carpool five days a week for the school run with another family on our street. Some take it in turns cooking their evening meal or preparing school lunches, passing Tupperware down the corridor or over the fence. Other neighbours chip in to buy certain ingredients or household cleaning products in bulk and divide them up, making them more cost-efficient. Exchanging clothes, toys, sports kits, books – there are many ways we can rethink our place in today's individualistic culture.

Buy local

When we buy at our local independent shops it keeps money in our communities, unlike when we shop online or from big chains, where our money flows away from our area. When funds stay local it benefits everyone, helping to keep communities thriving and even bringing regeneration to areas that need it. Supporting local businesses can also lead to more jobs being created and improved local infrastructure, and there are many environmental benefits too, including a reduction in packaging and carbon emissions.

I love to shop local when I can and am often pleasantly surprised at how reasonably priced many of the stores near me are, often beating the supermarkets in price. However, I fully acknowledge that it can sometimes feel quicker or more efficient to order whatever you need online, whether that's groceries or anything else. Similarly, unless you live in a thriving hub, you may not have much choice other than to default to bigger chains. The great news is that it doesn't have to be an all-or-nothing situation – every time we buy goods or services from a local business, we are investing in our community. Depending on your neighbourhood, many stores may even have a delivery service, allowing you to order your weekly fruit and veg or have milk delivered to your door.

Collective power

There are communities all over the world who, often despairing of government inertia, are coming together to stand for causes they believe in. Whether forming local economies to regenerate areas, implementing initiatives to get children away from screens and playing outdoors, or restricting car usage to help boost air quality, there is strength in numbers. Working in our community to enact change for the better allows us to live out our values, inspire others and set an example for the next generation to fight for what they believe in.

Forming interest groups can be the first step in rallying action. From climate action groups and neighbourhood improvement societies to groups that explore heritage, sexuality, disability or faith, whatever the focus, it can be really binding to meet local people who are passionate about similar interests. Don't necessarily aim for groups to be made of like-minded people. To avoid trapping ourselves in an echo chamber, let's seek out people who hold different views than our own (provided everyone is respectful). We don't all necessarily have to agree on everything to make positive change.

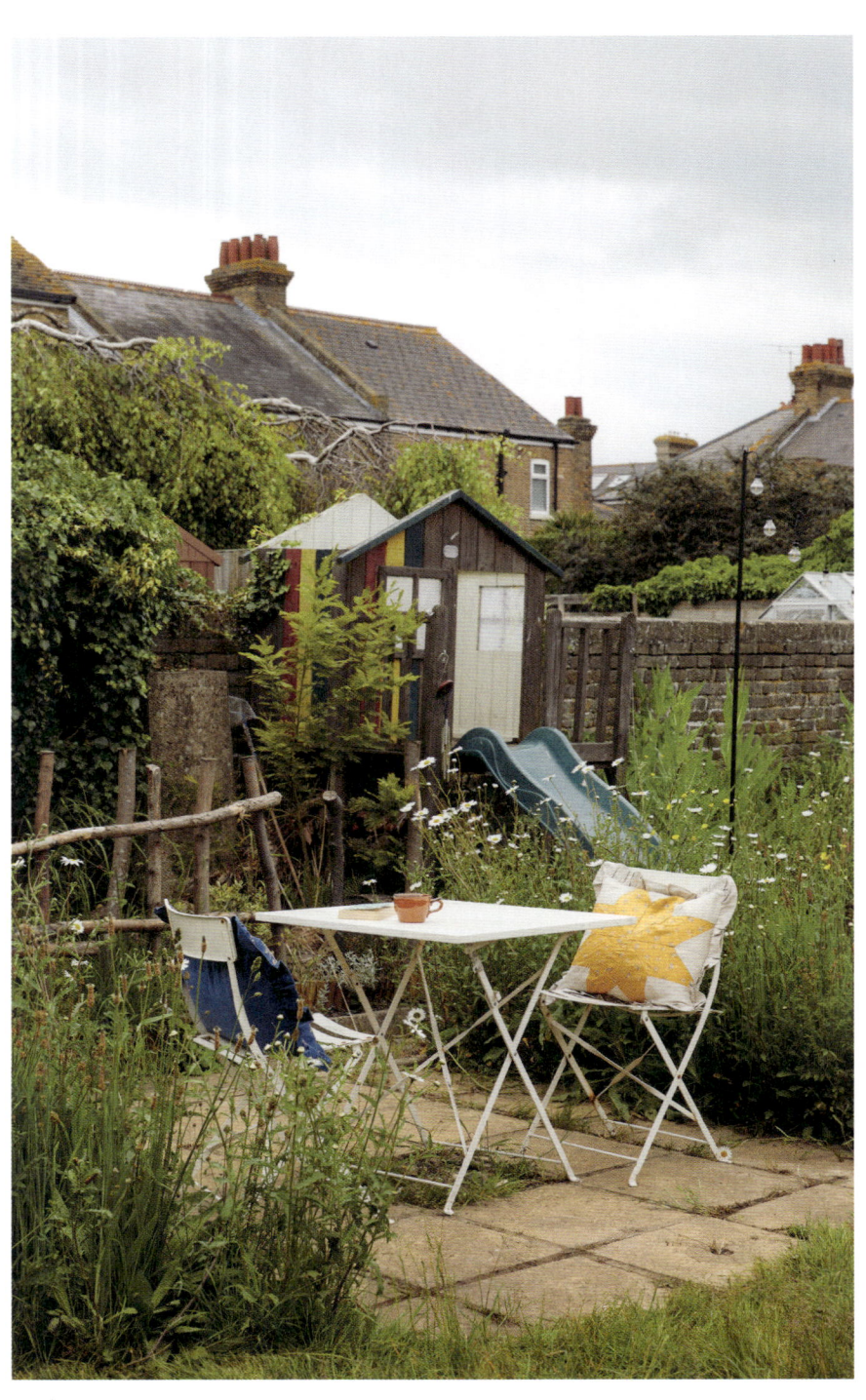

CREATE

Community greenery

There's something very grounding about gardening. There have even been studies that suggest putting our hands into the earth may release the happy hormone serotonin, helping to reduce stress. Whatever the reason, my husband and I have found that our attempts at growing flowers, fruit and veg have really boosted our mental health. I quite like the lack of control – the gardener does their bit and the rest they leave up to nature. It was a neighbour on our old street, number 21, who gave my husband his first tomato starter plant, completely unprompted, after seeing him try to maintain the shared communal garden plot out front. Little did she know that she would spark an entire new hobby for him, something that's brought him real tangible joy over the years!

In our industrialised world, having access to nature is vital – this should not be a luxury for the few, but a right for everyone. Collaborating with our wider community on outdoor initiatives makes a lot of sense. If you are fortunate enough to have a communal space near your home, like a public garden or a park, it may well be calling out for volunteers to help maintain it. Gardening together is so convivial, as are other outdoor activities such as litter picking – bring a flask and some gardening gloves and get stuck in.

At the height of lockdown, with three small children in a flat with no garden, we were struggling. When we had the idea to convert a bin area in the front garden into a tiny communal play space complete with a micro allotment and bug hotel, it was our wonderful neighbour at number 10 who assured us that we had the street's blessing and that every child had the right to play and to do so safely.

Low-cost ideas for making your neighbourhood a bit leafier

Sharing

Being able to borrow tools, swap seeds or obtain cuttings for propagation from neighbours can be a great incentive to start gardening. Before purchasing any garden apparatus, check with neighbours to see what can be borrowed.

Allotment divide and conquer

If you are lucky enough to be starting out with an allotment and you want to keep things simple in the early days, you might want to consider growing just a few crops in the first instance. Some new growers choose to co-ordinate with patch neighbours to start small and split their bounty, so for example one person may focus on leafy greens, another on root vegetables, and they will share out the results. As they gain confidence, so too does the variety of what they nurture.

Garden borrowing

I was often shocked in London at how many gardens are totally unused, looking like something out of *The Day of the Triffids*. Given that waiting lists for allotments were so often over-subscribed, this seemed crazy to me. Sometimes this neglect occurs through disinterest but at other times it's because residents are too busy or perhaps no longer have the physical capacity to tend to their gardens. So, many are coming round to the prospect of offering up their disused garden to someone who lacks one and is keen to get stuck in.

Guerrilla gardening

Living on a street alongside thriving pockets of nature can make a real impact on your quality of life, particularly if you live in a built-up area or lack access to a garden or nearby park. Some neighbourhoods have successfully petitioned their local council to 'gift' parking spaces so that a patch of road the size of a car can be transformed into a green haven. Whatever space you have – a window box or indeed a whole plot – consider keeping half of it wild.

Beyond the four walls of our homes, a supportive community not only contributes to a profound sense of security but also becomes a lifeline during personal struggles. As we embrace the fact that navigating life alone is harder than it needs to be, it becomes easy to see the indispensable role that community plays in our lives. In order to actively forge such connections, taking initiative is key. Investing in community initiatives not only fosters a sense of belonging but also aligns residents with a shared purpose. Through acts of kindness, active participation and a recognition of the value our neighbours bring, we weave a vibrant network that transforms houses into homes and neighbours into friends, truly embodying the strength of a thriving community.

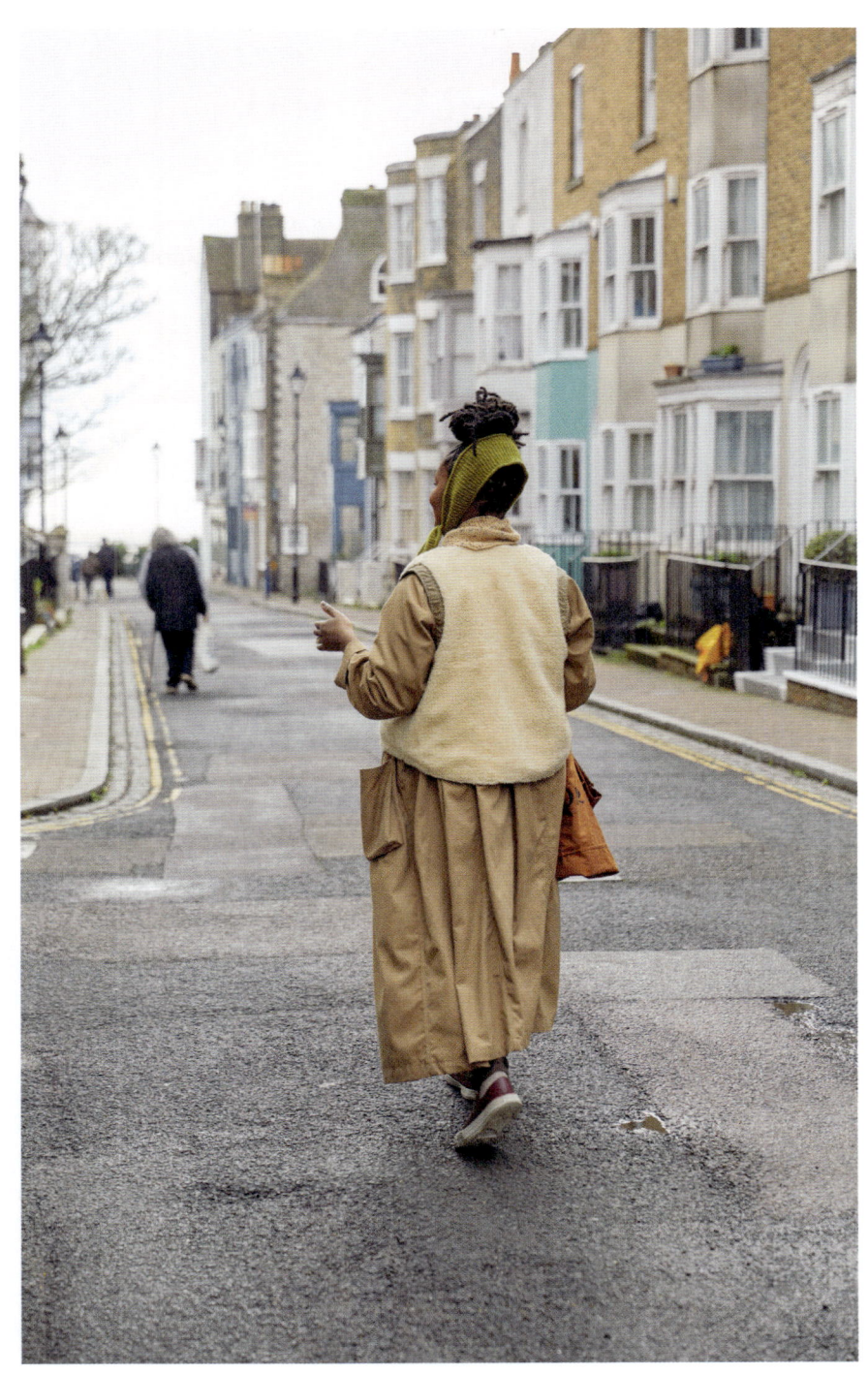

AFTERWORD

My concept of home has changed in recent months. As I continue to grieve for my papa, I'm surprised to find myself grieving also for my Caribbean homeland, Carriacou. This beautiful island that welcomed me on countless visits over the decades, now serves as a painful reminder of loss – a lost time, lost future, lost opportunities. How will I relate to this island home in the years to come now that the memories are marred and any joyous thoughts have been replaced with that solemn trip? Can it still be a home to me?

I recently learnt the Welsh word, *hiraeth*, that summed up so perfectly how I had been feeling – I'm told it describes a complex emotion that evokes nostalgia for something lost, homesickness or yearning for a place or a person out of grasp. In mourning for my father and for the place we both called 'home', I've had to re-evaluate what truly matters. My dad only got to enjoy five years of his longed-for retirement back in Carriacou. That tragedy has forced me to take a breath, to slow down a little and that's a good thing. Time isn't promised to any of us, so let's use it well.

As I look around my home right now, many tasks leap out at me from the to-do list. Two years after we moved in, one half of the house is still yet to be touched. There are uninhabitable parts of it in desperate need of work, and an endless snagging list for the parts that have been 'done'. The shabby exterior of our house badly needs painting. Our plumbing needs updating, both inside and out in the garden. Our en suite bathroom – which was started, then abandoned long before completion by our first builders – needs finishing. I know that the list will be whittled down over time – I tell myself that it must.

I have no doubt that every corner of home we breathe life into will have a positive effect on our sense of accomplishment as well as our everyday lives. More space to live, more room to play. Like life, choosing what to prioritise in our homes is a balancing act that often needs reassessing. Ultimately though, I believe you will create a home that nourishes, all in good time; the most important thing is that it continues to nourish you in the meantime too, not just once it's all 'done'.

I remind myself that forging a secure feeling of home for my children isn't about having a perfectly polished, finished space. And I know that in the blink

AFTERWORD

of an eye, they will be grown up, carving out lives of their own, embarking on relationships, settling in their own homes. Perhaps the four of them will stay nearby, or maybe they will establish roots in far-flung corners of the world. Time will tell. Wherever they go though, my wish for them is to live with an abundance of security and stability in all senses, and to leave our home secure in the knowledge of who they are and where they belong (everywhere – but especially with us). To know that the door of our home is always open, and that they can pass through it as often as they need to.

Life is simply too short not to put love into your surroundings. I hope this book has offered you some inspiration for creating a soulful home that bolsters your wellbeing. YOU are deserving of a home that feels special, a safe one that brings you peace.

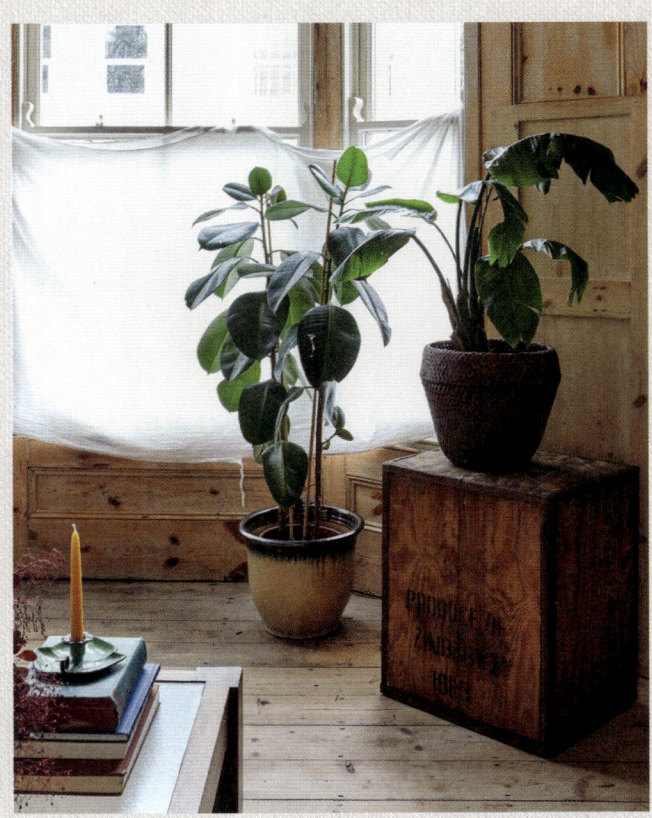

ACKNOWLEDGEMENTS

Writing a book is a journey that often feels solitary, but, in truth, it takes a village. I am deeply grateful to the following individuals whose support, encouragement and expertise have been invaluable in bringing this book to fruition.

First and foremost, I would like to express my heartfelt gratitude to my family, but specifically my husband, Jermel, for the unwavering support and belief in my dream of becoming a published author. Their love, patience and understanding sustained me through the highs and lows of the writing process, and at every step of the way I felt them rooting for me.

Without the talent and vision of my dear friend and colleague Kasia Fiszer, this book would certainly be a lot less colourful. Kasia's work has been instrumental in my career progression over the last six years. An unlikely friendship – if only for the distance – Kasia has seen our homes at their very worst and still managed to show them at their very best – taking the chaos in her stride and all

ACKNOWLEDGEMENTS

the while, being the loveliest colleague to spend my time with. Here's to many more projects together!

I am forever indebted to Tamsin, my researcher. Your warmth and wisdom shaped this manuscript in ways I couldn't have imagined. Meeting you over Zoom felt like fate – your chaotic radiance winning me over instantaneously and I'm deeply grateful for your guidance. We all need a Tamsin in our lives.

My deepest appreciation to my editor, Pippa, and the incredible team at Orion, thank you for believing in this project despite life's many interruptions to this project. Pippa, your calming presence put me at ease from the start and I knew my book would be in good hands.

A special thank you to my literary agent, Rachel (Rachel Mills Literary), for believing in my writing and tirelessly advocating on my behalf. Rachel trekked to my local park to meet me and my children for a socially distanced pitch what seems like a lifetime ago now, certain that I had this book in me, even when I doubted myself. Thank you for everything.

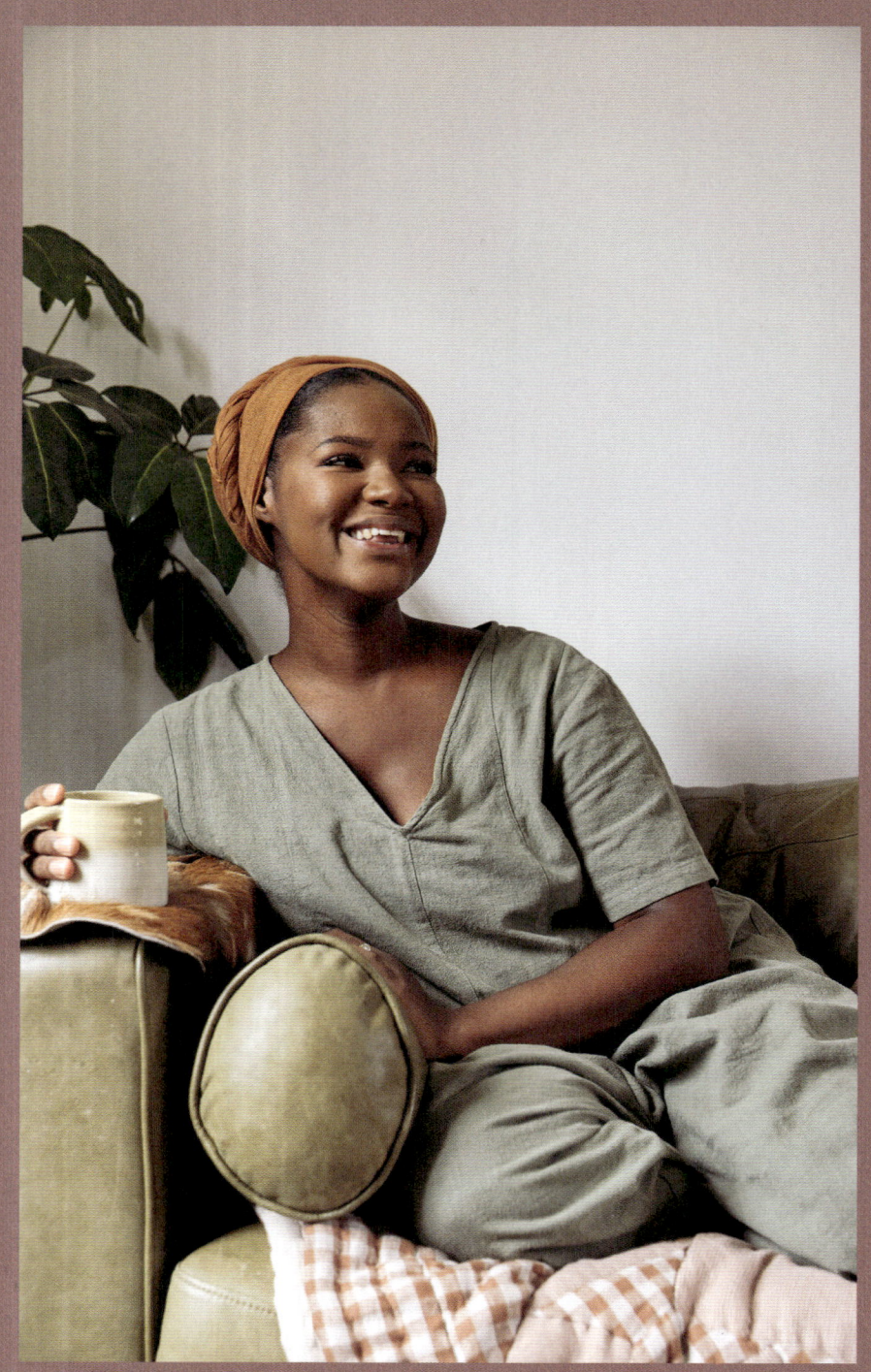

ACKNOWLEDGEMENTS

I would like to acknowledge the support of my first audience – the community within The Vitamin D Project. You stuck around and watched me bumble through early adulthood – allowing me the space to share my many thoughts (so many of which form this book) and have continued to champion me along the way. There would be no book without you.

Lastly, I want to express my gratitude to the readers. This is a book for anyone with a space and a longing for it to feel that bit more special. Please don't ever wait until you get your own room, move out or 'get on the ladder' . . . We should all feel empowered to make our current spaces both work for us and reflect us, and I'd love more than anything to see us as a society, putting that excitement and praise behind all living spaces in their many iterations.

May this book inspire you to make your spaces truly your own, no matter where you are in life. Thank you for your support and enthusiasm.

With love and gratitude, Africa

FURTHER READING

Heuman, Beata. *Every Room Should Sing.* Rizzoli, 2021.

Minter, Harriet. *WFH (Working From Home): How to Build a Career You Love When You're Not in the Office.* Greenfinch, 2021.

Ogundehin, Michelle. *Happy Inside: How to Harness the Power of Home for Health and Happiness.* Ebury, 2020.

Wiking, Meik. *My Hygge Home: How to Make Home Your Happy Place.* Penguin, 2022.

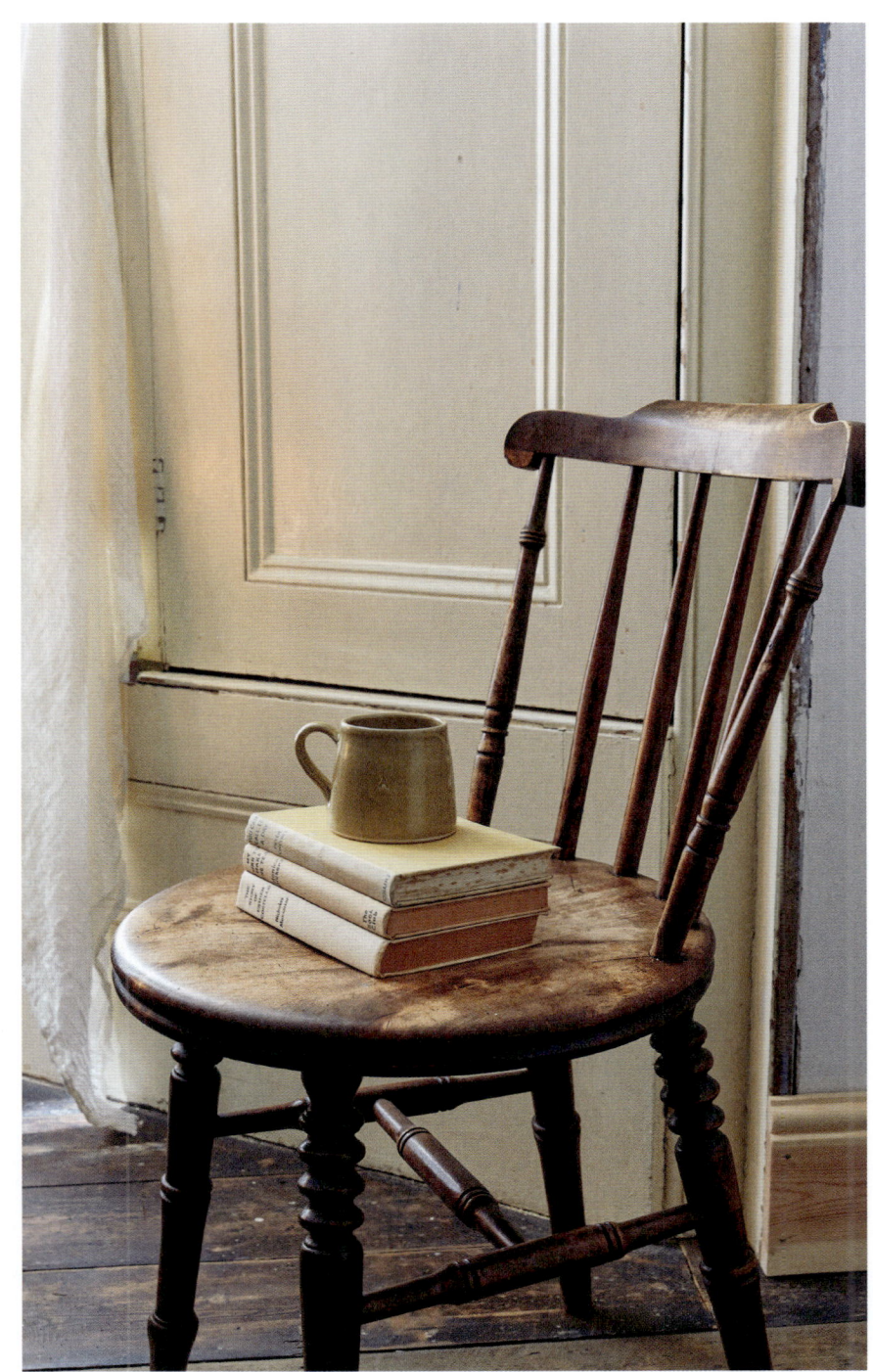

ABOUT THE AUTHOR

Africa Daley-Clarke is a freelance Art Director, brand consultant and writer. After over a decade managing high-profile fashion stores she ventured into interiors, working for a leading brand before becoming her own boss.

She launched her online lifestyle platform, The Vitamin D Project, with a focus on a more sustainable approach to interiors, childrenswear, and a real emphasis on social injustice. Africa has built an engaged community where she offers tips and tricks on how to slowly and thoughtfully cultivate a sustainable home that reflects not just your taste, but your values and your personal heritage.

Africa lives on the Kent coast with her husband and their four children.

Wallpaper designed by Africa Daley-Clarke in collaboration with Poodle & Blonde, scribbles added by her children

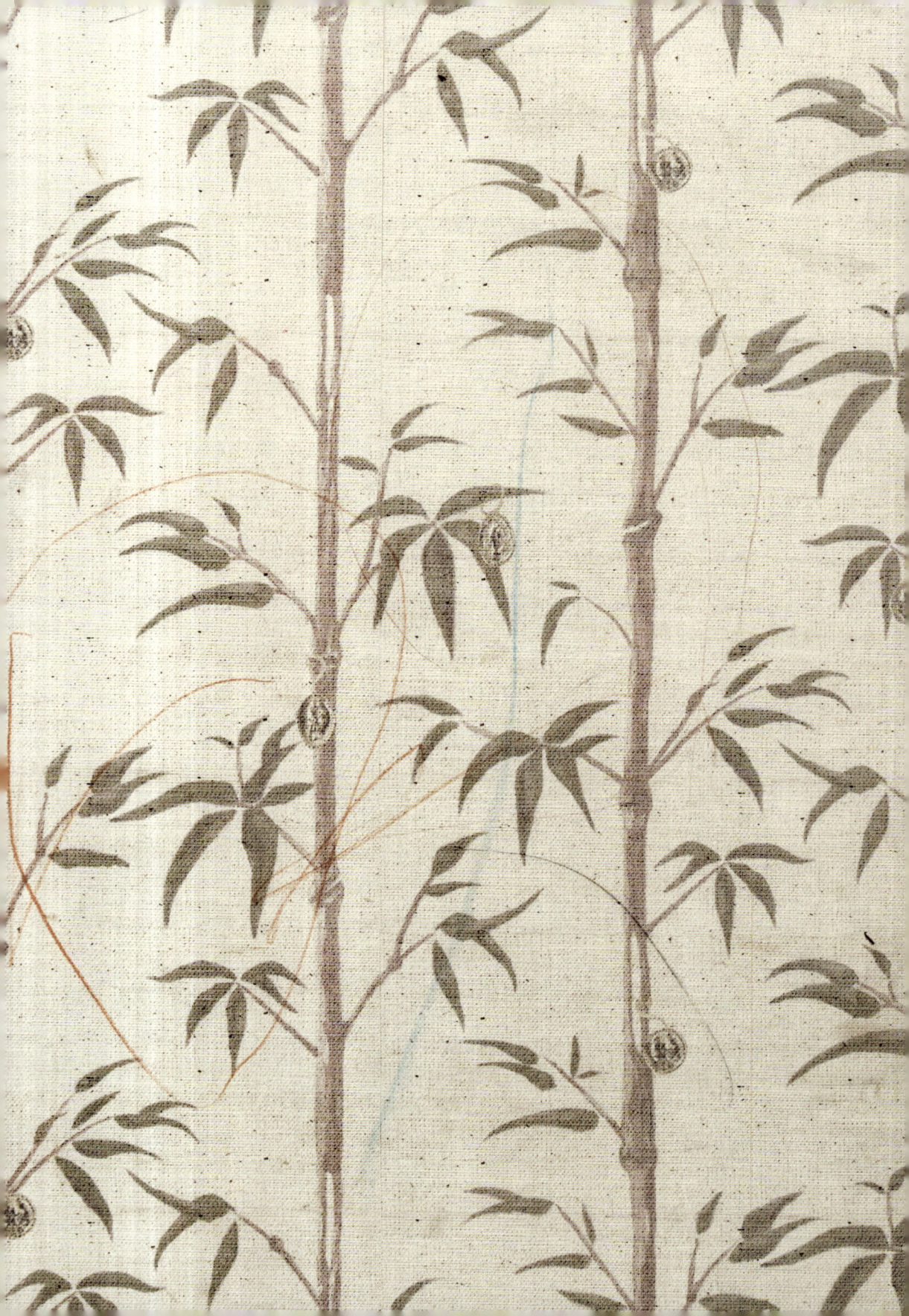